Fermentation on Wheels

Road Stories, Food Ramblings, and
50 Do-It-Yourself Recipes
from Sauerkraut, Kombucha, and Yogurt
to Miso, Tempeh, and Mead

Tara Whitsitt

BLOOMSBURY

New York London Oxford New Delhi Sydney

Bloomsbury USA
An imprint of Bloomsbury Publishing Plc

1385 Broadway	50 Bedford Square
New York	London
NY 10018	WC1B 3DP
USA	UK

www.bloomsbury.com

First published 2017

ISBN: HB: 978-1-63286-790-2
        ePub: 978-1-63286-792-6

Library of Congress Cataloging-in-Publication Data is available.

2 4 6 8 10 9 7 5 3 1

Designed and typeset by Elizabeth Van Itallie

Printed in China by RRD Asia Printing Solutions

To find out more about our authors and books visit www.bloomsbury.com. Here you will find extracts, author interviews, details of forthcoming events, and the option to sign up for our newsletters.

Bloomsbury books may be purchased for business or promotional use. For information on bulk purchases please contact Macmillan Corporate and Premium Sales Department at specialmarkets@macmillan.com.

For Noah DeWitt

my friend who believed that no dream
was too wild and that magic
could be found everywhere and in everyone.

CONTENTS

NAVIGATING FERMENTATION

Fermentation is one of the most fascinating, ever-present food processes, naturally occurring everywhere: the cheese in your fridge developing richer flavors; the yogurt left on your countertop overnight forming a layer of whey; the flour, water, and natural yeast intermingling to leaven dough. Microorganisms work hard, and they break down food matter whenever the opportunity arises. These hidden life-forms enhance food nutrients and contribute a diverse community of microflora to the miraculous microbiome inside you. And it all starts with a simple act in the kitchen.

You don't need sophisticated tools for fermentation. Only five years ago I was intimidated by home preservation, discouraged by pricey classes and kitchen apparatuses. One of the most difficult aspects of today's kitchen is the overwhelming variety of tools we think we need to master a home-cooked meal, not to mention the obscure tools we think we need for food preservation. Keep it simple. You don't need air-lock systems or fancy crocks for vegetable fermentation—your ancestors didn't fret when they packed twenty gallons of salty cabbage into a wooden barrel and left it in their root cellar to ferment in fall and enjoy through the next spring. The simple truth is that you can ferment one gallon of cabbage in a recycled glass jar with a rock as a weight and a tea towel secured on top. More isn't necessary.

Simplicity will be a running theme. But these pages will also explore fermented foods that require more commitment, practice, and kitchen means. I want to encourage you toward the rewards that come with such challenges. Most of the more complicated recipes in this book were first made with simple tools and by feel.

They're a testament to the deep intelligence of age-old processes and the eagerness of microorganisms to thrive. Where there is a will (which all microbes have, and you are mostly microbe), there is a way.

This chapter introduces a few concepts, supplies, and ingredients—compiled from workshops I've taught, both in starter-culture fermentation and wild-vegetable fermentation—that will bring more ease to recipes in the following pages. Some concepts are expanded upon within the recipes where they specifically apply; but let this serve as a well-rounded guide for getting started. Most important, I encourage you to embrace creativity.

What Is Fermentation?

Fermentation is a microbial transformation in which sugars are converted into acids, gases, and sometimes alcohol, transforming raw or cooked foods into a more preserved state and giving them complex, unique flavors. During this transformation, microbes proliferate and create a diverse microcommunity, so your food is teeming with beneficial microorganisms. Sauerkraut, miso, and yogurt are common examples of fermented foods packed with helpful bacteria. When you eat fermented foods, you introduce these beneficial microorganisms to your system, or your microbiome, located in the gut.

Why Fermentation?

Microbe-rich fermented foods and drinks offer a healthy alternative to the more widely available processed and preserved foods sold today. When you introduce beneficial bacteria to your body, you strengthen your gut, improve immunity, and better your digestive health. You also encourage a food culture that promotes diversity and health for your inner ecosystem, which like all ecosystems needs a balance of microbes to thrive. Microorganisms are essential—they're the underlying connection between all life-forms.

You can certainly go out and buy a jar of sauerkraut or miso from the store, but experiencing fermentation brings you closer to life forces that bridge communities of soil, plants, and animals. These small organisms are responsible for a healthy planet, too. Working directly with fermentation has taught me to appreciate the grandeur of the natural world at a more intimate scale—fermenting in your own kitchen is one of the easiest, most delicious, and fascinating ways to experience an ecosystem firsthand. Growing food has a similar effect. There, we initiate life; when we ferment, we cultivate and nourish ourselves with that life. It's an immensely rewarding and empowering process to achieve in a small home kitchen.

Wild Fermentation Versus Fermentation via Inoculation

When you allow fermentation to happen naturally, without the addition of microorganisms, such as bacteria or yeast, it's called *wild fermentation*. Vegetable fermentation is a perfect example of wild fermentation, for it depends on the organisms present on your vegetables; with the addition of a salty massage and submersion in brine, *Lactobacillus* flourishes. Though an exact flavor is unpredictable from batch to batch because vegetables from different sources will vary in microflora, vegetable ferments are reliably tangy and tasty. If you make something you find especially tasty, you can save the brine and use it to inoculate future batches. This particular method is called *backslopping*, and this brine is an example of a *starter culture*.

Starter cultures are communities of specific microorganisms used to inoculate foods—they jump-start fermentation and introduce desired fermentations and flavor profiles. Bacteria and yeast impact flavor, and when you work with a community of bacteria and yeast you know and trust, you're able to reproduce familiar flavors. Flavor profiles of starter cultures can change over time, though, based on environment and the ingredients you use to keep them going. San Francisco sourdough, for example, undergoes much change if you ship it to New York City and feed it with rye flour rather than white flour. Different microbes dwell in different environments and food mediums and quickly impart their own flavor qualities—that's part of the experimental fun.

All starter cultures, just like the backslopping brine, once had a botanical source. Today scientists produce starter cultures in laboratories, to mimic the unique communities of bacteria and yeast found in the wild. Some starter cultures are robust with long life spans (sometimes thousands of years), while others are less robust and will produce just two to three fermentation cycles. More often, the shorter life cycles are found in laboratory cultures. I have yet to work with a starter culture sourced from nature that has failed to infinitely reproduce when properly cared for.

This book includes a guide to sourcing starter cultures (page 12). Once you get your hands on a starter culture, it's important to care for it with regular feedings or store it properly when you aren't using it. Recipes in this book will guide you through the particulars of different starter cultures—each has unique needs.

In the Kitchen

The supplies listed below apply mostly to vegetable and alcohol fermentation, but they will also get you started with an array of other ferments. An incubation chamber, thermometer, and scale are included for accuracy measures, but aren't necessary for most of these recipes. Each recipe contains notes for the materials you will need.

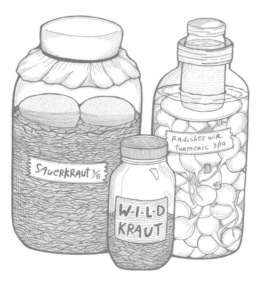

Fermentation Vessel. For three reasons my favorite vessel is a glass gallon jar: cost-effectiveness, visibility, and quantity. Glass jars are great when doing smaller experiments, too. The opening of a jar should always be wide enough for your hand to fit. When packing vegetables, make sure that they are fully submerged in brine. During fermentation, you may want to give the ingredients a push downward if you notice they're no longer submerged. This will prevent oxidization or mold growth. You may also use a ceramic crock or food-grade plastic containers, but I recommend starting out with glass containers so you can see what's going on and get to know your ferments better. Visibility will give you a sense of pace and let you know when the ferment needs maintenance. And, oh, the joys of viewing the color changes and carbon dioxide activity—the whole mesmerizing fermentation process!

Ceramic, Glass, or Plastic Bowls. A large bowl is the best vessel for massaging vegetables with salt or simply mixing ingredients. My favorite bowls are stainless steel and glass bowls, but use what you like so long as you transfer the ingredients to a proper vessel for fermentation. Steer clear of wooden bowls, as they will absorb the brine you're working to promote.

Weight. Many food fermentations, including vegetable ferments, are anaerobic—they require the absence of oxygen. Hence the need for weights to keep ferments submerged below brine. I use nonporous river rocks as weights—washed, scrubbed, and boiled in water for fifteen to twenty minutes. You may also use a flexible plastic yogurt lid and place a glass jar of water on top of it. With smaller batches (one-half gallon or less), I simply use the outer cabbage leaves or the ends of root vegetables, which would otherwise be compost, to pack the top of my ferment. If they oxidize or show mold growth during fermentation, I simply toss them.

Mold is a normal occurrence in fermentation. To discourage mold growth, check on your ferment regularly and push the ingredients below the brine. If you discover mold, simply scrape it off as a compost offering. Everything below the brine is fine. Think cheese: you wouldn't throw the block away due to a few spots of mold.

Cover. Once my ferment is properly packed and weighed in its vessel, I cover the jar with a tea towel and secure it with a rubber band. This keeps dust and bugs out. You can also use a plastic Ball-jar lid. Air-lock systems are also popular because they keep outside bacteria and yeast out of the equation. Steer clear of metal covers as they will corrode when in contact with high levels of salt and can introduce undesirable flavors to dairy and beverage ferments.

Bottles. When fermenting beverages, you will transfer them to a bottle for storage. Different beverages call for different bottles, but there are no strict rules. You can purchase bottles at a home-brew store, but I recommend using recycled bottles. It's much more cost-effective. I prefer *sling-top* bottles for varieties of fermented soda because they are airtight and thus also useful for secondary fermentation, which you can learn about on page 62. *Wine bottles* are great for wine and *beer bottles* for beer. You can learn about the wine bottling process on pages 138–39. This guide includes tips for cleaning and sanitizing recycled bottles, too.

Carboys and Gallon Jugs. Most beer and wine recipes in this book call for a gallon jug, but you can use a carboy if you'd like to scale up. A carboy is a large-quantity glass fermentation vessel with a narrow neck and mouth, for use with an air lock and bung. You can use a food-grade plastic carboy, too.

Air Lock and Bung. Air locks are nifty and sometimes necessary in alcohol fermentation. My recipes for cider, wine, and beer include the use of an air lock, which allows the escape of CO_2 but doesn't let oxygen in. These ferments are especially sensitive to outside bacteria and yeast, which can sometimes impact the flavor negatively. A bung is a rubber cork that secures the air lock to your vessel.

Bottle Brushes. These brushes are bendable, come in varying sizes to use with jugs and carboys, and are helpful for cleaning hard-to-reach spots of narrow-necked vessels.

Hydrometer. This inexpensive tool measures the alcohol by volume (ABV) of a beverage, which varies greatly depending on the sugar content. Most all of my recipes call for honey or fresh fruit—the sugar content of your ingredients may vary from mine, as different honey and fruit varieties will vary slightly in sugar content. If you're one for accuracy and knowing what you're going to get, a hydrometer is a must-have brewing tool. Noting your brew's potential ABV percentage is important for accuracy measures and because different yeast strains have different ABV tolerances. If you use a yeast strain that can only consume an ABV of 13 percent, and your hydrometer reads that your brew has the potential to ferment an ABV of 15 percent, the undigested sugars in the alcohol will result in a sweeter brew.

Tip: *Take notes!* This will help you achieve even better results as you move through your fermentation practice. Write down when you started the project, ingredient quantities, starting ABV percentages, and later ingredient additions. I write notes on tape or a tag and attach it to the fermentation vessel.

Home-brew Funnel. A home-brew funnel is the ultimate tool for fermented beverages. It has a wide opening, fits inside smaller-mouthed vessels, and sports a removable screen. Use it to strain off liquid from herbs, fruit, and starter cultures. It's useful for making beer, dairy kefir, kombucha, water kefir, and wine. These funnels are under $10 and available at your local home-brew store or online.

Racking Cane and Siphon. Use a racking cane to transfer a beverage from one vessel to another. This tool includes a plastic tip that discourages the sediment of your last batch from entering your new vessel. It's also a useful tool when bottling beverages.

Incubation Chamber. Incubation chambers are handy for the amazake, tempeh, and yogurt recipes. For years I used a cooler with either hot water directly in it or hot-water bottles surrounding the ferment. I built an incubator this year with a broken minifridge, a cheap thermostat, and a lightbulb as my heat source. Simple makeshift incubators call for more maintenance, whereas if you have the resources to build a more advanced chamber (or the money to buy one) much less maintenance is involved. I'll elaborate more on incubation on page 164.

Thermometer. A simple meat thermometer with a probe is inexpensive and will allow you to read temperature during incubation. I have graduated to an iDevices digital thermometer with two probes. It's Bluetooth compatible—this means I can program my phone to warn when the temperature is too low or too high. I love it.

Scale. A small, cheap spring scale is great. A lightweight digital scale that can read weight in pounds, ounces, and grams is even better.

Quality Control in Home Fermentation

Environment. Keep the scene clean. Quality often boils down to cleanliness and fresh ingredients. Wash your hands, wash your utensils, and rinse your produce. Sterility isn't necessary.

Temperature Stability. My ideal fermentation temperature range is 68° to 76° F, give or take. Higher temperatures will result in faster fermentation, and lower temperatures in slower fermentation. Keep temperature as stable as possible, and preferably lower than 76° F. I don't recommend temperatures over 90° F, as overly quick fermentation sometimes results in an undesirable texture, and very high heat can even be deadly to microbes. Fermented foods that require incubation, such as tempeh, are an exception and have certain heat tolerances, too. (See incubation on page 164.)

Time. Fermentation takes time—let it teach you the joys of patience. So you know what you're in for, all the recipes here note time frame. Some will ferment in less than forty-eight hours (yogurt, tempeh, water kefir), others may take weeks (many vegetables, kombucha), and a few a year or two (miso). All are worth the wait; in fact, you may find with time you develop an attachment to those ferments you've waited longest for, as they are some of the richest, most complex-flavored ferments to ever hit the palate. Great rewards come with time.

Ingredients

Dairy, Fruits, Vegetables, Legumes, Grains. Choose quality ingredients from a source you trust. Local and organic foods will contain the most desirable microflora—they're generally fresher and have been handled less. This isn't to say you can't ferment with Dumpster-dived or nonorganic ingredients, but I recommend going for quality. I also recommend you support your local farmer.

Water. Pure water can be difficult to source in the city since tap water is chlorinated. Boiling water will not diminish chlorine, but you may let water sit for a few nights and the chlorine will evaporate. I go for filtered, spring, or well water when fermenting, not because tap water won't work, but because it's best to use ingredients that are close to nature.

Additional Ingredients (Salt, Sugar, Fish Sauce). Again, stay close to nature. Unrefined, additive-free ingredients offer quality and are cost-effective. I refer to the list of ingredients on a package. Steer clear of any unrecognizable ingredients.

Salt

You may ferment with most any kind of salt. I usually go for cost-effectiveness and buy unrefined sea salt in bulk, but I'm happy to ferment with fancy Celtic sea salt on occasion. Iodized and pickling salt are not preferred choices because they have additives that might introduce unpleasant flavors or inhibit microorganisms, but based on my research they'll generally work.

Salt has many important functions, especially in vegetable fermentation. It inhibits the growth of undesirable bacteria and gives *Lactobacillus* the upper hand. In addition to being a *halophile* (salt-loving organism), *Lactobacillus* is a competitive organism—it keeps the undesirable bacteria at bay (see note on the resilience and competitiveness of *Lactobacillus* on next page). During vegetable fermentation, dry salting draws water and creates brine convenient for anaerobic fermentation. Salt also affects flavor. You can get away with using little salt if your ferment is in an anaerobic environment, below the brine. My vegetable fermentation salt spiel: if you don't like the level of saltiness before you ferment it, you probably won't like it once it's fermented.

When dry salting, I use roughly one tablespoon of salt per two to three pounds of vegetables. I start with less salt, massage, taste, and then add more salt as desired. See the salinity chart on next page. I ferment vegetables with a 2 percent brine ratio, which is roughly one and a half tablespoons per quart of water. A few of the recipes in this book call for higher salinity ratios, such as fermented burdock root on page 218.

salinity
salt brine percentages in vegetable fermentation

strength	percentage	PER QUART of WATER	
		grams of salt	tablespoons of salt
low	1%	9	½
	2%	19	1¼
medium	2.5%	24	1½
	3%	28	2
high	3.5%	33	2¼
	5%	47	3

Sister Noella Marcellino, a microbiologist and cheese expert, displayed the resiliency of *Lactobacillus* and other such beneficial bacteria in a 1985 experiment. Her study was motivated by the FDA's request that she ferment cheese in a stainless steel vat rather than a wooden barrel, with claims that the wooden barrel was more prone to undesirable bacteria growth. Marcellino made two batches of cheese—one in the FDA-approved stainless steel vat and another in her wooden barrel—and inoculated both with *E. coli*. Contrary to popular thinking, undesirable bacteria thrived in the vat while they died off in the barrel, which harbored years of beneficial bacterial growth—mostly of *Lactobacilli*—and easily outcompeted the *E. coli*.

Starter Cultures

One way to source starter cultures locally is to post a wanted ad at your local natural-grocery store or on Craigslist. Seeking out local events that focus on holistic healing or sustainable foods will likely point you toward a network of starter-culture carriers, too.

Sourdough. Make it (page 22) or visit your favorite local bakery and ask for a sample of theirs.

Koji. Koji is barley or rice inoculated with the fungus *Aspergillus oryzae*, used to make miso and amazake. You can purchase it online from rhapsodynaturalfoods.com or culturesforhealth.com. Cold Mountain koji is a widely available brand sold at most Asian grocery stores.

Dairy Kefir, Jun, and Tibicos. I've found online community marketplaces—specifically Craigslist, eBay, and Etsy—are the best sources for these starter cultures. I like to seek out communities of bacteria and yeast that have been passed down through generations so I know they will be long lasting once I integrate them into my kitchen practice. This requires a bit of research into the starter culture. If the sellers have been actively using the culture for a year or more, you can guarantee it is a well-loved and long-lasting starter culture. If they know the botanical source, it's a major plus, similar to knowing where your vegetables were grown. These age-old starter cultures come with rich stories. (You will discover more about starter cultures and their stories as you follow my journey in these pages.)

Kombucha. Purchase local kombucha from your grocery store and grow your own at home. Instructions for how to do this are on pages 73–75.

Vinegar. Purchase raw vinegar from your grocery store. Bragg apple cider vinegar is widely available at most stores. Key words for vinegar that will work for fermentation include *raw* and *with the "Mother"*—both inform you that live, active bacteria and yeast are present.

Yogurt. Mesophilic yogurts (page 215) are available at Etsy shops AnythingHealthy, Yemoos, and WellsofHealth. You can source thermophilic yogurt (page 216) from the grocery store. It isn't a given that commercial live-culture yogurt will last indefinitely, but it's good practice to start with. You can find heirloom yogurt cultures online through Craigslist, Etsy, or culturesforhealth.com.

Rhizopus oligosporus. This starter culture is a fungus used to make tempeh. You can source it from Indonesia—the brand Ragi tempeh is available on Amazon and eBay. Culturesforhealth.com and shortmountaincultures.com also sell tempeh starter.

Yeast. Yeast is immensely important to flavor when brewing wines and beers. Most recipes in these pages call for store-bought yeast, which you can purchase at a home-brew store. Wild yeast fermentation can sometimes result in off flavors and the alcohol tolerance of the yeast is unpredictable, so I generally ferment with store-bought yeast. However, wild alcohol fermentation has its perks, too—you never know what you're going to get, and if you have access to great ingredients and a good brewing environment, the results can be delectable. See beer, cider, and wine recipes for preferred yeast options, wild and store-bought.

I brew with champagne yeast varieties Lalvin EC-1118, Lalvin K1-V1116, and Red Star Premier Cuvée—all have alcohol tolerances of 16 to 18 percent and thus result in dry wine, or no residual sugar. If you prefer sweet wine you may experiment with Wyeast 4184 Sweet Mead (11 percent alcohol tolerance), which will result in 2 to 3 percent residual sugars.

Troubleshooting

Taste Along the Way. There is no harm in tasting these foods as they mature. For example, I like my sauerkraut fermented at room temperature for three weeks, but you may prefer yours fermented for one. This is part of the joy of fermenting at home!

How Much Time Does It Take? I have noted time frame, and its variance, for each recipe. Vegetable ferments and fermented beverages can vary greatly case to case.

What If My Ferment Grows a Layer of Mold? Mold, in green, blue, gray, or black, sometimes happens if your ferment juts above the brine for too long. Scrape the mold from your ferment and weight everything under the brine to discourage further mold growth.

How Long Before It Goes Bad? The short answer is—it varies. Fermented vegetables generally keep tasty for six to twelve months in the fridge, while other ferments have much shorter or longer life spans. Trust your senses. If the flavor, smell, and appearance don't appeal to you anymore, then toss it. More often the case is that your ferment is no longer tasty rather than "bad."

What Is Lacto-Fermentation? Lacto-fermentation refers to food fermentation using lactic acid bacteria, thus it applies to most all vegetable and dairy ferments. This term is popularly believed to refer to the fermentation of milk, in thinking lacto is short for lactose, the fermentable milk sugar. This, however, is not true!

Fermentation Is a Versatile and Forgiving Process. The recipes in these pages are meant to be approachable, inspire you to explore local ingredients, and encourage you to embrace creativity. Don't be afraid to substitute. Be experimental, explore, and have fun!

DREAMS & THE UNIVERSE

The only thing that makes life possible is permanent,
intolerable uncertainty; not knowing what comes next.
—Ursula K. Le Guin, *The Left Hand of Darkness*

I. In Pursuit of Myself

It's any morning at eight and I turn to the window with the best natural light in the house. It's on the west side of my communal Eugene, Oregon, home, Heart and Spoon, and I'm waking full of vivid dreams, featuring scenes from my past and flirtations with future possibilities. The room is crowded with fermentation projects—some bubbling through air locks, some hungry for their final feeding of something sweet, some ready to enjoy. The light coerces me out of bed and I move to the kitchen, with microbes on my mind.

In the kitchen Jesika starts coffee while her kids, Ash and Magnolia, scurry about. Her six-foot-four husband, Benjah, slithers through to the bathroom and back to their room. Noah raps while sautéing collard greens in a cast-iron pan. I toast homemade sourdough bread, check on the two-week-old sauerkraut, and grab miso from the fridge to spread on the sourdough. Lali makes her daily green smoothie.

Three-year-old Magnolia yells over the blender, "You make the best sauerkraut ever!" as she takes a big bite, and at least half the kraut topples from her toast. A few more people will file into the kitchen an hour or two later for their routines. I've never been more content than with this mix of creative chaos and social harmony in my community kitchen.

Fermentation, like my communal home, is a testament to how a community's unique parts work together to create something even greater. After decades of meticulously hygienic life in urban America (Houston, Philadelphia, New York City), I longed for sowed fields, sunsets by the river, and trees bearing fruit—a life where edible microbes presented themselves daily. Eugene satisfied my craving, from the mushrooms of the forest floor to homegrown cabbage to the apple, cherry, and plum trees that line the city streets. The Willamette River bicycle and path trail, also known as the Summer Highway, contributes to the magic that is Eugene. I found a family of friends there—a community—and since then my life path has taken an unpredictable route.

Food was never a political statement before I discovered fermentation; food was confusing. I didn't hail from cultures that valued food or had any kind of traditional cuisine. Early Dallas, Texas, memories include Welch's grape juice, smuggled half sticks of butter, and crying over well-done rosemary-saturated steak. I turned vegetarian at seven, received my first cookbook at nine, became independent in the kitchen by middle school in Houston, and at nineteen cooked in my own kitchen.

A year before autonomous kitchen life, I shared a modest dorm room with a sorority girl in Shreveport, Louisiana. I barely got by foodwise without refrigeration. I didn't yet have the tools to keep the sorority sisters at bay (kimchi, anyone?). Canned salmon became my mainstay protein; I moved to a pescatarian diet. The lifestyle at my private southern Methodist college didn't suit my tastes, so I jumped into an exchange program in Denmark. There I discovered pickled herring and rye sourdough bread from locals, as well as traditional miso soup and how to make perfect sushi rice from fellow exchange students. I made frog-leg pasta with a Slavic housemate. Cultural mingling broadened my palate and deepened my appreciation for food. When in 2005 my one-year visa expired, I felt a little lost, a little hungry— so I moved back to my more diverse, foodcentric Houston.

I worked evenings as a hostess at a Spanish tapas restaurant near Rice University and part-time for a petroleum geologist, copying archaeological logs at a downtown library. The Museum of Fine Arts, Houston, invited me as a photography student, and I continued my very ambivalent studies at the University of Houston, leaping from physics to linguistics to political science. I kept busy and traveled mostly by bike, often swinging through the Little Vietnam of my teenhood for bánh mì sandwiches. On special occasions, I would drive to the west side of town for South Indian food—curries, biryanis, and tandooris: a plethora of vegetarian spice and bright sticky sweets. Houston's Chinatown, in the far west of town, boasted a mile radius of authentic Szechuan cuisine. I traveled the world through food in my hometown, yet I was right back where I had started.

Not long after, on a trip to New York City, I discovered nearby Philadelphia— the charming cobblestone street leading to Benjamin Franklin's printing press, its Polish and Italian markets, and its visual and historical richness had me smitten. That was my last Houston summer. I left my studies, jobs, and friends for the City of Brotherly Love in 2008. It was a move toward the unknown, which always excites me even more than the specific qualities of a place—I want adventure. I want to be constantly surprised and inspired.

My Philadelphia apartment was at the intersection of Little Puerto Rico, a large housing project, and hip Northern Liberties. I accepted the first job I was offered: warehouse receiver for an independent entertainment company, Theater of the Living Arts. While my warehouse comrades lived on Philly cheesesteaks and cheese fries (secret ingredient: Cheez Whiz), I was relishing Mexican tacos with fresh Oaxacan cheese, Ethiopian injera, and an array of fish sauces from Spring Garden Market—the best cheap Asian food market in town and a five-minute walk from the warehouse.

A few years into Philadelphia I answered a call from my sister in Brooklyn. She asked me to move in with her, "Six month, tops," I said. I sold my belongings and moved into her Bedford-Stuyvesant efficiency. The Metropolitan Museum of Art, three Chinatowns, Coney Island's boardwalk, and the Brooklyn Bridge were all bike rides away. The city was rolling with cultural diversity and legendary nostalgia. Each neighborhood had its own flavors and unique character to explore. I walked most of Philadelphia in a few years. New York City would take decades.

Brooklyn had plenty of warehouses with seasonal work openings, and a retailer in South Brooklyn kept me on after a seasonal Christmas gig. It solidified Brooklyn as my new home. In time I was working in a sixth-floor Manhattan office, coordinating shipments with third-party warehouses in New Jersey. Shabby living situations and hour-long commutes became a thing of the past. I moved to Prospect Heights, then the Caribbean neighborhood of Brooklyn. The scent of roti wraps drifted into my apartment from above, while the sweet smell of pot and Trinidadian tobacco seeped up from below. The Brooklyn Museum was at the end of my avenue and I'd loop through Prospect Park by bike regularly. Between loving the city and working sixty-hour weeks, though, I neglected my carefully curated kitchen. It didn't help that I had no community of food lovers to share meals with.

The day in, day out of an office job offered stability, but blotted out everyday mystery. I was living a legit, you've-made-it life, subscribing to cultural norms and expectations because I didn't know how else to survive. I was struggling to find an identity that would satisfy my values. I craved adventure, human connection, and chance. I wanted new experiences in new places, accompanied by libations and good food.

Occupy Wall Street swept through the city in September 2011 and ignited a conversation that had long been neglected. In advocating for workers' rights, greater banking regulation, and above all income equality, the movement gave voice to the 99 percent of Americans currently shut out of the political system. A revolution was happening in Manhattan's financial district, a twenty-five-minute walk from my office. I visited Zuccotti Park weekly until it was cleared out by law enforcement two months later. The movement believed in, and some protesters lived by, values that spoke to me. It gave me hope after years of pushing, pulling, and fighting to feel comfortable in my own skin.

Fermentation fell into my lap shortly after Occupy set up in Zuccotti Park. My Brooklyn kitchen became a playground while the protest endured in the background. I split my time between deciding my next move, Occupy meetings in Brooklyn, and picnicking at Prospect Park. Then I met the man who'd become my first fermentation teacher. I was at the Prospect Park farmers' market when a stranger near the dairy booth noticed the Texas-silhouette necklace I was wearing. "Are you from Texas?" he asked.

His name was Giles. We had shared connections in Houston, where he had lived for a stint. He was a painter and invited me to visit his studio. We bonded quickly over art, pickles, and whiskey.

That October I made my first sauerkraut with him. He insisted I had to learn. Giles knew I loved fermented foods, claimed it was easy, and said I would love the process. All were true.

I'd always believed fermentation to be out of reach, because I couldn't afford to take a class, and then because I didn't have time for my kitchen. An earlier introduction to water kefir had left me perplexed. The recipe called for baking soda, molasses, and filtered water (in the following pages you'll find water kefir is actually much more flexible). Under Giles's guidance fermentation didn't require fancy kitchen tools. There was nothing strict about sauerkraut.

Sauerkraut was simple and versatile and fascinating. It made me feel more in tune with a greater community (the bacterial kind). As days passed and I watched the dark red and green cabbage transform to magenta and effervesce, I realized the invisible life forces working to predigest the cabbage. After seven days I tasted the kraut and was amazed by the unique sour flavor. It tasted better when I made it myself. It was also far more rewarding.

I failed at reviving the water kefir grains given to me, but I soon after mastered kombucha when I received a "mother" culture. I researched traditional kimchi recipes online and made a delicious, spicy Korean ferment on my first try. My small Brooklyn kitchen quickly filled with gallon jars of fermenting carrots, cucumbers, radishes, and more. Within six months I moved to Oregon to pursue my love of all things microbial—the rich soil and its constant harvest and the tangy gifts the harvest would bring.

In Oregon I plunged into uncertainty, trusting it would be better than the life I'd previously carved out. My first home was Alpha Farm, an intentional community fifty miles west of Eugene in the Siuslaw National Forest. Beyond the reach of cell towers and the Internet, it was home to a rotating set of characters, with 280 acres of woodland, salmon spawning grounds, and an owl refuge.

I had visited Alpha Farm the winter before and thought it was a perfect post–New York destination. Upon my arrival with Franklin, my slate-gray city cat, I cried. The forty-five-minute drive through immense receptionless forest was intense. I was overjoyed to free myself from my corporate routine but afraid to move into the new identity. I embraced it, though, eager for a homegrown self-sufficiency that the constant buzz of the city could never teach. I grew vegetables, fermented and canned them as they ripened, and managed the dinner menu for the community's restaurant, Alpha-Bit, in a nearby coastal town.

Though I was attracted to communal living, I didn't fully realize the challenges of the lifestyle, too. Alpha's model allowed us to work on the farm in exchange for residency. There was a discrepancy in work ethic among the residents, though, and there was little supervision. The model attracted rebels by the handful, all with unique baggage. (I was a renegade from city life with my own issues—I landed with a hint of snobbery, partly etched into me by my city-girl upbringing and partly learned in New York, that set me apart from most newcomers.) The biggest underlying problem was that people could get away with staying for free, without working in exchange for residency. This resulted in intense drama. Community doesn't work unless there's mutual commitment and understanding among all fellow communards.

I left Alpha but stayed in the Siuslaw National Forest, living in my tent, my 1989 Toyota station wagon, and a farmer's log cabin, helping with harvests in exchange for food to ferment through November. Though I was highly productive that fall— cases of wine and cider, kombucha, gallon upon gallon of kimchi and sauerkraut—I was still seeking a community that would embrace my fermentations and inspire me to pursue my lifework.

Oregon Coast crab claw

II. The Dream

At Heart and Spoon Community, in Eugene, I realized the importance of living and working out my dreams rather than flying through them. I'd spent a decade hopping from city to city, with such impulsive wanderlust that I'd neglected any long-term goals. The owners of the house and founders of the community—Jesika, Benjah, Lali—became my people, along with the other five dwellers then (Aaron, Ashley, Noah, Maggie, and Ash).

Heart and Spoon grew out of a love for two things: food and human service. The founders met while doing relief work in New Orleans after Hurricane Katrina, serving food to survivors and volunteers—every day, all day—for nine months. They opened a café and named it the Made With Love Café. After, they packed up together and decided to relocate to start an intentional community.

It was no mystery why I fit in: the most consistent bonding ritual at Heart and Spoon is its nightly communal meal. My housemates were activists plugged into social health care, saving forests, and do-it-yourself daily living, and from them I learned the importance of activism as a tool for changing the world. They inspired me to discover my own form of activism in my passion for growing and fermenting food.

I kept a regular fermentation routine in my household. In addition to monthly batches of sauerkraut, I learned to care for a sourdough starter and bake bread twice a week. My starter thrived when I baked often, which taught me to appreciate the connection between feeding the community of bacteria and yeast in my starter and feeding my community of friends. Both brought powerful sustenance and immeasurable joy.

Sourdough
how to build a community of bacteria and yeast

Experiment with whole milk or even sauerkraut brine for a unique flavor experience.

I love using rye flour for my starters. Brown rice flour is a great gluten-free option.

Equal parts flour and water

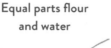

Add organic grapes or raisins to jump-start fermentation.

Store in a warm place and stir vigorously once a day for five to seven days until sourdough shows signs of life (growth and bubbles). Feed sourdough equal parts flour and water for a few more days to further activate.

The jar should be breathable. Cover it with a cloth and rubber band or plastic Ball-jar lid.

Use ½ cup of sourdough starter in place of instant yeast in any recipe and allow more time for the rise.

When not in use, store your starter in the fridge. Pour half out and refresh it with flour and water weekly. Otherwise, refresh daily and use often. Like all communities, sourdough starters require commitment, time, and love.

Seven months after arriving I had a dream featuring glass jars filled to the brim with microbe-dense foods and a converted school bus turned fermentation lab. I was its driver. The dream visited three nights in a row. Recurring themes included roving, generosity, curiosity, community, and the barter economy. Recurring scenes: me welcoming fellow food lovers onto the bus, me sharing my most recent wild wines, and me surrendering to the mercy of the road. The dream was questionable, but I fell for it: my subconscious beckoned me to take to the road. I was to spread the gospel of fermented foods, reinvigorate the open-mindedness of time past, challenge myself, and revolutionize the DIY food movement.

During my first year in Oregon, I lived off the meager proceeds of my bootleggings (hooch, sauerkraut, kimchi). I sold apples for farmers and had occasional illustration gigs. The plan was to stay inspired and steadily create, but I needed to work toward something that would financially sustain me, too. I wrote a business plan for a fermented-foods company, but the process was daunting, especially after crafting spreadsheets for start-up money. At the end of the day, I wanted to brew new herbal meads, process our excess veggies to kraut-chi, and bake a loaf of sourdough—all simply for the joy of kitchen-play and cultivating an appreciation for fermentation among my greater community. Fermentation was my tool for artistic expression.

Now I was dreaming about a lifestyle, an art project, and a way to pollinate people's minds nationwide—all as part of a unique business plan, too. The idea of driving a bus was laughable, and scary. I would need to get organized if I wanted people to take me seriously. The other scary part was how my friends would react—presumably with great skepticism at the grandness of it all.

At our monthly Heart and Spoon Community meeting I told everyone about my plan. Assuming I needed money, several housemates offered to buy the rest of my mead and sauerkraut. I explained I wasn't moving into a bus to save money—I was moving into a bus to build a nationwide fermentation community. Though it seemed wildly challenging, and perhaps a bit jarring to my communards, the project was inspired by the communal intentions at our home.

III. Onward

In those first urgent postdream weeks, I put the dream to paper—made a plan—and named it Fermentation on Wheels. My first mission statement reads strong and true to what it is today:

> Fermentation on Wheels is a year-long tour of farms and cities across the United States, in which we will work at farms in exchange for food and educational resources, and visit cities to hold free workshops on fermentation methods using locally harvested foods. By traveling the country, visiting farmers and connecting people to their food source, we hope to make a powerful statement and encourage the importance of strong, sustainable food practices and values.

I needed just one thing to get my journey off the ground: funding. (My housemates had that right.) I launched a Kickstarter campaign and in the run-up worked night shifts at a local grocery store. I used my spare time to refine the project plan, illustrate a logo, and make a film.

I also organized fermentation workshops, started a *Fermentation on Wheels* blog, and spent the last of my savings—$6,000—on a vintage bus. My friends were impressed with my optimism. Fermentation on Wheels was literally all I had to my name.

The 1986 International Harvester S-1800 Series bus was converted in 1991, complete with plumbing, propane, and electric. The bedroom housed a shower, toilet, and sink, all unused in the past decade. The kitchen was equipped with a sink and three-burner gas stove. A propane furnace, the sole heat source, sat between the kitchen and the driver's seat. It wasn't perfect but it was enough.

Two weeks into the campaign my younger brother, Seth, flew from Boston to Eugene to help me move into the bus before a family vacation on the Olympic Peninsula. Though both my siblings knew of my impending journey, I had yet to tell my parents. We expected they'd have minor breakdowns. Days later Seth and I took off for Washington State—the last trip in my station wagon. We met our parents and big sister, Edith, at a brewery in Seattle. I wasn't sure how to bring it up, so I did it casually.

"How was Eugene?" Dad asked. "What have you two been up to?"

Seth looked to me, and I responded, "Seth's been helping me prepare for a journey. I'll be teaching fermentation around the country out of a converted bus for a year. I got fully moved in late last night."

Dad said, "Hmm, okay."

Mom said, "Oh, honey. That's so cool!" Unsure what else to say.

We spent a week together and not much was exchanged on the topic after that. Finally, at the end of the week, my dad asked, "So what are you going to do when you get home? Sell apples?"

I wasn't surprised. "Remember, Seth helped me move into my bus," I replied. "I'm two weeks into a Kickstarter campaign. I'm moving to a farm tomorrow to finish the build-out."

"Wait. You actually bought a bus?" Dad asked.

My parents are well aware of my tendency to go against the grain, and I felt in their reactions they worried I was taking it too far this time. I expected it—it was why I broke the news to them *after* I bought the bus. Edith and Seth, on the other hand, seemed to fully accept the tour was a long-awaited calling.

Though Fermentation on Wheels didn't capture my parents' hearts, my campaign reached thousands of people and $11,000 in support. The momentum was encouraging, but the funds fell short of my $24,000 goal, which meant I would receive none of the funds. I would clearly need to get scrappy and seek donations if I wanted to stick to my departure date of October 2013.

Mid-September marked a strenuous monthlong countdown. I built a Fermentation on Wheels website and a PayPal donation site. Autumn brought abundant fruits and vegetables, so I fermented by the gallon, trading finished ferments for building materials while living at Rivers Turn Farm in Coburg, Oregon.

The farm was nestled in an elbow of the Willamette River north of Eugene. John Sundquist, the owner and farmer, has been a leader in Lane County's sustainable-agriculture movement since 1983. During my stay he held a celebration marking twenty years of the first Lane County spray moratorium. His friends came from all corners of the county, and a bluegrass band played. I invited people on the bus for a blackberry-mead workshop. I danced with forest defenders, drank with farmers, and chatted with progressive politicians.

Among the interesting characters I met was a pipe-smoking carpenter named Daniel Temple.

"Mind if I get a tour of your bus?" he asked. "I love skoolies."

"Skoolies?" I asked.

"A skoolie is a school bus converted to serve a live-in or working purpose. You can refer to the people who dwell in them as skoolies, too. There's a whole network of us—even online."

"Wait, so you're a skoolie?"

"My carpentry workshop is in an old school bus. I built it out myself. So, yeah, I'm more or less a skoolie."

Daniel blew my mind; I felt as if I were being let into a secret club, a holy baptism of sorts. I welcomed him onto the bus, a bit intimidated by a bus-converting connoisseur. To that point, it hadn't changed much, save for a wood-burning stove I'd installed a few weeks before. Lali, cofounder of Heart and Spoon and seamstress, had made curtains out of thrifted fabric for the windows.

It was a cozy home. The kitchen was rather functional: the plumbing didn't work but I had propane. A bookshelf, facing in the driver's direction, held books okay when the bus was stopped, but once in motion they flew forward. Opposite the kitchenette, bookshelf, and heater were three carboys and eight crocks filled with fermenting beverages and vegetables. The ferments were fitted in nooks among the legs of two chairs and a drawing table.

Daniel said, "You aren't really planning on driving around the country with these glass carboys on the floor, are you?"

"Well, it isn't ideal, but I have to work with what I've got. Eventually something will manifest."

"Do you at least have a vision? This is suicide."

I described a two-tier fermentation station to hold my five-gallon carboys and one-gallon jugs in the bottom shelf while the second shelf would house my crocks. It would span about six feet along the wall of the bus and accommodate all of my ferments.

"Good, I can work with that," Daniel said. "I think your project is really cool, and I like helping people, so I'm going to help you make this happen."

"Really? What do you want for it?"

"I want to see you live this out."

Two days later Daniel came back to the farm with three sheets of six-by-two-foot birch plywood, four birch legs, a gorgeous six-by-two-foot, two-inch-thick maple-wood block, and hardware. He made a list of the day's activities. We traced each of my vessels on the plywood, carved them out with a jigsaw, and sanded the maple piece for almost eight hours. The maple had been salvaged from Daniel's elementary school. He had been saving it for a worthwhile project.

It was Sunday. "Okay now, make 'er pretty. Sand down all the grit and find a paint color that pleases you," he said when he left.

It was the last week of September, inching into October. I spent it sanding and painting my fermentation station, making it pretty. Daniel came back Saturday and helped install the station, securing it with six-inch-long screws through the bottom of the bus. He secured it to the wall at three pivot points. My carboys, crocks, and Ball jars fit snugly into their new home.

Some people have referred to it as the brain, and some have referred to it as the heart, but clearly the station is the gut of the bus. And it is one diverse, robust, well-populated gut.

I wasn't scared of much, but traveling solo made me uneasy. Tyler Pell, Noah's best friend from college, showed interest in joining my trip. I gladly accepted him as my first long-term travel companion. He would join me in Grants Pass, 130 miles south of Eugene.

I would also need a bicycle. I found my match—a turquoise 1980s Peugeot mountain bike. Next I bought a four-bike rack on Craigslist in the hopes it would bring company. During that last stationary week I kept reminding myself, "You'll meet your people. You won't be alone."

Logistically, things were coming along. I raised just short of $7,000 in donations. It wasn't close to what I would need for the entire journey, but it would get me started. My last step was passing my Oregon driver's test. Having failed twice, I finally passed the day before my departure.

I organized a going-away potluck with the bus parked in front of Heart and

Spoon that night. We strung lights from the house to the bus, along the terraced front yard of wisteria, ferns, mint, and lemon balm. Crocks full of kimchis and sauerkrauts and plates of fancy cheeses and crackers covered the fermentation station. An unexpected guest, Guisepi, brought his Free Tea Party Bus and served hot tea. A bluegrass band named Biscuits and Gravy Costume Party played a set. Communards, neighbors, and friends from my year in Eugene filled the bus. It felt cozy and genuine. The party is a distant, bittersweet memory now.

LIFE IS
A POTLUCK

Being brave doesn't mean being unafraid. It means being afraid
and doing it anyway. —Paul Loeb, *Soul of a Citizen*

I. Oregon Fermentations

Heart and Spoon felt far away when I woke the next morning. And by eight it was time to head south for my first stop: Grants Pass, Oregon, where I would meet Tyler Pell and his family.

I filled up at SeQuential Biofuels, a gas station chain in Eugene with biodiesel at the pump and kombucha on tap. I purchased both, knowing I would soon leave such conveniences behind. I was distracted, already missing Eugene, and I swiped a stop sign on the sharp curve out of the gas station. The kitchen's cupboard doors flew open and I heard a crash.

At the first rest stop, roughly thirty miles down Interstate 5, I investigated the damage—a broken jar of molasses—and cleaned it up. I looked up at the cupboard, poorly constructed for travel, then at the congealed molasses on the carpet, then back at my driver's seat. Had there been a lesson, I wasn't aware of it yet. Driving the bus was difficult. I prayed for a swift learning curve.

Grants Pass is a town surrounded by mountains. I parked in front of Tyler's parents' home and was warmly welcomed with halibut dinner. His family charmed me immediately with kitchen talk and enthusiasm over the bus. Tyler's parents own a small grocer in Grants Pass called Sunshine Natural Foods, where they sell homemade ferments and have a passion for local food. I wasn't sure what to expect, but it became apparent Tyler was passionate about food and fermentation.

The next day we visited the Grants Pass Growers Market with a stack of Fermentation on Wheels flyers. At a farm stand where a young woman and an older man were selling vegetables, I feasted my eyes on daikon radishes. I purchased an armful and asked, "Do you like kimchi? I'm going to ferment these radishes. I have a project called Fermentation on Wheels. Maybe you'd be interested?" I handed the flyer to them. "We're looking for farms to work on and teach fermentation while we're at it. You wouldn't happen to be interested . . . ?"

The young woman turned to the older man, obviously the farmer, and pleaded, "Oh, please, Steve, can they come to the farm?" He agreed to it.

A day later Tyler and I made our way to Dancing Bear Farm, eighteen acres nestled in the Applegate Valley of southern Oregon farmed and owned by Steve and Patricia Florin.

The Florins' livelihood depends on the ancient yet increasingly vital practice of seed saving. Their thirty-plus seed contracts reach wholesalers and retailers as far away as Maine and Virginia; the seeds grown on Dancing Bear Farm feed people all over the continent.

Their daikon-radish field was overgrown. The daikons themselves each grew three to five feet in size. Though Steve and Leda, the farm intern, had brought several bushels to the Grants Pass market, the main function of the daikon crop was to provide cover and improve root growth for subsequent crops. Planting cover crop is an old practice common in organic farming today. Every fall I find farmers who gladly offer twenty pounds or more, out of the thousands of pounds they'll eventually till under, in exchange for daikon in delicious fermented, tangy form.

Cubed-Radish Kimchi

YIELDS 1 GALLON, 3–6 WEEKS

Cubed-radish kimchi is also known as kkakdugi and is a traditional kimchi variety in Korea. It has a crunchy texture and is slightly sweet.

INGREDIENTS
6 lbs daikon
1 leek
¼ cup salt
½ gallon water

INGREDIENTS FOR PASTE
6 cloves garlic
2 inches ginger

1 medium shallot
2 tbsp chili powder or fresh chili peppers
2 tbsp fish sauce or tamari

MATERIALS
Gallon glass jar or crock
Blender
Weight and cover

PROCESS
1. Chop daikon radishes in quarters, then cut into cubes; chop the leeks, too. Place the chopped vegetables in large bowl.

2. Combine the salt and water in a half-gallon container to make brine (3 percent salinity), then pour the brine over the vegetables in large bowl. Submerge the vegetables in brine using a large plate with something heavy on top.

3. Allow vegetables to soak for 6 hours or overnight. In the meantime, make the paste for your kimchi.

4. Peel garlic, ginger, and shallot and roughly chop into smaller pieces. Toss them into your blender bowl. Add chili powder or fresh peppers and fish sauce or tamari. Blend the ingredients and put aside until your vegetables are done soaking.

5. After the soak is done, strain brine from vegetables. Add the paste to your veggies in the large bowl, thoroughly covering them with the spicy goodness. You can use your hands, but you may want to use a large utensil to protect them from the hot peppers.

6. Pack the spicy vegetables into a glass gallon jar or ceramic crock until brine comes forth and the vegetables are completely submerged. Use a weight to keep vegetables under the brine, cover with a cloth, and store at room temperature.

7. Wait a week and taste the kimchi—it should be mildly tangy. Let it ferment for up to 6 weeks for maximum tanginess. Taste throughout the duration of fermentation and keep at room temperature until it reaches desired flavor. I recommend fermenting for at least 3 weeks.

8. Keep in cold storage when it's reached desired flavor and enjoy for 6 months, 12 months, or even a few years. Let your senses serve as your guide.

Tip: I like to triple the recipe for kimchi paste and store extra in the fridge for future kimchi and other ferments.

II. Mendocino Milestones

We parted with Oregon after our stay at Dancing Bear Farm, moving on to the Golden State. Our next stop would be the Dark Carnival in Boonville, but first we drove to Garberville, a small town off Highway 101, to meet with my forest-defender friends Erin and Aaron, also Heart and Spoon Community members. They had good, clean work, helping with a building project at a homestead, and could take one more person for the job. I decided I'd work for fuel money while Tyler camped out with the bus and cared for Franklin.

The detour to Garberville hugged the Trinity River, from Redding to Eureka. Though the scenery was epic, I received my first dose of road rage. My commitment to driving a clunky, slow, oversize vehicle meant accepting I would often infuriate other drivers, especially when I chose mountainous, two-lane winding roads. I knew then there are no simple detours in a forty-foot-long vintage bus.

We spent the night in Arcata, California, a few blocks from North Coast Co-op. It quickly became regular in our travels to park the bus nearby, sometimes even in front of, a food co-op or natural-grocery store. In our newfound primitive, roving lifestyle it was especially important to secure parking spots within walking distance of places that sold real food, had a toilet, and had a café with an Internet connection.

The next day, midmorning, we arrived in Garberville after a crunchy first driving experience for Tyler. The bus then sported a large dent on the lower right side, making the firewood storage inaccessible. Aaron and Erin met us at the local coffee shop, and at second glance Erin exclaimed, "T-Pell! You're on the fermentation bus, too?!"

"Hey, Girl Erin, hey, Boy Aaron," Tyler said, as they embraced.

"Ah, you two know Tyler?" I asked, surprised.

"Yeah, of course we know T-Pell!" Erin responded.

"Well, maybe he can join you for the workweek while I head down to Boonville and prep for the carnival. Are you planning to head down for it?" I asked.

"Yes, definitely! We'll come down for the rejoin!" Erin assured me.

"Perfect!"

The four of us walked back to the bus for Tyler's belongings, exchanged hugs, and agreed to see each other in a week.

I began my first switchback drive solo. That morning I dropped my phone exiting the bus and the screen cracked. Against all urges to be irresponsible and go on without a phone, I stopped in Ukiah and bought a cheap replacement. For years I had neglected mundane societal norms (insurance, Internet, being accessible by phone). I forced myself to stay on top of these things as much as possible now, for the sake of Fermentation on Wheels. My new way of being in the world would pose a special type of split identity, in which I alternated between going with the flow and depending on hard logistics. Both were requirements in making sure things ran smoothly.

New phone in hand, I made my way to Highway 253. It was getting dark and I approached what looked like a steep incline, though I couldn't make out how steep. I knew Boonville was only twenty miles west of Ukiah, and I pushed forward, jagged rock to the right of my narrow lane and a steep drop to the left. The bus chugged upward for half an hour before finally reaching the top. From there it would be a slow, brake-clenching descent into the valley town of Boonville below.

Half an hour later I crawled along an empty main street, toward the carnival site, where two organizers, Jeremy and Brooke, greeted me with a glass of home-brewed cider from a freshly tapped keg. Brooke was a town fixture, owner of Bite Hard Apple Cider and the son of the Boonville Hotel's owner. Jeremy was a local musician, carpenter, and close friend of a communard at Heart and Spoon Community, which was how I connected with the carnival crew.

The next day work began for those building out the carnival—there would be a haunted house, games, and a band stage. I got down to perfecting my theme: the Post-Apocalypse Bus. The inspiration had come to me weeks before, in my enthusiasm for self-sufficiency. I hoped the glories of less-is-more living and loving fermentation would shine through in costume.

Inspired by an apocalypse-themed issue of *Lucky Peach* magazine—which featured articles on the extinction of seafood, degradation of soil, cooking for zombies, and fermenting into the future—I wrote a narrative for the apocalypse I had been thrown into and made a sign for all carnival-goers to see:

> It is year 2023 and the apocalypse has dawned. Zombies Crazy Nico and Seth the Punk infiltrated our foods with micro–organism WHATABURGER, transforming most all the human race into environment–hating zombies.
>
> Insects are the mainstay protein, while most all plant and animal life is a thing of the past. Our bus is home to the company of a select few hard–core survivalists. We hope you'll enjoy our survivalist library, a very special exhibit of rare items we've collected since before the apocalypse, some whopping bargains, and limited edition ferments to adorn your brats with. You're on your own from here on out!
>
> —FoW

In the days before the carnival, I received help from several volunteers. Steve, the maintenance supervisor at the Boonville Hotel, took interest in the bus and helped me with my electric, teaching me the ins and outs of my water pump and trucker radio. We became quick friends. After discovering the large dent in my side storage, he helped me unscrew the door and smoothed the dent out with a sledgehammer before placing it back on.

Other projects through the week: painting FERMENTATION ON WHEELS onto a large wooden sign and strapping it to the bus; attaching a vintage outdoor lamp to a wooden pole over a makeshift shelf holding a week's worth of compost in a glass gallon jar, with beet juice poured over the contents, labeled HOLY COMPOST. Best of all, Jeremy helped build a bench that converted into a bed for traveling companions. Tyler would be stoked.

Aaron, Erin, and Tyler arrived the morning of the carnival, smelling like body odor and sawdust, and rushed to line up at the showers. Brooke set up the town's community apple press in front of the bus, accompanied by a few hundred pounds of fallen fruit we'd gleaned during the week at his uncle's orchard. I served the freshly pressed, sweet apple juice to kids. I agreed to do the pressing and serving, given that I could take the leftover juice on the road for later fermentation.

At dark I moved into the bus, offering sauerkraut and kimchi for people's brat-wursts, one ticket per serving. In addition to fermented samplings, which sold out by the night's end, the bus featured a prepare-for-the-future library, an exhibit of extinct vegetables and fruits, vintage photographs to peruse, dusty wine bottles, a scary stuffed bus driver, and whopping deals on soon-to-be-extinct items such as blackberry juice and olive oil.

I was light-headed from a cider-constant cup. Carnival-goers walked in and out at will—sometimes to dress their brats with sauerkraut and kimchi, other times to ask fermentation questions, and then most of all to sit and soak in the bus vibes and chat. The tips were good. They would be enough to fill my tank through San Francisco. After the carnival we made way to the after-party for all-night bluegrass, more cider, and sleeping on the floor.

The next morning Aaron, Erin, Tyler, and I shared brunch at a local restaurant. An enthusiastic man approached our table and said, "Great to see you guys this morning! Don't forget to join us down the street for yoga at one!" None of us re-membered him, though clearly we'd met the night before. The carnival was the first of many events where I would encounter more faces than I could possibly remember. "Cool," I said. "See you then!"

We said our final good-byes to Erin and Aaron. Tyler and I headed back to the bus to clean up the post-apocalypse remnants and prepare for our journey farther south. Our next event, a kimchi-and-sourdough workshop in San Francisco, was still weeks away. I stopped by the yoga studio, where I spotted the enthusiastic man from earlier. Our eyes met and he exclaimed, "I figured out what I can trade for your sauerkraut!"

Apparently we'd discussed a barter of some sort, so I responded, "Oh, nice. What's that?"

"Garlic. I grew tons of garlic this year."

"Wonderful—I can always use garlic."

"Why don't you bring your bus to my farm for a few days? My wife and kids would be thrilled to have you. Here's my info." He wrote *Roger & Ren* on a scrap of paper with their number below.

"Great. I'll come tomorrow. I have one more in my company, too."

"Sounds great."

We entered the yoga classroom. My mind was clear and I felt confident, happy.

Boonville had been our longest stay in one spot since leaving Eugene. I had a system now, though I wouldn't call it entirely efficient, and I'd learned a few things. For one, I got rid of the kitchen bookshelf, which faced the driver's seat and sent a sea of books flying to the floor each time I hit the brakes. I sold a clunky propane heater that was attached to the wall and replaced it with a high-lipped shelf for more kitchen goods. I attached hooks and screw eyes to keep the pantry doors secure and used bungee cords to secure the kitchen drawers.

Steve, the maintenance guy, visited the bus to say good-bye. He walked me through the bus's electric and plumbing once again. With Steve's help, I gained a better understanding of the livability of my bus. He wired my water pump to the bus battery, so I could wash dishes off-grid, too. I was grateful, but also more aware of how unprepared I was for the journey.

I asked him, "Do you think I can actually pull this off?"

"It's going to be really hard. Traveling the entire country for a year in this old thing is a little crazy. Call me anytime, though. I'll be here for you."

We forged a connection. He understood that my excitement to evangelize fermentation and live a little more freely was accompanied by a real and reasonable fear. Driving and maintaining the bus involved great risk. From the beginning I embraced and understood that my choices came with the territory, and that spreading the word—whether with post-apocalyptic imagery or teaching farmers how to ferment daikon radishes—was worth the challenges my journey brought, too.

As I made final preparations to leave—attaching bikes to the bus, checking my oil—I heard Jeremy call out in the distance.

"Leaving already?"

"Yep, I'm heading to Roger and Ren's farm."

"You know what they farm, right?"

"Sure I do—garlic?"

"Not exactly. More like marijuana."

Roger and Ren were sweet. And their farm literally fell in my lap (through a trade I still don't remember). Roger asked his twelve-year-old daughter to show me the garden. She introduced the fruit trees, greens, and alliums. I lifted her up to reach a few ripe figs and we wolfed them down.

Past the garden was a bigger garden, in two greenhouses each the size of a mansion. Roger's daughter smiled and trailed off knowingly, and Roger and Ren reappeared to give me a tour. (One of their proud claims for the year was that the kids hadn't been sent home once from school for smelling like marijuana.) Each plant was enormous, and there were hundreds, at least, between the two greenhouses. I learned about the legalities of pot distribution, lots of plant-strain names I will never retain, and that the trimming crew appreciated the farm's family-friendly environment.

The property backed up to Hendy State Park, known for its old-growth redwoods. In addition to snacking in the garden, the kids spent hours in the woods playing games (such as dressing as fairies and gnomes to hide out in recently discovered tree kingdoms). It was a contrast from the entrance of their farm, though, with two fifty-foot walls of solar panels and a long lineup on the front porch of weed plants, ready to be trimmed.

During their pot-circle moments, after breakfast, lunch, and dinner, Roger would take a freshly rolled joint, drag it below his nose with a deep inhale as a cue, then pass it for everyone else to do the same. Then they'd play a game of guess-the-strain.

"Coconut!"

"No, no—passion fruit!"

"You're on the right track . . . it's tropical . . ."

"Mango?"

"Pineapple," Roger would reveal.

I'm not usually one to partake, but the first time I stood to witness the circle, I thought I might take a hit. (I kept telling myself I should at least try it, since I was at a pot farm.) The second time, I took one hit of the mega-potent pot and quickly retreated to the comfort of my bus. Pot was never a social medicine for me.

Tyler and I stayed three nights. I was inspired by Roger and Ren's fabulous solar array. The morning we departed, I decided we should visit the Solar Living Institute in Hopland, California, which I had noticed on a tourist map in Boonville a week before. It was unlikely we would actually install a solar system, but I was curious.

We arrived on a perfect California day. It was November but the sun was bright and we wore light sweaters. I remembered the previous November in Eugene—constant rainfall, muddy boots, sunless days—and felt grateful for California and being on the road.

The institute was designed like a museum and sprinkled with plaques offering statistics on the awesomeness of solar and sustainable living. (A sign in the bathroom read TWO GALLONS OF WATER IS USED EACH TIME YOU FLUSH A TOILET.) There was a store filled with solar-system parts, maximum-compatibility solar appliances, and locally crafted goods. I soon found myself at the information desk, where I began a long conversation with the solar salesman, Eric.

"I've been looking into solar systems and am struggling with where to begin," I told him, diving right in. "I have a largish home on wheels. I don't need an immense amount of power, but starting out, I'd like enough to operate my lights and charge my computer."

"Well," Eric replied, "there are many components involved here, and they're all important, but you can spend less if you decide to operate with less wattage, which would mean a more affordable charge controller. Say, something with 540-watt capacity."

I tried to follow along but after what seemed like an hour of wattage talk, he sensed I'd gotten lost. "Is the vehicle here? I'll take a look at it if it is."

We walked to the bus and I unlocked the battery compartment. I pulled out the rusty heavy battery tray, where my two twelve-volt marine batteries sat—with an empty space next to them.

"You have room for another battery," Eric said. "That's a good place to start.

Would you like to take part in a class this weekend?" He proposed a deal. I would buy materials, he and the class attendees would install the system at half price, and I could sit in free of charge.

Without hesitation I responded, "Yeah. Let's do it."

It was Wednesday and the class was three days away. Eric guided me to a corner of the parking lot with a plug-in, where we could power the bus via the institute's solar grid. That night Tyler and I met the institute's five interns. Each evening they convened at a large yurt two hundred feet from the bus and would comprise Saturday's class; most were already experienced in solar systems. I feasted on their wealth of knowledge. To compensate, I invited the interns to the bus Thursday night to learn about fermentation—first with Jerusalem artichokes, which were plentiful in the garden, and then for a cyser lesson. We fermented the apple juice pressed in Boonville, all six gallons, with a little help from our dear friend honey.

Cyser

YIELDS 1 GALLON, 13 PERCENT ABV, 3–6 MONTHS

Cyser is hard cider on steroids. By adding honey or other sugars to fresh-pressed juice, you provide more food for the yeast to feast on, which gives cyser a higher alcohol content than hard cider. Cyser is a relative of mead's. Mead is also known as honey wine, "the ancestor of all fermented drinks," as the food writer Maguelonne Toussaint-Samat called it. An upside of cyser is that it requires less honey than mead does, on account of the sugars from the apple.

I first discovered cyser in Brooklyn—it was the first wine I ever made. It's simple, delicious, and one of my favorite summer beverages. If fermented in the fall, when apples are dropping from the tree, your cyser will reach dryness by late spring, and you can enjoy it through the summer. I've traditionally offered apple-harvest help every fall and in exchange asked for apples to press fresh, usually five gallons' worth. With this method you can literally enjoy the fruits of your labor.

INGREDIENTS

1 packet Lalvin EC-1118

6 cups water

2 lbs honey

½ gallon apple juice

MATERIALS

2 one-gallon jugs

Air lock and bung

Home-brew funnel

Hydrometer

Siphon and racking cane

PROCESS

1. Activate the yeast a few hours before adding it to the wine. Dissolve the packet of yeast in 1 cup of lukewarm water.

2. Gently heat water in a pot and add honey, stirring until the honey is liquefied.

3. Transfer the honey water to your gallon jug using a home-brew funnel. Add the apple juice and top off with water.

4. Use a hydrometer to test and take note of the specific gravity. The hydrometer will help you determine the ultimate ABV, which may vary slightly from mine depending on the sugar content of your apple juice. (This recipe should yield roughly 13 percent ABV.)

5. Add the yeast and seal jug with an air lock and bung. Give the jug a few swirls to aerate and distribute ingredients evenly. In 1–2 days the yeast will feed on the sugars and your wine will take off. You will notice by the movement inside your air lock.

6. After 1–2 weeks, when the movement in your air lock slows, rack your cyser into another jug using a racking cane and siphon (page 8). This will separate your cyser from the sediment. You can rack once more before bottling for a clearer cyser.

7. Taste along the way. When the wine is dry and the hydrometer reading is at zero it's ready to bottle. If you're impatient you can drink it immediately, but the flavor improves as it ages—I recommend waiting at least 3 months and for optimal flavor 6 months. Read about how to bottle wine on pages 138–39.

Depending on the honey and the juice you use, your ABV may vary from mine. Add more sugars to aim for higher ABV or dilute to aim for a lower ABV. Note that if you aim for an ABV over 18 percent, the yeast won't digest the remaining sugars and your cyser will be sweet.

Saturday morning I was wrapping my brain around the fact that I would have something of a solar system at the end of the day. After going over the costs with Eric, I decided we would install everything except the solar panel and the inverter, so the most labor-intensive and expensive parts—battery, charge controller, and breaker box (lovingly called Big Baby Box)—would be out of the way. It wouldn't be functional yet, but I'd figure out the rest as I went. Besides, we were heading for winter and there wasn't a rush to catch the sun.

In addition to the interns, there was one character in the class I hadn't yet met. He was in his late sixties and appeared to be a friend of Eric's. He had a heavy Yiddish accent and a habit of blurting out factoids. Each time, Eric responded with a smile and went on. I decided to forgive the interruptions until I got the full story.

Hours sped by, and before we broke for lunch, I announced that anyone hankering for sauerkraut or kimchi should come by the bus for a serving. The older man stood and looked my way. "Heading to the bus, now!" he declared.

He, Tyler, and I walked to the bus.

The guys sat down while I brought out my crocks, presenting a variety of krauts and kimchi for our guest. "What would you like to try? We have an arame-seaweed kraut, pink cumin-caraway kraut, mustard-green kraut, daikon kimchi, and traditional kimchi."

"I'll try all of them!" the older man said.

As I dished out small piles on a large plate, he told me his name was Myron. He and Eric were jazz friends. Myron was a drummer from Wisconsin who had been in the Bay Area since 1969. I passed the plate his way and he gulped down each type, praising them in between, his mouth full.

He insisted on buying three quarts, which I sold for $20 apiece. Pulling out a wad of cash, he continued to praise the kraut. He called me a philanthropist; he insisted my work was of utmost importance. I thanked him, probably blushing.

"You are welcome to park at my house in Walnut Creek, north of Oakland," he said.

"Okay. I'll think about it," I responded.

"No, I really insist. My wife and I would love to have you." He handed me his business card. "So, are you going to eat that pepper?" He pointed at a pepper sitting in my compost bin.

"Well, no—that's why it's in my compost bin."

"I have to eat it. I'm going to eat it." And with that, Myron picked it out of my compost bin and took a huge bite.

I winced, not sure of the Scoville scale, and upon seeing Myron's face, I put my hands to my heart. "Oh, God. I only have water. May I pour you some?"

Red in the face and barely able to speak, he whimpered, "Gotta run. Call me."

As Myron walked off the bus, I watched him open one of the kraut jars and take a big gulp of brine.

III. Electric Friendships

The shared meal elevates eating from a mechanical process of fueling the body to a ritual of family and community, from the mere animal biology to an act of culture.

—Michael Pollan, *In Defense of Food: An Eater's Manifesto*

It was one A.M. when we reached Walnut Creek, and I was inching the bus down a narrow suburban street. I couldn't make out any of the house numbers and was feeling self-conscious about my loud engine when my phone rang. It was Myron. "I hear you!" he shouted. "I'm up! I'm running out to the street. Look for waving arms behind you." I looked in my mirror and saw a flailing body thirty feet behind me. I backed up and parked, and Myron greeted us with open arms.

A few minutes later we were sitting at Myron's kitchen table, and in no time he brought us each a glass of merlot, a bowl of lamb stew, and sliced persimmon. He asked if we needed anything else and told us to stay until our journey would move us farther south. "Myron, this is unprecedented generosity," Tyler said. I couldn't agree more.

The week was productive. I vacuumed the bus and scrubbed the carpet with water and baking soda. The fermentation workshop we held in San Francisco, on kimchi and sourdough, was well attended. We joined Myron for his seventieth birthday party that night at his friend Rita's in Oakland. It was dreamy: Rita's penthouse featured two walls of windows overlooking Lake Merritt, while Chinese antiques and assorted musical instruments filled her apartment. Myron and a couple friends went to town on the piano, a stand-up bass, and some drums, and I admired the two large paintings hanging in the dining room. The paintings were of Rita's great-grandparents from nineteenth-century Hong Kong.

Rita and I bonded in the kitchen as we roasted a large bird for the guests and band. She was a fellow food lover, and in no time we were finishing each other's sentences. By the end of the night we were practically holding hands.

A few days later, Rita called and asked if I'd be interested in parking by the lake and staying at her apartment the next week. I accepted.

Meanwhile Myron had become a father figure and friend. We sat up late drinking wine, talking in Yiddish, and playing drums. I made a large batch of kimchi our last night there. While chopping the radishes, I noticed a tapping at the kitchen table where Myron sat—he was tapping in rhythm to my chops. He kept with it as I moved from cabbage to leek to carrot. Myron clicked along as he gathered pots and pans for a full kimchi percussion set, with a wild smile planted on his face. No words were exchanged for an hour and a half—just music and fermenting. It was understood: we got each other.

The next morning I ate eggs, collards, and sauerkraut. Myron stuffed persimmons into a bag for me and I consulted my oversize trucker's atlas. It was my reference manual for big-rig driving challenges, especially low-overhead clearances. I found an easy route, poured a small glass of wine, and geared up to leave.

Tyler and I parked on the north side of Lake Merritt in the early afternoon, near Rita's. Rita suggested I bring Franklin upstairs so she could have a cuddle companion; I obliged. Seeing Franklin in that apartment sitting on the expansive windowsill with downtown Oakland in the background brought me right back to Brooklyn. Franklin had grown up in the city, moved to the country, and was beginning to discover a nomadic life.

Rita had a long shopping list, so we drove to Chinatown to scout out the goods. Our first stop was her herbalist; they spoke in Cantonese as he gathered five herbs for her upcoming five-spice chicken soup: astragalus, goji berry, Chinese yam, lotus seed, and burdock. We left and walked along, window-shopping—taking detours for sticky rice wrapped in lotus leaves and mung bean buns—until we came to the Peking duck stand. Rita expertly took an order for two ducks, lightly chopped. She was a woman after my own heart. Her love for flavor was unmissable; her body language and utterances clearly expressed her commitment to tasty food. (When one recommended a delectable flavor combination or she discovered a difficult-to-track-down ingredient, Rita would bring her hands to her cheeks, her lips with a full smile, and let out an "Mm!" or "Oh …!"—experiencing a holy synesthesia.) Our final stop was a Chinese grocery, where we bought Chinese broccoli, chicken, shiitake mushrooms, ground pork, and dumpling wrappers.

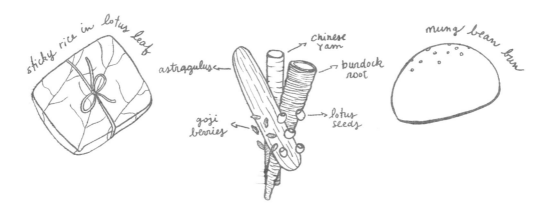

We cooked for hours. Rita was determined to show me the Chinese way of cooking—such as not cutting the chicken down before throwing it into the stockpot (which I immediately did), but leaving it whole and letting the chicken fall apart in the pot with the herbs. She also taught me how to fold dumpling wrappers flower-bud-style, so they had a finger hole and cute triangular tail. We filled the wrappers with a traditional mixture of ground pork, shiitake mushrooms, and soy sauce. Not to be forgotten were the Peking duck and steamed Chinese broccoli. Our menu fed the three of us. No words, just chewing.

While Tyler hitched a ride to Grants Pass to spend Thanksgiving with his family, I continued to lounge at Rita's, taking advantage of the swimming pool and sauna, as well as cooking loads of good food.

One day Rita exclaimed during lunch, "I simply must introduce you to my neighbor, Nik! He's interested in food and sustainability. The two of you must have so much in common."

We left a note under his door. Coincidentally I had e-mailed him only a month earlier asking if he might help host a workshop. Nik is an ecologist; he taught at the San Francisco Art Institute and managed gray-water recycling at a public-serving learning center in Oakland, A PLACE for Sustainable Living (also known as PLACE), that showcases sustainable-living practices. Two hours after our leaving the note, Nik knocked on Rita's door. We invited him in for leftover fermented green tea salad.

Fermented Green Tea Salad

YIELDS 8 OUNCES OF FERMENTED TEA, 1–2 WEEKS / SALAD OF 16 SERVINGS, 1 HOUR

Burmese cuisine was another favorite of Rita's, specifically laphet thoke, or fermented tea-leaf salad. Fermented green tea is a staple of Burmese street food, fermented from scratch with a fresh Cambodian variety of green tea. After making the dish with a store-bought package of the fermented tea one evening, we were inspired to try our hand at fermenting the tea ourselves. This is one of the most delicious and unique dishes I've ever had, and fermenting the tea on your own is simple.

This dish has fishy elements and is heaven for anyone who loves umami. But you can omit the fish sauce if you'd like and use tamari instead.

FERMENTED GREEN TEA INGREDIENTS

½ cup dried green tea leaves (whole)

1 inch ginger

3 cloves garlic

2 tbsp fish sauce (or tamari)

1 Thai chili

juice of ½ lime

2 tbsp sesame oil

1 tsp salt

SALAD INGREDIENTS

2 lbs cabbage

2 large tomatoes

3–4 scallions

1 cup peanuts

½ cup sunflower seeds

½ cup yellow split peas

¼ cup sesame seeds

MATERIALS

8-ounce Ball jar

Weight and cover

FERMENTED GREEN TEA

1. Soak dried tea leaves for 1–2 hours at room temperature, drain then rinse, remove the tough twigs of the tea, and soak overnight.

2. After the overnight soak, lightly chop the tea leaves and combine them with the first set of ingredients. Press ingredients firmly into an 8-ounce Ball jar and add a weight. Let sit at room temperature for 1 week. The flavor is already intense, but you can deepen it by letting it ferment for longer periods. I like to let the mixture ferment for a few weeks.

SALAD

1. Chop cabbage, slice the tomatoes, chop the scallions, and in that order place onto a large serving plate. Toast the peanuts, sunflower seeds, yellow split peas, and sesame seeds each with sesame oil on medium-high heat. Toast separately, as they have different toasting times. The nuts and seeds will give off an aroma and deepen in color once they are well toasted. Be careful not to burn them. Add the toasted seeds and nuts to your salad.

2. Dress the salad with fermented green tea and toss the ingredients half an hour before serving to meld the flavors and soften crunchier elements. Season with fish sauce, lime, and chili.

Nik connected me to a greater community of fermenters focused on social practice. With him I toured PLACE's gray-water facilities, gardens, kitchen, and tiny homes. We shared lunch at Ghost Town Farm, an Oakland urban farm and the focus of *Farm City: The Education of an Urban Farmer*, a memoir by farmer Novella Carpenter. He connected me to the sustainability coordinator of Esalen Institute, a dreamy coastal mecca in Big Sur for all things communal, educational, and renegade. The intentional community had long been on my radar.

Timing was close to perfect when I left, two days before Thanksgiving. A warning from the Oakland police on my driver's window, posted that morning, informed me I'd get a ticket if I didn't move soon. One of Rita's jazz friends, a burly bassist from Chicago, helped me move my belongings back into the bus, and Franklin and I made our way toward Santa Cruz. It was my first long leg of traveling solo.

Thanksgiving morning the sustainability coordinator at Esalen responded to Nik's e-mail and invited me to a leftovers feast the next day. Her name was Kat. Though I knew the harrowing drive down coastal Highway 1 would be a challenge in my rig, I was excited to connect more deeply with California's sustainability community. The prospect of soaking at Esalen's Pacific Ocean cliffside baths, known to intentional communities far and wide, was also appealing. I wondered if Kat would have advice for taking a dip there, which seemed duly guarded by the community.

I parked at a large turnout next to Big Sur Bakery—*the* spot in Big Sur to sip coffee and eat pastries (I was into it). Kat picked me up and we drove up the hill to her house. I was the first guest by a few hours. We occupied the time with small talk about my project and her work at Esalen. I felt shy. I was worried I'd be the only outsider at the gathering.

I wasn't, though. A diverse group of people joined—college students visiting from the Bay Area, local food producers, an arborist and his daughter, and more. The feast was potluck style, so leftovers from everyone's household were brought to share. I brought sauerkraut and kimchi from the bus.

At Heart and Spoon, we have a nightly dinner ritual called the Together Hug—a dozen or more of us hold hands with the people to either side of us, and we say, "One, two, three . . . *together hug*!"—long and drawn out. Then we squeeze hands and exchange smiles before letting go. This type of ritual has always satisfied my style of gratefulness for my food and my people.

At Kat's house we had a Thanksgiving-style ritual. We sat in a circle and each person shared a little bit (or a lot) about what he or she was grateful for. "I'm grateful to be with company for the holidays," I said. "I've been traveling—driving and living in a bus the past month—and it gets lonely."

After the circle came to a close, the arborist, Lee, took an interest in my travels. We talked about traveling and loneliness. We bonded quickly. He offered to drop me off at the bus on his way home, so I left the party with him and his daughter Sonja.

We pulled into the turnout by the bakery, and they were surprised by the size of the bus. Most people were, including me. I invited them in and they liked my setup. I was fermenting stuff and I was obsessed—it was clear. In that hour I developed a fondness for the free-spirited tree-loving professor and his daughter. We agreed to meet for coffee at the bakery in the morning, before I headed south.

Coffee with Sonja and Lee led to a trip to the Big Sur Harvest Craft Fair, an annual fair featuring handmade crafts by local artisans. The fair led to a trip to the beach, where I found a Monterey pinecone the size of a baby's head. The beach trip led to Franklin and me camping on a cliffside a hundred feet outside Lee's yurt, which he had built himself. I learned about the local flora of Big Sur, especially its oak trees (Lee's specialty) and cooked often with Sonja and Lee. The week with my new friends moved quickly.

Lee brought me to Esalen one evening for "locals night." When we drove toward the institute, I thought it was too good to believe. I finally bathed in those rock barren baths with the sound of waves splashing in the distance below, while I gazed at the stars. Lee had taken me in as one of his own. My community of friends now extended to the woods of Big Sur.

I would miss Lee and Sonja. They drove me back down the hill to my bus the next morning. My right rear tire had a slight tear. I went to the closest gas station to add a little air—a stopgap measure till I could get to a tire shop sixty miles south of Big Sur. I hit the gas.

"Okay, boys—stand away from that tire! It could blow! These tires are like bombs!"

Mechanics never hesitated to make me feel like a dope. It seemed reasonable to spend my dwindling funds on items that would save my life in the long run, so I bought two new front tires. I pressed on, nearly to Paso Robles, and spent the night at a rest stop.

The next morning the temperature had plunged forty degrees. (I rarely checked the weather forecast in California, assuming permanent warmth.) I woke to find Franklin on my stomach per usual, but shaking. I quickly wrapped him in blankets, made a fire, and sat in front of the stove, rocking him for nearly an hour. At last he stopped shaking. I brought his face to my chest for a squeeze, feeling guilty, and then fed him a heaping serving of canned rabbit.

After coffee and eggs, I dampened the stove to get back on the road. My next host was expecting me in L.A. soon, so I got behind the wheel, turned the key, and—nothing. The bus wouldn't start. I brought my head down and thought this could be the end of my journey, right here.

IV. Patience

AAA arrived three hours later and strapped the bus up for tow. Not long after, I watched a mechanic in Paso Robles pop the hood and without the help of tools start the engine right up.

"Wait—how did you do that?" I asked.

He unscrewed a cylindrical piece on my fuel injector. Once the piece was unscrewed, it popped outward and could be pumped in and out, to "prime" the engine. The technique would be necessary on especially frigid days, when my diesel fuel gelled. It seemed like a trick anyone driving a rig such as mine should know before departing for a yearlong journey.

California was filled with lessons on patience and humility. The more I learned about the bus and its idiosyncrasies, the less I felt I knew. The knowledge would come slowly, and by necessity, and I would never learn it all. Acceptance was my only recourse.

Midday I was finally Los Angeles–bound. I crawled up the on-ramp to Interstate 5—and the bus stalled. Cars began to line up far behind me, accompanied by honks and yells. The engine needed priming but I couldn't do it alone—one person needed to rev while the other primed. I called the shop, only to hear elevator music. Then a man in a construction uniform who was working nearby appeared at my window and asked if he could help out.

"Yes! You definitely can. Will you pop open my hood? My bus needs to be primed while I press the gas."

"Okay, well, I—"

"You got this, trust me. It's easy."

With a little guidance he primed, I revved, and soon I was off again.

I arrived at Bernard and Nancy's Atwater Village home in Los Angeles late Thursday night. The couple was a connection from a New York friend. During my stay with them, they introduced me to their friend Karen Atkinson. Karen is an artist and teacher, and the founder of Side Street Projects, a mobile educational program of school buses housing woodworking workshops. She expressed interest in my project, a novice one next to hers, and joined us for lunch. Once seated, Karen quickly got down to business and asked how I was supporting Fermentation on Wheels. I told her about my failed Kickstarter, the here-and-there workshop donations, and that future finances were hazy.

Karen's work, like mine, is a rare kind of enterprise with the purpose to make positive social impact through art. It benefits the common good, and because it does that, nonprofits such as Fractured Atlas (Side Street Projects' fiscal sponsor) will get behind a project to make sure that impact sustains. Because I favored barter over dollars and adhered to the values of the "food is free" movement, I had neglected financial logistics. Karen encouraged me to stay true to my principles and helped shed light on the advantages of a nonprofit sponsor.

What were the advantages, exactly? With sponsorship, I could apply for grants with 501(c)(3) tax status, which would make Fermentation on Wheels eligible for tenfold the number of grants. It also meant I could offer tax-deductible receipts for donations of money or goods. Both would incentivize larger donations and perhaps be the maker or breaker of my staying on the road. It had already proven difficult to get a foot in the door with my alternative—very casual—business model. I realized that if a nonprofit had my back, it would bring legitimacy. I needed a reputable source to stand up and say, "Fermentation on Wheels is the real deal."

During the holiday week, I had another realization: I would need to let Tyler go. When he'd first joined me, I had felt the universe was on my side—help was jumping out of the woodwork when I thought I needed it most. But the scope of Fermentation on Wheels had grown in unexpected ways since then, and I needed a fully committed travel companion. At first, not knowing exactly how to propel the project forward, there was no way I could prepare another person for what it might become. The work it involved continued to grow—I knew this was a big ask for Tyler. When we next spoke, I told him I thought we should part ways.

I had a newfound confidence in traveling alone after the intense trek down to

Los Angeles. And I had work to do. In the midst of my grassroots ideals, I knew Fermentation on Wheels needed to gain recognition in the long year ahead. My next acquaintance would prove invaluable in that undertaking.

A twist of fate veered the bus south after Austin Durant, the chief fermenting officer (CFO) of Fermenters Club in San Diego, invited me to town for a collaborative workshop. He was the first fellow fermentation fanatic to reach out. We were to hold a potluck, and I was fired up for all the tangy things I'd taste and fermenters I'd meet.

Austin embraced my microbe-dense bus moments after I pulled onto his street. He just hopped on, directing me where to park. No one had ever *just hopped* on my bus before, so I was beginning to feel initiated into the club. Austin was a well-preserved man in his late thirties. He wore well-fitting jeans and a T-shirt, conventional at first sight.

Once parked in front of Austin's condo, we stepped out of the bus when a salesman, from out of nowhere, approached us and asked, "Hey! Would you two like some free water?"

"I'd love some free water!" I said.

"Okay, which one you want—the alkaline, reverse osmosis, or spring?"

"I'll take the reverse osmosis."

Austin looked over and said, "Yeah, the pure stuff. Water for your ferments!"

I smiled at our mutual understanding.

Food and fermentation books covered the coffee table in Austin's home. We drank homemade eggnog while Brent, second-in-command at Fermenters Club, made pastrami. Guests slowly filed into the apartment, accompanied by jars upon jars of fermented vegetables. There was nothing ordinary about the enthusiasm in San Diego—Austin had organized a loyal tribe of fermentation nerds. After we'd stuffed ourselves, the party crammed into the bus. All appreciated the dimly lit and cozy vibe. The bus was so youthful at that time, with not much more than a few books, lots of wine, fermented vegetables, and my beloved sourdough-starter culture.

Fermenters Club and Fermentation on Wheels held their first collaborative workshop that weekend. We taught students how to make sauerkraut with one of Austin's favorite recipes: sauerkraut with fennel, ginger, caraway, and juniper.

I followed the sauerkraut lesson with a short workshop on culturing bread with sourdough starter.

The day before heading east—also my last day on the West Coast for two years—Austin and I made adzuki-bean miso. This miso is close to my heart. A wonderful thing about miso is that the flavor becomes deeper and richer with age, like community and friendship. Every time I eat this miso, I'm transported back to my first fermentation project with Austin.

Adzuki-Bean Miso

YIELDS 1 GALLON, 3 HOURS KITCHEN PREP AND 12 MONTHS FERMENTATION

Contrary to popular belief, miso isn't always made with soybeans. Miso is great for fermenting all kinds of legumes, grains, and other ingredients into a rich and complex paste. It's a simple ferment to make once you source the starter culture, *Aspergillus oryzae*. More commonly, one can find the *Aspergillus oryzae* already inoculated on barley or rice, which we refer to as koji. You can source koji online or at your local Japanese market.

This long-term miso is a standard recipe and can be used with a variety of other ingredients; thus I've included all ingredients in grams as well as their weight percentages in relationship to one another. Long-term miso (one year or longer) calls for 50 percent koji by weight of the legumes and 13 percent salt by weight of the legumes and koji combined. I use 65 percent water by weight of legumes and koji in both short-term and long-term miso. For more on short-term miso, see pages 184–85.

INGREDIENTS
2 lbs / 910 g adzuki beans
3¾ cups / 885 g conserved bean water (65 percent, by weight of legumes and koji)
175 g salt (13 percent, by weight of legumes and koji)
1 lb / 455 g koji (50 percent, by weight of legumes)
1 tbsp mature miso

MATERIALS
Gallon jar
Large bowl
Hand blender or potato masher
Weight and cover

PROCESS

1. Soak the adzuki beans a few hours or overnight. Drain water, rinse beans, and cover with fresh water—roughly two inches above level of beans. Bring to boil on high heat, then reduce to medium low for a 60-minute simmer, or until the beans are tender.

2. Drain the bean water and conserve 3¾ cups for brine. Add salt to the bean water and transfer adzuki beans to a large bowl.

3. Add 1 cup of brine to the beans and mash with a potato masher or blend with a hand blender. Mash to your desired consistency. Allow the beans to cool to at least 140° F, the tolerable heat requirement for *Aspergillus oryzae*.

4. Once the bean water is warm to the touch, or below 140° F, add the koji (and optional mature miso) and stir.

5. Add the salty koji mixture to the adzuki beans once they have also cooled to at least 104° F and distribute the ingredients.

6. Rinse your fermentation vessel and leave wet, to lightly salt the walls of the container. Add a few tablespoons of salt and quickly turn and agitate the jar, so the salt catches.

7. Form balls of the final mixture with your hands and toss the balls hard into the jar. The trick is to have as little air space as possible. This method of slinging tightly packed balls into the jar slows you down, so you can focus on tightly packing your mass of ingredients.

8. Distribute a thin layer of salt on top of the paste.

9. Place a flexible plastic lid from a quart container or plate on top of the paste and weigh down with a few rinsed and boiled river rocks or another heavy object, prefer-ably glass or ceramic, that will keep the paste submerged in brine throughout the 12 months of fermentation.

10. During fermentation, store the miso in the dark (I keep mine in a brown paper bag when fermenting in a clear glass jar) and check on it every 2 months. If mold forms on top, simply scrape it off and replace with another layer of salt and your weights. When the flavor is to your liking, pack into jars and store in the fridge. You may want to pack half and let the other half ferment even longer, to develop even richer, deeper flavors.

CULTURING
THE SOUTHWEST

Do not go where the path may lead,
go instead where there is no path and leave a trail.
—Ralph Waldo Emerson

I. Milky Fermentations

Never having worked with goats, but having always been smitten by their cuddly and childlike demeanors, I was excited to travel to Crow's Dairy, just west of Phoenix, for my first farm visit since southern Oregon.

Before heading there, I made a pit stop at Phoestivus Holiday Market, wanting to get my name out and network with local food lovers as well as do some holiday bartering, ferments in hand.

At the market I met the Killer Bee Guy (nationally renowned for his killer bee honey, I discovered); scored some Mayan coffee alternative extracted from the Maya nut native to Jalisco, Mexico; and I befriended a goat-dairy farmer who referred to Crow's Dairy as "corporate" and invited me to her farm. I was interested but declined. I had plans. An hour later I drove west.

Upon my arrival, Rhonda and Wendell Crow greeted me warmly, along with their dogs. It was late in farmer time, so I settled in and we got better acquainted early the next morning while milking goats.

I didn't milk many. Instead, I listened to Rhonda's stories and made cheese with boisterous Wendell. The Crows grew up on family dairy farms and had mastered large-scale industrial cow-dairy management and grunt work alike by their mid-twenties. They got married and opened their own cow dairy. (This alone would give anyone in the agricultural community a "corporate" reputation.) The Crows were old-school. They sold their cow dairy in 2006 and shortly after moved to goats for the good life. Rhonda knew all 150 of their goats by name. During birthing season, in February, she rarely slept, helping her goats deliver their kids for a month straight. I was in awe of their dedication to and understanding of their animals.

I drank my first raw (or unpasteurized, fresh, straight-outta-the-animal) goat milk, which I discovered had a clean flavor and creamy texture I loved. And it had microbes! I would start to scout out raw milk in every state, regardless of its legality—some for drinking and some for fermenting.

Raw milk is not only creamy and delicious; it's a more compelling option for fermentation. Fresh, raw milk—as opposed to the pasteurized milk from your supermarket—comes packed with microorganisms that introduce fermentation without the addition of bacterial cultures, whereas inoculation of some sort is necessary when fermenting pasteurized milk.

Wondering where you're going to get raw milk? Yes, of course you are. The two best references in the USA are Real Milk Finder on www.realmilk.com or through your local Weston A. Price chapter.

What It Is : Dairy Fermentation

In dairy fermentation, milk is microbially transformed via *Lactobacillus*. While increasing the shelf life, fermentation also enhances the digestibility of milk, introduces microbes to our inner ecosystems, and gives a more acidic, delicious taste.

In dairy fermentation milk sugars, also known as lactose, are ingested by bacteria and yeast, which in turn produce lactic acid. The starter cultures we play with when we make yogurt or kefir produce different body, texture, and flavor depending on the bacteria and yeast we integrate with the milk. The starter cultures known for milk fermentation, *L. bulgaricus* and *S. thermophilus*, live in our digestive tracts, too. Many other bacterial species present in yogurt also help balance and nourish our gut flora.

Wendell was the cheese guy of the operation, as Rhonda put it. I love cheese. You know that thing Benjamin Franklin said about wine being proof God wants us to be happy? Well, that's how I feel about cheese, whether it's in the stinky realm (blue cheese and Camembert) or mild-flavored (Swiss, Gouda, and Brie).

Raw Soft Cheese

YIELDS 2 CUPS, 54–74 HOURS

Cheese making varies from simple to highly complex, as some cheeses take years to mature and specific environments. Softer cheeses are relatively simple; it's a faster process and thus specificity is less significant. The flavor is mild and the texture is creamy. You can spread soft cheese on your favorite breads or crackers and adorn it with other items such as sauerkraut, olives, capers, sardines, and hot sauce for a hearty, well-rounded snack stack.

I've learned much more about do-it-yourself cheese making since my trip through the Southwest, mostly through literature and watching others. This soft-cheese recipe uses a simple process with accessible ingredients.

INGREDIENTS	MATERIALS
1 qt raw cow or goat milk	Glass quart jar
1 tsp salt	Cheesecloth
	Wooden spoon
	Deep, widemouthed pot or jar

PROCESS

1. Let the milk sit in the jar for 24 to 48 hours, until it has thickened and becomes *clabber*—a rustic, old-school word for thickened raw milk.

2. Line a bowl with cheesecloth and pour the clabber and whey onto the cheesecloth. Gather the cheesecloth and tie it to the center of a wooden spoon handle. Hang clabber to strain off excess whey. Conserve whey for later fermentation (see note).

3. After 24 hours, bring the cheesecloth to a bowl and salt the cheese. Mix the salt thoroughly—the salt will improve the flavor and help remove moisture from the cheese.

4. Hang the cheese for 4 to 6 more hours, then untie and store in a glass or plastic container. Enjoy up to 2 weeks.

Note: Whey can be used as a starter culture in beverage and vegetable fermentation. This liquid leftover from dairy fermentation is yellow and slightly cloudy. In addition to jump-starting fermentation, it's a traditional starter in some recipes, such as the Guyanese ferment sweet-potato fly (on page 83). Whey is great for soaking grains, too. Refer to page 229 for a cultured oats recipe that calls for whey.

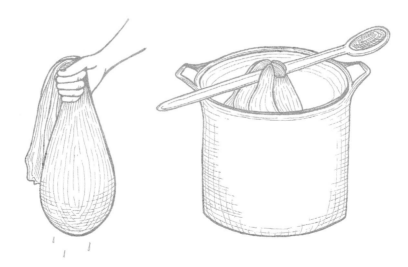

Dairy Kefir

YIELDS 1 QUART, 24–48 HOURS

Midway through my stay with the Crows, Rhonda and I secured some kefir grains from her friend Lylah. Wendell and I quickly set up a dairy kefir station in the cheese room using the "grains" (technically they are a community of bacteria and yeast). Dairy kefir is supersimple, arguably the simplest of dairy fermentations. Raw goat milk fed my starter culture for years, but pasteurized milk works fine. Refer to page 12 to source dairy kefir grains.

INGREDIENTS
1 qt milk
1 tbsp dairy kefir grains

MATERIALS
Quart jar
Strainer

PROCESS

1. Add ingredients into quart jar. Let sit for 24 to 48 hours and agitate the jar occasionally to discourage curds and whey from separating. The cooler the temperature, the longer fermentation will take, while the warmer it is, the speedier.

2. Once the milk kefir smells and tastes pleasant to you, pour it through a mesh strainer over a quart jar. It may take a bit of effort to push the kefir through, so use a spoon. Your dairy kefir grains, the starter culture, will remain. Healthy grains will double each time you ferment. Keep some and pass the excess grains on to a friend.

The Crows introduced me to dairy and its nourishing and delicious qualities when handled with love. Their goats produced great-quality milk because there was a sense of deep respect. That respect, from farmer to animal to milk, helped me appreciate the medium more. I had never been interested in milk, put off by images of industrial dairy farms. Now I would seek it out in my travels. I would think of the hardworking farmer, the animals, and the collaborations that brought their life forces to the table—in raw, play, and fermented form.

II. Holy Holiday

Christmas was approaching and I was eager to move on. Rhonda recommended I contact an intentional community south of Tucson called Avalon Organic Gardens & EcoVillage. Their website was sparse, but I wrote them and was invited to stay a week, during Christmastime, in exchange for a daylong fermentation intensive.

I drove to an all-night diner in Tucson to awkwardly and slowly update my website, which skill I was learning with encouragement from Austin, the CFO of Fermenters Club. I worked until I could no longer focus on the screen and retired to my bus, parked on a downtown side street. Sleep was especially restless in the city. After five hours I woke with the sun and made my way toward the border.

It was midmorning when I arrived, and to my dismay the polyvinyl chloride pipe leading to my water tank had broken during the drive, releasing water all over the back carpet. The center of my cabinet had started to sink from the ceiling, and I worried that it might fall at any moment—sending molasses and all smashing to the floor. I thought about Steve in Boonville, and how I longed for his help.

Avalon came just in time. A greet team met me at the gate. A tall man jumped in and introduced himself as Anyan. He asked me how the drive was, and I expressed my concern. He ushered me to my spot for the week and said they'd check out the damages.

Forty-five minutes after I parked what I thought was a run-down mobile home, the cabinet hardware was reinforced and secured to the metal ceiling, probably in better shape than it had ever been. The PVC pipe leading to my water tank had been replaced, and my bed frame was mounted to the floor, to discourage movement. (The piping had broken because my bed had shifted and taken the rigid pipe with it.) All this with the help of a few dudes; I started to regard the Men of Avalon as heroes.

Everyone was genuine and bighearted. DeleVan Erba, one of the founding daughters, was my hostess. She showed me the house where I would dine and offered her vacuum, with a smile. We had our first heart-to-heart outside the dining hall at a picnic table, and she asked, "Are you spiritual?"

"No, not really. Are you?"

She responded incredulously, "Well . . . we're a spiritual community."

Communards of Avalon Organic Gardens & EcoVillage are followers of *The Urantia Book*. The community's leader and founder, Gabriel of Urantia, was partly responsible for the growth of the spiritual following, which first took root in Chicago in 1925. *The Urantia Book*, published in 1955, unites concepts of religion, science, and philosophy. Avalon, with 120 residents, is in a desert oasis twenty miles north of the Mexican border. The level of sustainability practiced there qualifies them as perhaps one of the most self-sufficient communities I've ever encountered. They have an elaborate rain catchment system, and an array of immaculate cob houses made of clay, water, and straw. Most impressive, they produce up to 75 percent of their own food.

As a Catholic Church dropout from the age of nine, I was uncertain how to feel about their spirituality. Organized religion had made me feel servant to a specific higher power; I didn't have a choice in my youth. One day, in Sunday school, I was told I would need to memorize a prayer and recite it onstage wearing a white dress for a First Communion ceremony. I was boyish then and the soccer field had my heart. I wouldn't touch a white dress. I protested with such intensity that my family, save my father, never routinely went back to church.

In my adult years I've learned to appreciate spirituality from afar. Avalon was organized around their spirituality, and though it initially made me wary, much of their philosophy was aligned with my own. They were lovers of the earth and they nourished that love by growing and making good food.

The food- and herb-processing rooms were a paradise for food lovers. Starter cultures and fermentation projects adorned every square inch of shelving space of the food room, and a large island in the middle of the room proved a perfect work surface. Buttermilk, dairy kefir, tibicos, sourdough, sauerkraut, green beans, and a variety of other vegetables were neatly packed in jars of brine. In the adjoining room used for herb processing, sweet desert lavender and common dandelion filled one corner, and various wild-harvested herbs hung from shelves.

Tibicos: Storage and Tips

YIELDS 1 QUART, 24-48 HOURS

I took special interest in the tibicos starter culture one member claimed came from an *Opuntia* cactus native to Mexico. Tibicos comes in different varieties, and it is more commonly known as water kefir. The grains make nonalcoholic fermented beverages, simply and quickly. These favorites from Avalon became my prized grains for their unique flavor profile—they have a cheesy aroma and look like small glass beads.

INGREDIENTS

1 qt water (hard water and spring water
    are best—avoid water with chlorine)
¼ cup unrefined organic sugar
5 thin slices of ginger
1 tsp molasses

1 tbsp tibicos
½ crushed shell of egg

MATERIALS

Quart jar
Strainer

PROCESS

1. Gently heat water and thoroughly dissolve sugar. Thinly slice ginger to expose as much surface area as possible and add to the warm water. Add molasses and stir.

2. Allow the water to cool to 100° F or less (comfortable to the touch) and add tibicos.

3. Add ½ crushed shell of egg and cover your container with a cloth and rubber band or use another method to allow air flow.

4. In a day or two, depending on temperature, you'll notice effervescence. Your tibicos is feasting.

5. Add more sugars for secondary fermentation (see note on next page). You can simply purchase a natural fruit juice (no additives or preservatives) at the store, add your grains, and then adjust the sweetness with sugar for your grains to consume.

6. When you aren't making delicious elixirs, add other nutrients to your tibicos to keep it in good health. I add sugar to strained bean water and feed it to my tibicos. The tibicos perks up within hours. Make sure to store the tibicos in the fridge with a loose lid (I use plastic Ball canning lids) when you're not conducting experiments and feed once a week to keep in good health.

In secondary fermentation you ferment a beverage with a second round of sugar to flavor or carbonate it. We achieve carbonation by adding something sweet, such as a few tablespoons of sugar or simple syrup (pages 212–14), before bottling in an airtight container. The bacteria and yeast feed on the sugars and produce CO_2, naturally carbonating the beverage.

Note: *Dairy kefir and water kefir are not related.* Although results may be interesting, possibly even delicious, I don't recommend feeding your water kefir milk sugar (lactose) or your dairy kefir cane sugar to keep them in good health. By all means experiment—provided you have extra culture to play with. Refer to pages 153 and 222–24 for fermented-soda recipes.

A Note on Fermented Sodas

These guidelines keep kefir bubbling through summer heat and winter cold. My tibicos culture has weathered both extremes and remained happy, but it is an aggressive fermenter in warm temperatures and can be unpredictable. This also makes for a somewhat dangerous ferment—if you bottle a tibicos-fermented beverage in an airtight container and leave it on your counter for too long, the rapid CO_2 buildup can explode the bottle. Therefore, as soon as you bottle tibicos, transfer it to the refrigerator. It's also a good idea to open fermented sodas with caution. My friend Ken in New York City taught me a useful method for opening soda with care while taking care to not lose any of the beverage—he places the bottle in a bowl, covers the top of the bottle with a plastic bag, and opens it. If soda should fly, the plastic bag prevents it from flying high and the bowl catches it.

Christmas Eve Day the community stood in a circle on a grassy hill by the dining hall in the sun holding hands, giving thanks and love. Everyone, save myself, was dressed well. (As a bus dweller, I always had an excuse to dress like a rag doll.) Residents lined up in the hall. Lunch was a variety of salads, roasted vegetables, grains, legumes, and roasted goat.

I carried my full plate out to feel the winter sun and sit with people still strange to me. As I walked toward the picnic tables, a woman named O'Breean ushered me to sit at hers. We spoke mostly of my travels and goal to pollinate people's minds with the mysteries of fermentation. O'Breean said, "You remind me of a quote by Ralph Waldo Emerson, 'Do not go where the path may lead' . . . something like that." She invited me to a puppet show that evening called *The Godchild Came*, written by the kids.

That evening I sat by the wood-burning stove with the residents of my host home, listening to passages read from *The Urantia Book*. One stood out most—the story of Joseph and a very pregnant Mary seeking shelter during their visit to Bethlehem. It was an appropriate enough story to share with a visitor; I felt lucky my travel companion was a cat rather than a pregnant wife.

I was also lucky to be with spiritually stimulating friends who fed me like a queen and told stories by a fire. The entire visit was story-glorified. Residents asked what I was doing, why I was doing it, and how I got started. The people of Avalon loved a good story.

Christmas was a busy day. I was chauffeured by several different residents around the community. I joined Anyan, my greeter and the community's sourdough expert, for brunch at one of the more formidable homes, judging by the enormous kitchen and living room. I received gifts—a hand-knit scarf and earrings threaded with heirloom corn and turquoise. I helped prepare brunch, and when we finally sat down to eat, a woman walked in and every person at the table rose. I looked up at Anyan for guidance and from his glance decided I should stand, too.

The woman was Niánn Emerson Chase, Gabriel of Urantia's first wife and DeleVan's mother. When we sat back down, Anyan explained, in a whisper, that she was a spiritual mentor to them—a woman of utmost importance. She joined us and we ate. I passed no judgment on their spiritual formalities. I felt a kinship with the group as I mentally prepared for our hands-on fermentation workshop the next day.

Five students attended, Anyan included. Four of them were deeply involved in the community's kitchen, where I had eaten beyond-impressive meals during the week. Many of them were chefs in former lives and knew a thing or two about fermentation, too. At the time I didn't think about their level of experience compared to mine. We had fun, and they adored the bus. I didn't have to be an expert.

After my last dinner at my host house, I asked each person to take the spotlight and share where he or she came from and how he or she arrived at Avalon. The stories were riveting: from a party-girl journalist in Philadelphia to an introverted indigenous woman in rural Mexico. Each person had stumbled upon Avalon by chance, and each had been there a decade or more. Like my microbial creations, all from diverse botanical sources, these stories wove the community into something richer than its parts.

Community can be a holy thing. There's nothing commonplace about finding your people.

Arizona obsidian

HOME, SOUR HOME

Perhaps the best resolution would simply be to act on resolve.
It's easy to talk the talk, hard to walk the walk. Here's to a year of walking.
—Joel Salatin, New Year's letter, 2014

I. Birthday Wishes

The Texas Panhandle threw me into a snowstorm so intense I had to pull over until it passed. The plan was to meet with my maternal grandparents and aunt in Dallas, but the trek from Albuquerque was dragging on. My birthday was three days away and I was determined to spend it with family.

The evening before I turned twenty-eight, I arrived at my grandmother's house, where I'd spent much of the first decade of my life. Now it was for sale, and empty. My grandmother—Gamby—and her husband had already moved to a home in the nearby suburb of Plano. I thought of all those stories I knew about my mother's teenage years here—of her headbanging to Led Zeppelin, and dancing to Bowie with her queer friends, and sitting in the tub with new jeans so they'd fit skintight. The only trace of life now was the Internet connection.

That night I took full advantage of it, e-mailing farms and potential venues, and scouring food publications, looking for a journalist who might take interest in my project. I wrote the founder of *Civil Eats* and the editor in chief of *Vice*'s food site, *Munchies*. Then I tucked in with Franklin and thought of all the foods I would cook and ferment in my childhood kitchen.

On my birthday I woke late to a mild Texas winter day and unpacked ingredients for a five-spice Chinese chicken soup. Gamby, Aunt Karin, and Grandpa Jerry visited for birthday lunch. Rather than go out for my birthday, I wanted to shine with a home-cooked meal, which I felt would be a treat for my family.

I tend to avoid Texas—the climate and culture don't mix well with my microbes or lifestyle. As a result I hadn't seen my Dallas family for a few years. They were curious about my decision to trek around the country in a large rolling fermentation lab—how strange! They were supportive, too. Despite being different on so many levels, my maternal side has somehow always gotten me.

Gamby talked about her new suburban mammoth of a house. Aunt Karin asked about fermented foods as a possible aid in her struggles with multiple sclerosis, an autoimmune disease. Grandpa Jerry was fascinated by Franklin's chill attitude toward our trip and was curious to know if I'd read *Cat Sense*, a recent book about feline science. An academic, historian, and bookworm, Grandpa Jerry misses no opportunity to squeeze a recent bestseller into the conversation.

After lunch we made plans to visit more before I moved on. I was planning a workshop by White Rock Lake's historic bathhouse and performance venue and encouraged them to join. They were curious how I managed to pull off a workshop at the bathhouse. I explained I was simply planning to pull into the parking lot and open my doors, guerrilla-style. Sometimes, that was the only option. Besides, the bathhouse and I had history—as a child I would bike to the lake every other afternoon, little to my parents' knowledge, and watch the geese. These were fond memories from my first decade of life—worth celebrating on my birthday.

Gamby and Aunt Karin like sauerkraut, but they hadn't eaten microbe-dense kraut until I shared mine with them. Pickled vegetables can be confusing. Not all pickles are fermented, but all fermented vegetables are definitely pickles. How does one know if they are fermented or heat processed, anyway? Fermented foods will always be available in the refrigerated section of your grocery store. Without slowing down the process (the refrigerator is also known as the pause button), vegetable ferments will keep breaking down until they are inedible.

Canned or heat-processed pickles on the other hand will store for years and are known as shelf stable. They are more widely available in grocery stores across the United States and can also be delicious, but these pickles lack the nourishing benefits of fermented pickles.

Canned Pickles Versus Fermented Pickles

CANNED PICKLES

- Pickles are made with vinegar and spices and then heat processed or sterilized.
- The pickled flavor comes from vinegar (see page 71), which is a product of fermentation.
- Heat processing wards off all organisms—good and bad—and creates a shelf-stable product that can keep for years at room temperature.

FERMENTED PICKLES

- Pickles are processed with salt and submerged in an anaerobic environment, encouraging lactic acid fermentation, or the growth of beneficial microbes.
- The pickled flavor comes from a unique selection of bacteria, grown right in your jar during fermentation.
- Fermented pickles will continue to ferment at room temperature, so it's best to store them in the fridge long term.
- Why choose fermented? Because the organisms are beneficial for your gut—your body craves it. Also, it's delicious.

The Midwestern food culture of my relatives, by contrast to cultures rich with fermented foods (such as Japanese cuisine), is hardly healing. In fact, most of it, TV dinners and fast food alike, is the opposite, with its embrace of preservatives and high fructose corn syrup. Fermented foods promote good gut health and a more resilient immune system. Sauerkraut easily converts newbies such as Gamby and Karin to fermentation.

Classic Sauerkraut

YIELDS 1 GALLON, 1–4 WEEKS

I recommend starting with sauerkraut to give your gut a good dose of microbes. Sauerkraut is simple, delicious, and fun. Sauerkraut workshops are my most rewarding workshops. Students often share stories of going to the grocery store immediately after the workshop, so they can make a batch as soon as they get home. That's what I'm trying to do. Get you back in your kitchen to take control of your food and health.

INGREDIENTS
7 lbs cabbage (2 medium-size heads)
2 tbsp caraway seeds
1 tbsp juniper berry
2–3 tbsp salt

MATERIALS
Gallon glass jar or crock
Weight and cover

PROCESS
1. Cut cabbage into quarters and finely chop. Place chopped cabbage into a large bowl. If you have outer leaves of cabbage, rather than compost them, place them aside.

2. Add caraway seeds and juniper berries to the bowl of chopped cabbage.

3. Add 2 tbsp of salt and massage the cabbage for 5 to 10 minutes. Your cabbage will release water, which will serve as your kraut's brine. Taste the cabbage—you may want to add more salt to your liking.

4. Check for a puddle at the bottom of your bowl and squeeze a handful of cabbage above the bowl to check whether it has produced enough brine. Once gently squeezed, brine should drip with ease from the cabbage.

5. Pack the cabbage into your gallon jar until it's submerged below brine. Take the cabbage leaves you set aside from earlier and layer them on top of your kraut, pressing down.

6. Add a weight, such as scrubbed and boiled river rocks or a small jar filled with water, on top of the layer of cabbage leaves. Secure a tea towel to the mouth of your jar with a rubber band to keep dust and bugs out.

7. Wait a week and taste—you may want to keep it going another week, but it's good practice to try your ferments along their journey. Vegetables will ferment at different speeds depending on their environment—the warmer it is, the faster it will ferment, while the colder it is, the slower it will ferment. Most vegetable ferments thrive best between 68° to 76° F.

8. When the sauerkraut is to your liking, cover it with a lid and store in the fridge. Keeping your new kraut cool slows fermentation, so you can more or less enjoy the fermented flavor from when you sealed the jar.

Back at my grandmother's after the workshop, I found an e-mail reply from the *Civil Eats* editor, asking if I'd write a blog post about my experience teaching fermentation. I said I'd love to, and for the next few weeks that would be my focus, along with my Fractured Atlas fiscal-sponsorship application. Both felt like gateways—chances to spread more awareness of the growing fermentation movement.

II. HausBar Urban Farm and Vinegar

After the monotony of the suburbs, Austin was a relief—no more Dallas strip malls, no more Dallas traffic. I arrived at HausBar Urban Farm midmorning. Farmer Dorsey and her wife, Susan, raise rabbits and chickens for meat and maintain an acre of land in East Austin. I parked in front of their fence and peered at the setup; beyond the garden was a processing facility, chicken coops, rabbit pens, and a home with an outdoor educational kitchen and aquaponics.

HausBar had drawn considerable controversy in recent years, of a sort increasingly familiar to urban farmers. A local activist group, People Organized in Defense of Earth and her Resources (PODER), concluded HausBar was a neighborhood nuisance. There was an uproar over Dorsey's slaughtering rabbits and chickens in a residential zone. PODER complained of compost smells, too. And gentrification—Dorsey's farm appeals mostly to race- and class-homogenous young foodies and four-star chefs. On the other side, Dorsey has done a tremendous job including the community in farm education. With HausBar she has built a diverse and thriving ecosystem in the middle of the city.

Dorsey's right hand, Lola, could clean a chicken in 240 seconds. With Lola and Dorsey, I ate my first tripa de pollo (tacos filled with crunchy fried chicken intestines)—a delicacy in Mexico.

Another first: I witnessed my first chicken slaughter and butcher. I was mesmerized by Lola's meticulous cleaning of bird after bird. Dorsey loved her chickens, and even in death they were an extension of her farm family.

Dorsey and Susan threw a party to get me acquainted with the food lovers of Austin, including Kate Payne. I knew of Kate as Austin's go-to girl for fermentation and the author of *The Hip Girl's Guide to Homemaking*. She was helpful and organized an event with the bus at the Mueller's Farmers Market that weekend. She brought homemade shrubs to Dorsey's party. I was immediately enticed by these sweetened vinegar-based syrups and asked Kate if she would teach me how to make vinegar, so I could try my hand at do-it-yourself shrubs, too. She invited me over the day before my departure.

When I arrived at Kate's, she brought out an array of homemade vinegars accompanied by sparkling water, and we tasted each. I brought an organic grapefruit from Arizona and smudge sage from Oregon to turn into vinegar. Though Kate was concerned the high acidity of the grapefruit might stunt fermentation, after researching, we decided to double the sugar to assure plenty of edible interest for the microorganisms.

Fruit Scrap Vinegar

YIELDS 1 QUART, 1–3 MONTHS

Vinegar is also known as acetic acid, the primary bacterial component. It adds a complex, acidic flavor and has many uses in food, from salad dressings to sauces to deglazing a pan to making canned pickles. In fact, we call canned pickles *pickles* because vinegar introduces tanginess—a tanginess that originates from fermentation.

Vinegar is simple: the primary ingredients are sugar, water, and air—fermented to alcohol and further fermented with the addition of acetic acid bacteria. The addition of air introduces *Acetobacter* (acetic acid bacterium), but I recommend inoculating with raw vinegar for more consistent and reliable flavor. You can source raw vinegar from your local grocery store. Bragg apple cider vinegar is a brand that contains live, active bacteria and yeast. (Read more about sourcing vinegar on page 12.)

INGREDIENTS
1 qt water
¼ cup sugar
1 cup fruit scraps (berries, apples, and more)
¼ cup raw vinegar (optional)

MATERIALS
Quart jar
Strainer
Cover

PROCESS
1. Gently heat 2 cups of water on the stovetop and dissolve sugar.

2. Transfer sugar water to quart jar and add fruit scraps. Top off with water and cover with a cloth and a rubber band or a plastic Ball-jar lid.

3. Let the mixture naturally ferment. Once the ferment shows signs of activity and has a boozy scent and flavor, after 1–2 weeks, simply let it ferment wildly or add the optional raw vinegar to minimize the possibility of off flavors.

4. The warmer the temperature and larger the surface area exposed to air, the faster it will acetify. The final fermentation for one quart can take anywhere from 1 to 3 months.

5. Once the alcohol is fully converted to vinegar, store it in a sealed container. Oxygen will cause the vinegar to spoil. If you are patient enough, you can age your vinegar for a year or two, which I like to do. The flavor develops deeper, richer notes with age.

Tip: If the fruit yields less than 5 percent ABV, the vinegar will yield less than 4 percent and be prone to spoilage. This is why the addition of sugar is important. If you have a hydrometer (page 7), you can check the ABV beforehand, making sure that your vinegar will yield at least 5 percent ABV and not spoil.

III. H-Town

Brooklyn comes close, but no place fills me with as much nostalgia as Houston, where I spent my teenage years. So many feelings from my young life are mixed up in that nostalgia: worry, fear, longing, self-discovery.

This might explain my first anxiety attack on the bus.

I was on the outskirts of Houston, heading east toward my parents' house on the familiar Highway 290. Traffic was absurd. As I passed the suburbs and approached the city, my heart raced and my thoughts flurried. I couldn't focus. I could barely drive. I'd crash if I didn't figure out how to pull my behemoth over, but the traffic was making it impossible.

Finally, after what felt like half an hour, a median appeared. I pulled into it. Neutral, boom. I lurched out of the driver's seat and threw myself on the floor of the bus, hands on my head, taking a few deep breaths. Franklin rushed to me, nudging his face into mine, checking my vitals with a wet nose. I drank water, breathed, drank again.

Ultimately, the only way to get through these things is convince yourself it's not that bad. Laughter helps. I try to laugh at least once per drive. After all, it's funny: I'm driving a vintage school bus filled with forty gallons' worth of glass jars filled with fermented foods around the entire United States. "You've made it this far; you're doing great, baby."

That afternoon I pulled into the driveway of my parents' pale green inner-city home and opened the iron gate to the backyard garage. The small but spacious house was quiet when I entered, both of my parents still at their respective oil-and-gas-industry jobs. Mom had remodeled the entire place a decade ago: tore down walls, lined it with hardwoods, decorated with Danish modern furniture. She is a projects woman, with good taste. I spent the rest of the afternoon unloading and setting up ferments on my mother's metal IKEA table, which she had bought for my ferments two years past.

When they arrived home three hours later, Mom wanted a tour of the bus; Dad went straight to his study, once my bedroom. "There isn't anything you could do that would surprise me," he'd said to me years ago, and that statement has always seemed to satisfy his curiosity.

The next three weeks were full of power tools, sawdust, Home Depot, and Mom's cooking. Bus-renovation plans included yanking out the never-used/useless shower, expanding the closet attached to the ex-shower, putting down wood floors, resizing the bed, and building a shelf.

Building closet frames and putting down wood floors takes time and focus. I did it all on a tight budget and with the help of YouTube tutorials. On occasion I called my friend Daniel for expertise. Daniel was the mastermind behind my fermentation station, the gut of the bus, so naturally I declared him chief architect of Fermentation on Wheels upon my departure.

Kombucha

YIELDS 1 GALLON, 1–3 WEEKS

Whenever stationary, I start a large batch—or three—of kombucha. Ferments involving SCOBYs do better when they're not in motion or otherwise agitated. Kombucha is also less stinky than kimchi, and my mom barely noticed the batch until she opened the pantry doors and stared deep into the cellulose blob floating at the top of a liquid. Mom's used to concoctions of this variety; she's a chemist. Dad doesn't open pantry doors.

On the road I frequently encounter people seeking a kombucha SCOBY (symbiotic colony of bacteria and yeast)—they are disk-shaped starter cultures consisting of cellulose and acetic acid bacteria that reproduce during vinegar and kombucha fermentation. Kombucha, the beverage, is crucial for inoculation, though. The kombucha SCOBY assists in fermentation, providing the bacteria and yeast with her nutritious microbial presence, but she is the by-product of their action.

Thus, you can grow your own SCOBY at home. If you purchase a bottle of kombucha, preferably something small batch or local (to provide a more familiar environment for the culture), you can transfer it to a widemouthed jar, cover with a cloth (in a stationary space), and wait one to three weeks. Ultimately, you will have a SCOBY to start larger batches of kombucha in your kitchen. Or you can find a kombucha SCOBY and some starter from a friend who brews at home.

Note that SCOBYs are also known as mothers—so appropriate! They are a reproductive life force. Food-science writer Harold McGee says of their life force, "It really does take a village to make these things. A single mother is not enough. A father isn't enough. It takes a community. All of these things are communities of microbes and that's the cool thing about them."

Kombucha relies on caffeinated tea—varieties of *Camellia sinensis*—and sugar for fermentation. You can add other herbs in addition to caffeinated tea for flavor or remedy. I have known some people to wean kombucha off caffeinated tea—however, not all SCOBYs will take to the elimination of *Camellia sinensis* with ease. If you decide to take on this task, start slowly—by using less caffeinated tea in each batch. Make sure you have an extra SCOBY in case your experiment doesn't succeed.

My favorite herbal remedy for well-being is 2 tablespoons Saint-John's-wort, 2 tablespoons oatstraw, and 2 tablespoons licorice, while some of my favorite herbs for taste are 4 tablespoons of mint or lavender. As you get into your kombucha routine, you'll find creative ways to integrate herbs for remedy and flavor. Herbs with high oil content will stunt microbial growth, most notably chamomile, so use such herbs sparingly (or steer clear of them).

INGREDIENTS
¾ to 1 gallon water
1 cup organic unrefined sugar
4 tbsp black, white, or green tea
4 tbsp herbs as you see fit for flavor and /
    or remedy (see above)

1 cup kombucha
kombucha SCOBY

MATERIALS
Gallon jar or ceramic vessel with spigot
Home-brew funnel

PROCESS
1. Heat half of the water in a pot with the sugar. Dissolve the sugar as your water comes to a boil; once it reaches a boil remove from heat.

2. Steep your tea and other herbs for 10 to 15 minutes.

3. Add the remaining water to your pot. This should allow the sweet tea to cool to a temperature that is comfortable to the touch. It's important that your tea not be above 100° F when the culture and SCOBY are introduced.

4. Pour sweet tea through mesh strainer into your fermentation vessel, a glass gallon jar or ceramic vessel with spigot (see note). Use a funnel to prevent tea from missing the container. Make sure you leave enough room for your culture and SCOBY.

5. Add the culture and SCOBY. Keep your soon-to-be-kombucha in a temperature-stable place, away from direct sunlight. Cover it with a tea towel, secure with a rubber band, and taste every 7 days or until a new SCOBY forms a layer at the top.

6. Taste your kombucha weekly as the flavor intensifies. Less time will result in mild and sweet, while more time will lend a tangy vinegar-like flavor. When it's to your liking, bottle and refrigerate. Keeping your kombucha cool will pause fermentation. Don't forget to save the SCOBY and 1 cup of kombucha for your next batch. Pass the other SCOBY on to a friend!

A ceramic vessel with a spigot allows you to taste the kombucha without disturbing the newly formed SCOBY. It also makes "continuous brewing" easy—you can simply leave the SCOBY and some kombucha in the vessel and add the sweet tea once it's cool to the touch.

After three weeks of my following YouTube tutorials—and the ups and downs of my parents' perplexed reception of my new life—the bus had a new mood. A parade of good fortune followed: *Edible NOLA* took interest in my upcoming visit to New Orleans, booking a gig at the Southern Food and Beverage Museum and advertising in various city publications; *Civil Eats* asked a freelance journalist to cover my story; and Fractured Atlas accepted Fermentation on Wheels as a sponsored project. I moved forth from my childhood home feeling truly like an adult. It was nothing like the nine-to-five-workweek adulthood of my early twenties. It was an adulthood in which I felt I was making it with my passions. I was growing—moving forward.

I still remember how engaged I felt with my life in that moment. It was a time of embracing *doing*. The way I see it, you can't feel your way into doing; you have to do your way into feeling. Whatever it is that you want to achieve, the conditions will never be perfect. The time is now. Or, as beatnik traveler Jack Kerouac would put it, "Climb that goddamn mountain."

THE DEEPEST SOUTH

For what gives value to travel is fear. It breaks down an inner structure we have. One can no longer hide behind the hours spent at the office. (Those hours we protest so loudly, which protect us so well from the fear of being alone.) —Albert Camus

I. Fear Is the Fuel for Exhilaration

Truck drivers eyed me as I pulled in to a truck stop in East Texas, near Beaumont, my father's hometown. Though I'd visited family there dozens of times, I always felt out of place in the strangely familiar town. When I emerged from my bus, big, tall, bearded trucker-hat bros pointer-fingered their glasses down their noses. I was proud of my ride. "Just don't call me sweetie," I thought.

The line between two states blurred. As I approached Louisiana for the next milestone, I kept my chin up and looked straight ahead, my confidence bolstered by my big-rig expertise and Fermentation on Wheels' new validity.

Though hippies fear Texas because of its conservatism, harsh drug laws, and love of firearms, I've always felt comfortable there. I'd been a rebel in Texas from when I was a beef-loathing six-year-old. The Deep South was less familiar territory, and

I felt a fresh chapter of my project emerge as I drove forward. A fear swam inside me, per usual, as I floated farther from the West Coast.

That fear always brought exhilaration, too. I was excited to be afraid. It reminded me I was in for surprises. Anything could happen. And though I was behind schedule, I embraced my last dose of familiarity at my uncle's house in Vidor, twenty miles west of the Louisiana border. We spent the evening drinking Budweiser, being loud chatty Texans, and boiling crawdads. I got on the road at four the next morning, with the aim of making my New Orleans workshop on time.

The southern Mississippi watershed brought misty dreamlike roads. An occasional break in the fog peaked into Louisiana swamp dwellings—numinous little homesteads that had always fascinated me. I imagined the extraordinary resilience of people living in such watery circumstances, and the feasts of well-seasoned frog legs, alligators, and crawdads. I raced through the winter fog, determined to make my first well-promoted event with ample time to spare. I still needed to source vegetables.

In New Orleans, my new bookshelf proved no match for the potholes. By the time I got to the Southern Food and Beverage Museum, books covered the floor of my bedroom. I had thirty minutes to spare—I wouldn't make it to the market. I opened the door of the bus to fifteen people. Class still hadn't started and I already had a full house. I skipped vegetable fermentation and went straight to discussing starter cultures. The crowd was wooed enough by the aura of the bus to not mind that we didn't get to fermenting vegetables.

―――――――――

I camped at the Mississippi River for two nights on the recommendation of a gastronome-poet, Sebastian Knight. Sebastian was my first familiar face from Eugene and had dropped by my workshop the day before. He professed to be my biggest fan. Some part of this must have been true. He was two thousand miles from Eugene, insisting that I let him join the journey. He had asked the same upon my departure, too.

I hadn't been so sure about taking on a travel companion, but I thought twice now. I was, after all, wavering each day between lonesomeness and uncompromising independence.

Some lovely aspects of Sebastian: He enjoys a good walk and getting lost in thought. He appreciates dirt, trees, and sun. And he's an eccentric, known to sit on the sidewalk, at times of heavy foot traffic, with his clunky typewriter, composing poems on small sheets of paper, perfect for attaching to a small vole or pigeon.

I'd never known Sebastian to hold down any bill-paying job, and it was unclear how he supported his lifestyle, which included, but was not limited to, fine dining and traveling from fantastic city to fantastic city. I had always sensed he depended on others to get by, and I was not in a position to be further depended upon. My starter cultures were enough.

As long as he was willing to work, though, he was welcome. I offered my guest bed, given we would wake up and get straight to it.

Next day, I rose early to research farms and nonprofits in Alabama and Georgia. An hour later, Sebastian crawled out of bed. I made breakfast and coffee for us. He sat on my workbench, which was still in bed mode, staring blankly into space, sipping his coffee. Then he got off the bus.

Upon his return an hour later, he said, "Darling, I had to meet the river for my morning poetry-writing session."

"You're not coming with me on the next leg," I said.

His final plea was the suggestion that Fermentation on Wheels make contacts with the fine-dining realm—restaurants focused on sustainable-food practices. Having connections with influence, power, and money would be helpful, he argued.

I pushed back. Fermentation on Wheels is for all people. Fine dining is for those who can afford it.

The next day, I parted ways with Sebastian and continued to Mississippi.

———————————————

Sebastian had been a useful distraction, preventing me from getting nervous about my Jackson elementary school classes. They were my first kids-only classes, arranged by Lauren, a blogger who'd set me up in a partnership with FoodCorps, the food branch of AmeriCorps. I would teach at four public schools over four days.

My first youth class was a group of second-grade boys at Magnolia Speech School. We talked about community (the people kind) and then about other, smaller, bacterial communities. We followed that by smelling starter cultures and tasting sauerkraut. They went around in a circle, each taking a taste.

"I . . . hey, I actually *like* it!" the first student declared.

Next taster: "I *like* it, too!"

Taster No. 3: "Hey, me too!"

As the tasting continued, every student cheered and clapped for their classmates, exchanging high fives.

Best first youth class ever—not to be confused with one of my most unsuccessful youth classes ever, which took place two hours later at Rowan Middle School. Each and every sixth-grader walked to the door of my bus and spat out that very same sauerkraut.

I held my first adult workshop sans bus at Rainbow Food Coop. I visited the Jackson farmers' market to find fresh, local vegetables. The options were sparse—all root veggies. My eyes turned to the rutabaga, my second-favorite vegetable after radishes, and not one where I'd triumphed fermentation-wise. There was also ample turmeric, a new market find.

If I'm unable to break boundaries, experiment, and adapt old projects, then I'm not mastering the art. I make something fresh at every workshop. It proves to myself and my students that fermentation is versatile.

Fermented Turnips and Rutabaga

YIELDS 1 GALLON, 1–2 WEEKS

Turnips and rutabaga pair well together, and neither has too strong of a flavor, thus they are great to ferment with spices that will infuse extra life into them. Rutabaga, to boot, is an especially nutritious root vegetable packed with vitamin C and potassium.

INGREDIENTS

1½ lbs turnips

1½ lbs rutabaga

3-inch turmeric root

1 large shallot

3 tsp dried poblano pepper

2¼ tbsp unrefined sea salt

6 cups water

MATERIALS

Gallon jar

Weight and cover

PROCESS

1. Prep your turnips and rutabaga by cutting them julienne-style. I measure each of my cuts at 2–3 bites per pickle. Toss them in a big bowl.

2. Thinly slice the turmeric and shallot and add to your ingredient bowl.

3. Add the poblano pepper. If you like more heat, be more generous in your addition.

4. Toss your vegetables and evenly distribute all your ingredients. After they're all mixed up, pack them snug in a gallon jar.

5. To make the brine, dissolve the salt in water. Pour the brine over your ingredients and seal tightly with lid, then give the vessel a few quick flips to distribute the spices. Take the lid off.

6. Add a flexible plastic quart-container lid and add a weight on top of it that will keep your root vegetables underneath the brine, such as an 8-ounce Ball jar filled with water. Cover your vessel with a cloth and rubber band, to keep bugs and dust out.

7. When your ferment is to your liking, cover it with a lid and place in the fridge.

Lauren hosted Fermentation on Wheels' first fermentation-themed potluck at her house. Potlucks would quickly become part of my event repertoire. The small gathering of eight people was mostly service members of Jackson's FoodCorps along with a few attendees from the adult workshop and the head fermenter from the food co-op. The sweet-and-sour spread included a garlic kefir dip, three types of vegetable ferments, roasted vegetables, and a loaf of sourdough bread flavored with sauerkraut juice. After the potluck we packed into the bus, visited with Franklin the cat, and drank my home-brewed herbal meads late into the evening.

The gathering marked my last night in Jackson, and I would miss the enthusiasm and optimism of the FoodCorps crew, who dedicated their time to teaching kids who lacked access to good food. They were an inspiration. Lauren later wrote a blog entry about my visit to Jackson that warmed me. So rarely am I able to describe the feel of the bus and do it justice. Our homes, no matter how special they are, feel commonplace when they become a day in, day out aspect of our lives, sewn into our existence. Other people can feel the magic more than we can.

Lauren described my home, also my work space, in her blog entry as feeling like the "cozy kitchen of an artistically-inclined mad scientist." I'll gladly take that.

Yokna Bottoms Farm outside Oxford, Mississippi, invited me to speak at a monthly potluck in conjunction with the Mississippi Sustainable Agriculture Network. It had been a big week. The day before my departure from Jackson, the *Civil Eats* piece went viral on the Internet. In one day I'd gone from awkward fermenter to badass bus-driving fermentation lady.

"Excuse me, will you please stand there, right there—pose in front of your bus?" a photographer at the event asked. "And then will you please stand with these gentlemen so I can get a shot of the three of you together?" The hype from the article was partly responsible, but the southerners I met also seemed to have a natural appreciation for my renegade, roving do-gooder project. If *Civil Eats* wouldn't make me a face of the food movement, maybe the South would.

Before my next arrival at the Mississippi Modern Homestead Center, in Starkville, I had leads for workshops all the way up the East Coast, as far as Maine. It was February and I would soon be booked through June.

Marion, founder of *Southern Cultured*, greeted me at the Mississippi Modern Homestead Center before my afternoon workshop. She asked how she could assist, and I asked if a shared lunch might be something we could work in.

She disappeared and arrived an hour later with lunch accompanied by curtido, a Salvadoran vegetable ferment.

Fifty people attended the workshop. It was a great knowledge-sharing session and spurred thoughtful conversations. After the talk students lined up to chat and get starter cultures—tibicos, sourdough, dairy kefir. And for the first time my tip jar was loaded.

I stayed four nights. The next morning a workshop attendee brought a gallon of raw goat milk in thanks. To take advantage of the luxurious kitchen, I made goat cheese (see soft cheese on pages 56–57) and a batch of cultured oats, learned from Austin of Fermenters Club.

Sweet-Potato Fly

YIELDS ½ GALLON, 24-48 HOURS

I also made sweet-potato fly, a beverage traditionally fermented in Guyana using sweet potatoes, spices, and whey, a by-product of cultured dairy (page 57). I wanted to try it with another culture medium: tibicos (pages 61–62). I was also curious how the recipe would turn out if I roasted the sweet potatoes with a little fat. This fizzy and spiced beverage with a roasted aroma is best served cold and titillates the palate on a hot day.

INGREDIENTS

1 large sweet potato (roughly 1½ lbs)
1 tbsp coconut oil
1 inch ginger, chopped
2 cinnamon sticks
1 tbsp nutmeg powder
1 tsp cloves
¾ cup sugar
3–4 cups water
1 tbsp tibicos or ½ cup whey

MATERIALS

Grater
Roasting pan
Gallon glass jar
Quart jar

PROCESS

1. Grate the sweet potato and rinse it in a colander to relieve some of the starchiness, which can add an unpleasant texture during fermentation.

2. Melt coconut oil in a saucepan and toss with grated sweet potato in a roasting pan. Roast the sweet potato for half an hour at 350° F.

3. Once the sweet potato has cooled to 100° F, place it in gallon glass jar with ginger, cinnamon, nutmeg, and cloves.

4. In a quart jar, dissolve sugar with warm water and add to the rest of the ingredients.

5. Add tibicos or whey to the ingredients. I place tibicos in a tea bag, for easy removal after fermentation.

6. Fill the gallon jar with water and give the ingredients a good stir with a large spoon. Cover the jar with a cloth and a rubber band and let the mixture ferment for 24 to 48 hours, until the beverage is fizzy and to your liking. The shorter the fermentation time, the sweeter it will be, while lengthening the fermentation time will introduce tangier elements. Strain the beverage, bottle, and store in the fridge.

With its open-door kitchen policy, people regularly dropped in to the homestead center. One visitor, Hiroko, brought me a jar of rice-bran miso.

She and Marion had been cultivating the bed of rice-bran miso, also known as nukadoko, essential in making nukazuke, which translates to "rice-bran pickle." Marion had studied a recipe and made the concoction, but struggled to get it right. Hiroko adopted the nukadoko from Marion in hopes of approximating the Japanese rice-bran pickles of her homeland. Not until Hiroko's mother visited and worked with the nukadoko day in and day out did they arrive at an authentic flavor.

I dined with Hiroko and her daughters my last two nights in Mississippi. We made traditional Japanese dinners with natto, mountain yam, seaweed, nukazuke, and miso soup. She taught me how to make nukazuke and work it into my kitchen routine. Her bed of rice-bran miso lives in a two-gallon crock. Every morning she buries fresh whole vegetables in the rice bran and unburies them before serving dinner. She juliennes and slices the pickles after digging them out. The flavor is earthy-umami.

Nukazuke

YIELDS 6 CUPS NUKA BED; 3–4 WEEKS STARTER TIME, 10–12 HOURS PICKLING TIME

Starting your own nuka bed is easy, though it helps to learn from someone who has worked with the medium; the texture and flavor are specific and take practice to get down. I started a bed of rice-bran miso in Georgia and inoculated it with Hiroko's nukadoko sample. It was especially helpful to have her years-old starter as a reference for texture and taste.

Nukazuke requires commitment because you must feed it with vegetables regularly to develop the bed's flavor. The bed also needs to be aerated daily by hand. If you can inoculate the bed with a sample of nukadoko, I encourage you to do so. If not, you can still achieve delicious results starting it as a wild ferment.

INGREDIENTS

90 g / ⅓ cup salt (15 percent salt, by
    weight of rice bran)
2½ cups water
610 g / 7 cups rice bran
130 g nukazuke culture (optional)
¾ cup fresh shiitake
¼ cup hydrated kombu
1 slice sourdough bread
2 inches ginger
1 cup dried bonito
1 tbsp ground cayenne

FOR CARE

Rice bran and salt
Additional ingredients for flavor
    (ginger, bonito, seaweed, etc.)

MATERIALS

Blender
Deep glass or ceramic vessel
    (for long-term use)
Tea towel

PROCESS

1. Dissolve salt in water on stovetop and set aside to cool.

2. Lightly toast rice bran for 5–10 minutes in a large pan on the stovetop, stirring occasionally to make sure the bran doesn't burn.

3. If you have a nukazuke starter, add it to the brine once it has cooled and mix well.

4. Lightly chop mushrooms, kombu, bread, and ginger and puree with bonito, cayenne, and ½ cup of the brine. Then add pureed ingredients to the brine and mix well.

5. Combine the hearty brine with toasted rice bran and mix together by hand. It will feel and look like wet sand.

6. Transfer the ingredients to a deep ceramic or glass container. Make sure to choose a container in which you can comfortably bury whole vegetables into the rice-bran bed.

7. Bury an array of vegetables in the bed. Vegetable suggestions: carrots, radishes, quartered cabbage, and cucumber. Starting out, it's a good idea to add more neutral vegetables that won't alter the flavor too dramatically—keep it simple. Cover the container with a tea towel.

8. Unbury vegetables 12 to 24 hours later. If your environment is warm (80° F or higher), I recommend taking the vegetables out after 6 to 12 hours. Rinse and chop the freshly pickled vegetables and enjoy. The flavor may not be fully developed yet, and it might take weeks to experience delectable pickles pulled from your nukazuke bed. Again, it's commitment and patience! Note that if you leave vegetables in for too long, it will create a sour flavor (for the vegetables and the nukadoko).

FOR MAINTENANCE

1. The vegetables deplete your nukadoko of salt. Thus each time you bury more vegetables, aerate the nuka bed with 1 teaspoon of salt. Alternatively, you can rinse and then sprinkle your vegetables with salt before burying them.

2. Aerate every day by hand and offer vegetables to the bed daily to develop good microbes and keep the nuka from spoiling. The texture and salt content of the nuka bed will change based on vegetable feedings. If the bed becomes a little too wet, add more toasted rice bran. Hiroko likes to add a light layer of dry soybeans on top of her bed when it becomes too wet, to soak up the water.

3. If you desire, integrate more ginger, bonito, shiitake, cayenne, and seaweed for flavor. You can follow the first 6 steps and scale down the rice bran, salt, and water quantities.

4. When not in use, store your nukadoko pot in the fridge.

My overhead was low while I was on the road, and the donations from my workshops in Mississippi tallied up to nearly $500, twice the amount of what I had been spending in an average month. I knew exactly what I wanted to invest in: a solar panel.

So Marion referred me to a solar-panel dealer and suggested I take her truck for the transaction. I arranged to pick up the panel my last afternoon in Mississippi, in the small town of Louisville. I was directed to the "only Mexican restaurant in town." In the strip-mall parking lot of Mi Rodeo, Fermentation on Wheels got its first solar panel. It would lie on the bus floor for the next thousand miles. I had no means or skill to install it, yet.

II. With Affettuoso

I made a quick stop in Birmingham, where I taught a workshop outside a trinkets shop called the Painted Shovel Mercantile and held a potluck at Jones Valley Teaching Farm. Otherwise I raced through Alabama, stopping once more to restock on supplies before heading to Georgia.

Restocking on supplies was a challenge for my obsessive standards. Local food co-ops became rare after I left the West Coast, and faceless mega-supermarkets were not my first choice shopping-wise. I did what I could, often going out of my way. I researched the grocery stores in each region, state, and city, seeking spots that would benefit the local economy, had large parking lots, and sold goods that were sustainably sourced and available in bulk.

I was lucky to befriend farmers in my travels, who gifted fresh vegetables, so these trips were mostly for the sake of my ferments: salt for fermenting vegetables, sugar for my tibicos and kombucha, flour for sourdough feedings, drinking water for my cultures and myself, tea for kombucha, and milk for my dairy kefir. As I cared for my dependents, they proliferated. In addition to being serious obsessions of mine, bartering and selling cultures would soon become a viable source of income.

Paul and Terra, brother and sister-in-law of my Eugene communard Jesika, awaited my arrival in Georgia. Their spot, Full Life Community Farm, is a primitive farm in Carrollton, sustained by a modest solar system. The buildings were made of cob, and we pooped in a hole in the ground.

Paul and Terra had fifty chickens. I helped move chicken fencing and we shared every meal. Their daughter, Zinnia, was just five months old and diaper-free. She'd been trained to relieve herself on command, with a gentle *tiss* or fart impression in her ear. I was impressed.

I helped with odd here-and-there chores as I always did during farm stays, and Paul asked if I would help dip the chicken's feet in oil, a cure for mites. The evening before I left, when the sun went down and the chickens were at roost, we began the hour-long process. I wore my bright yellow rain jacket and held a five-gallon bucket of peanut oil near Paul, who gracefully grabbed each chicken and dipped their feet in the oil before returning them to roost. As we moved through the coops, Terra followed us with a flashlight, Zinnia strapped to her torso.

With few tools, we pulled it off with finesse and minimal squawking. The process felt more like love than business. It was the closest I've ever felt to chickens.

I rolled into a suburb of northwestern Atlanta midmorning, where I had earlier scouted out the state's largest Japanese grocery store, whose lot belonged to a typical suburban strip mall. The sun shone beyond a scattered cloud formation, giving warmth on the cool winter day. In the store I bumbled aimlessly, per usual and with great pleasure, carefully eyeing the meticulously arranged shelves of salty sauces, packaged wagashi, and boxes crowded with Japanese script before filling my basket with three quarts of koji and a large bag of rice bran.

After my grocery store meditation, I approached the bus. It took up two spots, and the machines surrounding it were tiny by comparison. Would I ever find myself here again? I hoped I would summon the energy and courage to make such a trip again, but even if I did, what were the chances I would end up in this parking lot a second time, approaching my fermentation bus with armloads of koji before taking to the road again? Each parking-lot scene was a unique moment in space and time.

Not long after, I arrived at my host's home in Decatur, Georgia. It would be a grueling few days. My weekend workshop Get Cultured! had a hundred reservations, so I organized two more events to relieve the crowd, which nevertheless swept through the booked-up venue that weekend. I introduced my workshop with a bit of Fermentation on Wheels philosophy to fifty attendees:

> I drive a mobile creative project equipped with a fermentation lab that serves as an educational space. It's also my tool to inspire people to live more simply and sustainably, as well as encourage people to prepare their own food.
>
> Thriving communities realize the interconnectedness of education, food, and health. If we don't have access to good food, we won't have the energy to discover solar energy or think up the next Google. Our industrial food system disregards the sacredness of and destroys living things—plant, animal, or microbe—and desensitizes our palates.
>
> I'm trying to show people, with my alternative lifestyle and love for fermented foods, there is a way to thrive in the current education, food, and health systems. My line of work began and has flourished thanks to solid community. Thank you for continuing to show up and grow with me!

Atlanta was my last chance for repairs before heading to the mountains, and I'd had an oil leak at my back rear wheel since Northern California. (I know, I know—I've been hiding this from you.) According to all the smart mechanical people I knew, the worst-case scenario was a tire fire. Somehow this didn't terrify me much until the impending Appalachian mountain range. I ordered the parts and had them shipped to a guy in Mechanicsville, a neighborhood in Atlanta.

Before heading for the mechanic's garage lot, I bought a six-pack of microbrews, some coconut milk, and smoked fish at Dekalb Farmers Market, a grocery store worthy of its own zip code. It would be a long two days of auto shops and strip malls.

Coconut Kefir

YIELDS 1 QUART, 24–48 HOURS

I decided to drink beer and play with my food—typical. I inoculated the coconut milk with dairy kefir grains, and the results were luxurious: thick, fluffy, coconut-flavored yogurt. Refer to page 12 to source dairy kefir grains.

INGREDIENTS

1 can of coconut milk
1 tbsp dairy kefir culture (make sure you
   have extra grains first)

MATERIALS

Quart jar

PROCESS

1. Shake canned coconut milk and pour into a quart jar.

2. Add dairy kefir grains to the coconut milk. Make sure you have extra dairy kefir grains before you add the tablespoon—coconut milk tends to eat up the grains.

3. Agitate the milk and kefir 3 to 4 times a day for 24 to 48 hours until thick and creamy. It should have the texture of Greek yogurt, but slightly thicker. Stir, refrigerate, and enjoy. Coconut kefir will keep for 1 to 2 weeks.

My schedule pulled me to Charleston, South Carolina, a week later, for a workshop at GrowFood Carolina. I felt slightly stressed when Franklin crept off the bus beside some railroad tracks. He'd been known to slip away on occasion, but he always came back. At the farms we visited he had free rein—I tried to be much more cautious of his whereabouts while in the city, but his stealthy self could be difficult to keep tabs on.

I kept my cool, joined by three chefs and a family of five. Of the family, the Scholls, four sported dreadlocks—this included three girls under the age of twelve. They were also school bus dwellers and had driven eighty miles into town after hearing about my workshop. We quickly became friends, Franklin reliably returned from his foray, and Jody, the matriarch of the Scholl bus family, invited me to their friend's farm where they were parked.

The farm was on seven hundred acres, kept in one family since the early 1800s. The Scholls cultivated mushrooms with the farmer—they even offered a few shiitake logs for me to take along on the bus. I decided against it, fearing it would spark a new obsession on top of my trillions of microbes.

One afternoon Jody, her two youngest girls, and I crammed into a golf cart and rode through the fields, through the woods, and around old structures. We came to a spring, forcefully pushing its way through the dirt to form a sizable pool at our feet. This led to a creek that ran through the property. It was my first clear view of a spring source—mesmerizing. I felt rescued, transported by the abundance and clarity of the country after the narrow chaos of the city.

The visit was too brief. I longed for friends who truly understood my lifestyle— the beauties of it, but the challenges that came with it, too. Though I was surrounded by people, teaching day in, day out, I craved a greater nomadic community, with whom I felt kinship.

Traditional Kimchi

YIELDS 1 GALLON, 3-6 WEEKS

We made kimchi our last evening together. Kimchi has a reputation as difficult because of its megafunk, and perhaps because it hails from a faraway land, Korea, where it's sometimes buried underground. I informed the Scholls it was nevertheless easily made— if you can make sauerkraut every month, you can get kimchi down. This palate stomper is worth the extra work. Though kimchi is generally spicy, you can adjust this mild recipe to suit your tastes. It is also renowned for its pungent aroma and will fill the boundaries of any room (or small home, such as my bus).

Kimchi has hundreds of varieties. You can follow this recipe in a strict sense, but don't be discouraged if you can't locate some of the vegetables here. You'll want roughly seven pounds of veggies to make one gallon. This recipe calls for an overnight soak in brine, which is the traditional Korean technique—it lifts bitter elements in the vegetables. You can find a quick version of kimchi on page 123.

INGREDIENTS
3 medium napa cabbage (4 lbs)
1 bunch carrots (1 lb)
2 bunches radishes (1 lb)
2 bunches turnips (1 lb)
1 leek
¼ cup salt (3 percent salinity)

INGREDIENTS FOR PASTE
6 cloves garlic

2 inches ginger
1 medium shallot
2 tbsp chili powder or fresh chili peppers
2 tbsp fish sauce or tamari

MATERIALS
Gallon jar
Blender
Weight and cover

PROCESS
1. Chop napa cabbage, carrots, radishes, turnips, and leek and place into a large bowl.
2. Follow instructions 2 through 8 in the cubed-radish kimchi recipe on pages 31–32.

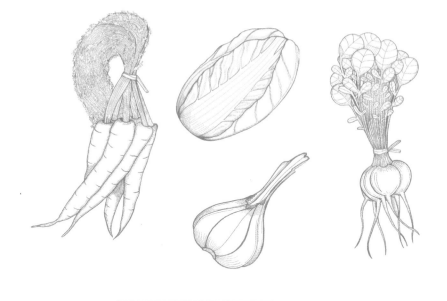

Waking from the kimchi party, I hustled to strap down and make my way to North Carolina. I had an after-school class scheduled in Wilmington with FoodCorps member Timothy's class. Upon arriving that afternoon, I lined up behind yellow school buses, ready for the daily rush of children and my fermentation class.

The school buses scooted forth after pickup, I parked where directed, and the after-school kids packed in, eagerly snacking on my bus-made concoctions. Then they chopped, massaged, packed, and squeezed their own homemade sauerkraut.

Teaching was easy; finding a comfortable place to park was hard. It was March and cold fronts had been hitting the South since February. My wood-burning stove barely warmed my bedroom space and I was resorting to a "poor man's heater"— two clay pots on top of a bread pan containing three tea candles.

I took the stove for its first spin at a farm not far from the elementary school. I had a week to kill. Timothy introduced me to Margaret, the head honcho at Shelton Herb Farm in Wilmington. The visit started out fantastic—I moved a pen for a sounder of swine, harvested pounds of microgreens, and made a cozy space in my bus—but then a slump set in. Maybe it was the dreary weather or maybe I felt stagnant. I've found that fear grows out of nothing. I worried about not living up to other people's expectations, not being funny or charming enough, waving my hands in the air too much, not delivering as exciting or expert of an experience as everyone hopes for when I come to town.

I ate several dinners with Margaret. We drank cheap beer, in the spirit of my southern upbringing, and talked late into the evening about family, her apple farm in Virginia, and cider. After dinner we retired to the living room, where we fell asleep to the Weather Channel.

Margaret and her farmhand assisted in scheduling two events for the weekend. A workshop at a local community garden had a staggering turnout. On this spring day, though the flowers were a month late, our spirits were on time. Fermentation on Wheels always brought me back to a mental clarity—teaching reminded me I was meant for the journey. With my intention to empower and inspire others and my love for the art of fermentation, it doesn't matter how high my hands fly or how conversational and heart-to-heart my approach is. A clear passion for knowledge and sharing it ignites curiosity and enthusiasm—that's why I'm in this business.

After the workshop, an attendee offered to help fix my plumbing, which had two broken pipes. I hadn't washed a dish while on the bus since Texas. We met in a Home Depot parking lot and worked all day, revamping my plumbing system. On

a break, I made a few calls to solar companies in the Charlotte area. One salesman offered to mount my solar panel for $100. It was a good deal. I would make the trip.

The next morning I drove until I reached Accelerate Solar in Charlotte, where the solar panel installation would go down. The owner was a young man from upstate New York. We spent the day together having not only a panel-mounting ordeal, but an inverter-installation party as well. He accepted sauerkraut as part of the final payment.

I left Charlotte as soon as we were done. I finally had my first mounted panel and was a fully functional off-grid fermenter.

EVERYONE PRAYS IN APPALACHIA

Each friend represents a new world in us,
a world possibly not born until they arrive, and it is
only by this meeting that a new world is born.
—Anaïs Nin

I. Soul and Guts

My home station for the next three days was a parking lot across from Green Hill Urban Farm in Asheville, North Carolina. The Blue Ridge Mountains loomed in the distance from the corner of the lot, which belonged to a cheap seafood restaurant. I appreciated the split identities of people and place and immediately took to my colorless parking spot accompanied by far-off epic scenery. I had a few days to myself and biked the small town, which had similarities to Eugene. Like my hometown, you couldn't tell who was rich or who was poor—people didn't seem to value fancy rides or high fashion—and there were enough eco-activists to balance out the mainstream folk.

The city had me, and I was excited to host my first guest since California. Austin Durant of Fermenters Club would join me for a weeklong trek, starting with a workshop at the urban farm. I'd warned him a month before that my living situation was rough for the average city dweller, assuming I wouldn't have plumbing or

electricity. Those concerns were smooth now with the recent renovations, and I felt proud and prepared to share my space.

Austin arrived by cab a few days later and settled in with ease. Our Asheville workshop rallied a crowd, and he took over in the speaking department. Not until then did I realize I needed a break from talking. Though a little chaotic during the hands-on portion, it was nice to have two instructors, with his more formal approach mixed with my casual tone. Austin kept the students engaged while I brought eight people on the bus at a time. Bonnie Young was among the last people hanging out in my bus after the workshop. A road warrior herself, splitting time between Georgia and Virginia, she had been trying to catch a workshop of mine since Atlanta. She gave me her number and told me to be in touch if I ever felt in a rut. She had connections all along Interstate 81 in Virginia.

The next evening we hosted a potluck at the urban farm. A mix of beginner, just-getting-started, and advanced fermenters joined the outdoor gathering staged on picnic tables, with a bonfire thirty feet away. Among the dishes my favorite was a feast of edible flowers and trout lily leaves on top of sauerkraut. Austin and I made a much-loved miso mayo accompanied by roasted sweet potatoes.

Miso Mayo

YIELDS 8-OUNCE JAR, 30 MINUTES

Miso is a versatile food, best consumed when raw because the bacterial cultures are eliminated when heated over 140° F, which is often the case when people make miso soup in the Western world. These two recipes are just a few creative ways to integrate miso into your daily foods.

This recipe calls for black garlic, a sweet and savory caramelized garlic with hints of balsamic vinegar. It's processed at low heat for several weeks and sometimes mistakenly believed to be fermented—it does not actually involve any microbial action. Black garlic is becoming more widely available, but you can buy it online or simply omit it from the recipe. This first recipe also has raw eggs in it, thus I recommend using eggs from small-scale-farmed, pasture-raised chickens when fresh. If you aren't sure about working with raw eggs, I've included a sesame miso-dressing recipe below, too. Both are tasty ways to integrate raw miso into your diet.

INGREDIENTS

3 egg yolks (room temperature)

2 heaping tsp miso

3 cloves black garlic (optional)

2 tbsp cider vinegar

2 tbsp balsamic vinegar

½ cup olive oil

MATERIALS

Large bowl (for whisking)

Blender

PROCESS

1. Put egg yolks into a medium-size bowl, good for whisking up a storm.

2. Blend miso, optional black garlic, and vinegar at high speed until all ingredients are well mixed.

3. Slowly pour half the blended ingredients into the bowl with the egg yolks while whisking. Once the mixture becomes nice and thick, add the rest of the blended ingredients, continuing to whisk.

4. Slowly drizzle olive oil into the mixture while whisking until you have a smooth, thick, and creamy mayonnaise.

Sesame Miso Dressing

YIELDS 1 CUP, 10 MINUTES

INGREDIENTS

2 tsp miso

2 tbsp sesame oil

1 tbsp apple cider vinegar

1 tsp sesame seeds

1 tsp tahini

1 tsp honey

PROCESS

1. Combine all ingredient in a quart jar and shake vigorously.

2. Spruce up a bed of greens.

We drove along the Smoky Mountains to Knoxville, Tennessee. Our vegetable-fermentation workshop took place in a restaurant recommended by the local food co-op, Three Rivers.

Two attendees invited us to park at their house for the evening, but their driveway was too narrow for the bus. After several tries, I gave up and drove on. At last we came to a dodgy-looking abandoned convenience store. We pulled into the lot, made our beds, and stepped outside to pee. The next morning Austin insisted we stay the night at a campground, something I'd never had the funds to do. Even with a solar panel and expert plumbing, bus life didn't suit everyone. And no wonder—random lots for sleeping, showerless days, driving around teaching fermentation in a big metal box. What was I doing anyway? My uncertainty was buzzing as I made my way past Knoxville. I was about to meet the master of controlled rot.

Sandor Katz had altered many fermentation enthusiasts' lives, including my own. His groundbreaking book, *Wild Fermentation*, introduced the simplicity and joy of DIY fermentation to the modern home kitchen. After being introduced to his work, I unearthed more tools to expand my own repertoire. His inspiring anecdotes joined by easy-to-follow recipes have provided invaluable literature for the fermentation and food movements.

He lived in a modest home in the Tennessee countryside, roughly an hour southeast of Nashville. I pulled into the driveway. He greeted us with humble, warm hugs and responded favorably to the bus. Relief washed over me. It didn't feel like such a chaotic big metal box after all—it was alive. He invited us to a potluck at the nearby community where he lived while he wrote *Wild Fermentation*. The community is part of the Radical Faeries, a queer countercultural movement, and offers safe haven for lesbian, gay, bisexual, transgender, and queer people.

He walked us around the two-hundred-acre property; we passed goats grazing along the hillside, half a dozen buildings, a bathhouse, a modest solar array, and a large garden just starting to bud. The kitchen was bustling, similar to Heart and Spoon's, and I felt at home. The sweet potatoes we'd originally planned to roast wouldn't fit in the already stuffed oven. We easily resolved to boil them in a pot on the stovetop instead. During the potluck, we introduced dishes, held hands around the table, gave thanks, and shared news and information.

Sandor had moved to the community from New York City in 1993, sometime after discovering he was living with HIV. The diagnosis shifted his priorities and deepened his interest in nutrition. After moving to Tennessee, he fermented the excess cabbage from the community's garden to make sauerkraut, a staple of his youth. He was immediately drawn to its flavor, its simplicity, and its microbial benefits. He considers fermentation to be an important part of his healing and inspires others to reclaim the age-old tradition in their home kitchens. He has taught hundreds of workshops around the world. So great is his influence that, after he posted a photo of Austin and me on the bus the next day, traffic to the Fermentation on Wheels website exploded. Sandor delivered a whole new level of legitimacy.

Austin and I drove on to Nashville, where we stayed with Nick and Nicole of Double N Urban Farm. Austin had found the couple a month before while admiring their photos of homesteading and plant magic on Instagram. They practice community-supported agriculture on the east side of town and have recently expanded to herbalism, too. Nicole grows all the herbs on-site and develops remedies for aches and pains and general rejuvenation. They have busy lives—with side jobs in addition to their farm—and commit their time to making their big dream work.

The day after our arrival, we had a workshop at Hands On Nashville, a five-acre educational farm and nonprofit south of Nick and Nicole's house. Our students were jovial, helpful, and excited for water kefir and sourdough. One woman brought an injera starter—used for making Ethiopian pancakes. Another attendee brought a dairy kefir culture sourced from the Caucasus Mountains. A couple in their fifties drove two hours from a small town in Kentucky and went home with tibicos, sourdough, and kombucha starters.

Austin and I wrapped up our collaborative week with a potluck at Nick and Nicole's farm. Austin made sourdough pancakes with kimchi blended into the batter. I made a pie with bacon bits, red cabbage, apples, maple syrup, and apple cider vinegar—a savory specialty of mine from my Eugene days. Kimchi, sourdough bread, yogurt, and several different fermented dips accompanied our dishes.

The weekend was easygoing with Austin at my side. How perfect it had been to spread myself a little less thin, I thought, to travel with another fermenter whose skills complemented my own. Austin was always on. He spoke in front of crowds with immense confidence, and he allowed me to focus my attention on sharing starter cultures and having more intimate conversations on the bus. It was a much-needed mental vacation as I continued to pour energy into upcoming tour logistics, driving the bus, and caring for eighteen starter cultures. He would be missed.

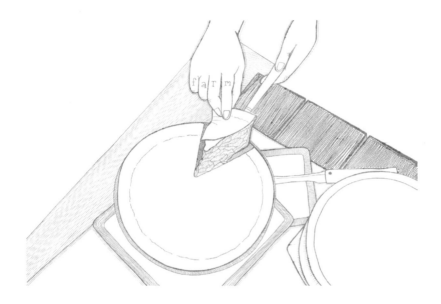

II. Appalachian Spring

Welcome to Floyd. We have a bus that is converted too. It is from California. You can call us if you like. We live in Floyd. We are Bob & Gayle. Our phone # is . . . We like your bus.

—Note left on bus, April 22, 2014

I called the number scribbled on the index card placed under my windshield wiper, after a long day of answering e-mails over coffee in town. I had planned to park on a side street to get some shut-eye, but the voice on the line urged me to park at her and her husband's place for the night. They had land ten miles north-east of Floyd, Virginia.

The farm was hard to miss. Their bus, a purple 1956 double-decker, was parked out front. Gayle and Bob rode to various renaissance festivals to sell handmade jewelry out of their bus-converted-home-and-studio and had recently bought land. They spoke of a time when roving in converted buses forged a bohemian nomadic community. Most of their fellow nomads from the 1970s were stationary now, and a handful had landed in Floyd. Their friend and bus owner Grateful Steve would later tell me, "We're the minority now."

Bob said they had made their last trip when they traveled to Florida the previous winter and had to spend a few grand on the engine coming back up. He was a quiet guy inching toward eighty years, made elaborate gothic jewelry adorned with precious crystals, and practiced yoga three hours a day. It was Bob's idea to buy land in Floyd, a complement to their rent-controlled apartment in Manhattan. When he wasn't in his studio or practicing yoga, he was in the garden.

Some of their friends dropped by to check out the "new generation" of skoolies—me. Grateful Steve told me I should bring my bus to a big party in Floyd that fall, FloydFest—"give the kids something to get excited about, respark the movement." I wondered what that would look like and couldn't help but wish for the skoolies of Steve's generation, or the diverse crew of nomads—musicians and jewelers and scientists—Gayle and Bob traveled with in the seventies and eighties. To all of us, the bus gave the option to design our spaces (and lives and work) from a clean slate. I was with the very people who revolutionized the lifestyle I love.

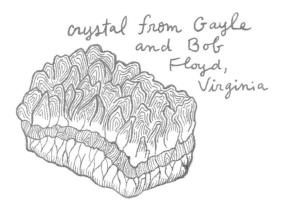

crystal from Gayle
and Bob
Floyd,
Virginia

It was almost noon by the time I left Floyd, with a mix of wistfulness and anticipation. I'd spent the morning bottling Concord-grape tibicos and putting together a gift of mustard-seed kraut for a local farmer who had gifted me raw milk. As I backed out of the driveway, I looked at the good-luck crystal adorning my control panel, a gift from Gayle's studio. Gayle blew a kiss, I blew one back, Bob held the peace fingers high, and I was off.

I was feeling as if I'd found a second family—I would miss the nomadic-kinship connection I stumbled upon in Floyd, and a part of me wished that I had more time to embrace such connections while on the road. Still, there was so much to look forward to. My next destination was Polyface Farm, the epicenter of sustainable animal farming.

Though we had never met, Polyface's Joel Salatin had a hold on my food heart. His farming philosophy has had an enormous impact on my diet and life as an activist. Like many others, I discovered Joel in Michael Pollan's book *The Omnivore's Dilemma*. Pollan described Joel's methods as an answer to many of our agricultural problems. His antibiotic-free, free-range "symbiotic, multi-speciated synergistic relationship-dense production model" was a revelation. Eating meat from a ranch such as Joel's allowed a person to be an omnivore *and* an environmentalist. I'd never known such a thing was possible. Joel is a philosopher, too. The Polyface website reads, *We are in the redemption business: healing the land, healing the food, healing the economy, and healing the culture*. My kind of evangelizing.

After discovering Joel, I went (slowly but surely) from a lifelong vegetarian (ages six to twenty-six) to an omnivore. No small thing. Growing up vegetarian in Texas, especially with my conservative, meat-equals-meal family, was akin to civil unrest. The response was even worse at school. Lunches packed with carrots, greens, toasted peanut butter sandwiches, and yogurt—that might fly in California, but not in Texas. My nickname in fifth grade was Carrothead.

Returning to meat after all that time was a confrontation with all of my former selves. Perhaps that made the impending visit to Polyface feel bigger.

I planned a pit stop at Harvest Moon grocery for some pre-Polyface shopping. It included good porter, fresh kale, raw cheese, and topped-off coffee. Grateful Steve, bus dealer and ladies' man, was at the grocery store, too. He helped carry my groceries to the bus and, to my delight, handed me $50 and cleaned me of the last year's kraut: a red-and-green classic kraut with mustard seed and a ginger arame green-cabbage kraut.

He offered to take a look at my engine, and while I wanted to get on the road, I knew I shouldn't pass it up. Steve knows buses.

"It looks like someone replaced your fuel filters in December. That's great."

"Yep," I replied, the road on my mind.

"Your air filter looks clean, but the indicator says it's clogged. I've reset it, so if you start up your engine, the indicator will give a true read."

I got in, started up, and indeed it was not clogged.

"Wow, I guess you know how to take care of a bus."

"I've learned a few things," I responded, clearly uncertain of my abilities.

He laughed and I wished him the best. He told me to call him if I ever needed mechanical help while on the road. I didn't take him for granted. Steve would offer important advice through the remainder of my journey.

It was late April and in the past week the landscape had finally turned a spectacular green. It felt like the spring we'd been waiting for since the equinox. The hills were rolling, and cows munched grass along the road; trees were showing off their green bouquets. Where I once dreaded the scrape of branches along the roof of my bus, lush greenery was now petting it. I was venturing deep into untouched Virginia terrain, the way I once ventured deep into the rural Oregon landscape that beckoned me two years back.

When I pulled out to let people pass, they smiled and waved, which was a rarity for me in my slow-moving oversize rig. On the final approach to Polyface, I stopped before a small wooden bridge and contemplated my size. There was no way it couldn't hold my bus if trucks filled with cows and pigs crossed it regularly. Still, I wasn't sure and didn't want to be the one to break Joel Salatin's bridge. I pulled over and got out, just as a contractor was making his way toward me. "Can this bridge hold twenty-two thousand pounds?" I asked.

He laughed. "Yes, definitely. Try fifty tons! This bridge isn't going to break." I returned, revved up, and pulled slowly over the bridge into the farm. Almost immediately an energetic man in overalls ran up to the bus, waving his hands.

I swung open the door.

"Hi, I'm Joel!" He hopped in and took a seat in the stairwell. He was an amiable dude. As he guided me to my parking spot, Franklin emerged from under my seat to nudge him, and Joel petted him nicely. He complimented Franklin's calm and sweet demeanor, then described all the cats on his farm and the ways in which he admired their unique personalities.

Though he was in the midst of packing for a trip, Joel and I talked for what felt like an hour. Teresa, his wife, walked over, and Joel gave her an excited tour of the bus. I was exhausted and thrilled and proud and glad to be in the presence of this man. "Chores start at six thirty A.M.," he announced, as he backed out. "People will be bustling about, just so you know."

"Yes, of course. No problem!"

Next morning I woke, bumbled to the farm store, and picked up bacon for breakfast. In the two days that followed, I would help corral sixty giant pigs; bend an ear toward Joel's mother, the Polyface matriarch; herd, lose, and then reherd cattle; collect and wash hundreds of eggs from Polyface's egg mobiles.

I'd also save Franklin from air attack. After one long and dirty day I arrived back at my bus to be greeted by Joel's eight-year-old grandson, Andrew, the farm's unofficial feline narc. He was standing beside the bus with his slingshot.

"Is that your cat?"

"Yeah." Franklin is often mistaken for a feral. He's tall and long and athletic; nothing average about him.

"I thought he was a panther, or a bobcat, or some other animal that's a danger to my enterprise, so I just wanted to make sure he's a house cat."

Andrew's enterprise was ducks. He was already a serious businessman.

He walked away. As welcome as we were, we were still strangers here, and tomorrow we would be strangers someplace else.

III. Luxurious Interlude

The Northeast megalopolis was a week away. I had yet to find a landing pad before departing Polyface, so I reached out to Bonnie, who had mentioned her list of bus-friendly cohorts along I-81. She came through and connected me with two of her high school friends: Bibb and Dolly of Harrisburg, Pennsylvania.

I was initially intimidated by the Fraziers' estate—it was huge, fancy, and immaculate. I second-guessed their wanting a scrappy, poorly painted old bus in their front yard. I sensed they had long ago evolved from young urban professionals to making-it-in-a-serious-way land-owning adults. I can appreciate expensive taste and luxurious living, but a tiny home on wheels keeps me in check, assuring a small footprint on the planet. It is also much easier to maintain. I tried to imagine the logistical challenges that accompanied a megahouse. I couldn't.

I parked in the driveway and had barely knocked when Dolly opened the door, greeting me with her big blue eyes and ushering me inside. I was filthy from farming and realized I hadn't showered in over a week. Living on the road had dramatically changed my hygiene habits, and my body had begun to keep up with it. I no longer needed to shower as often as I had—self-cleaning mode had kicked in.

Dolly, Bibb, and I ate meals together every night. During the days Bibb was at the quarry, and Dolly kept busy with chores and riding her horses. Occasionally we'd venture into town or visit their friends in the countryside. Though Dolly had a dedicated dislike for sauerkraut, I taught them fermentation.

Bibb had a wine cellar, perfect for fermenting. A newly converted enthusiast, he decided kombucha would be his first project. Meanwhile Dolly discovered she loved garlic sauerkraut. We worked as many fermented foods as possible into their already healthy vegetarian diets.

Potomac Vegetable Farm in Purcellville, an hour outside Washington, would be my first stop in the Northeast, and the beginning of big-city traffic and a full schedule.

Indo-Thai Sauerkraut

YIELDS 1 GALLON, 1–3 WEEKS

To prepare, I cleaned and rubbed my fermentation station with beeswax and made my last Appalachian ferment: Indo-Thai sauerkraut. This mild to spicy sauerkraut is made with carrots, chili, caraway, and cumin. The cumin and caraway give way to smoky and earthy flavors reminiscent of some of my favorite Indian curries, and the Thai chilies bring the Thai spice.

INGREDIENTS
5 lbs cabbage (green or red)
2 lbs carrots
1 tbsp caraway seeds
1 tbsp cumin seeds

3 dried Thai chilies
2–3 tbsp unrefined sea salt

MATERIALS
Gallon glass jar or crock
Weight and cover

PROCESS

1. Quarter and thinly slice cabbage and julienne the carrots. Put them in a big bowl. If you have outer leaves of cabbage, set them aside to use as a top layer between your kraut and your weight.

2. Add 1 tablespoon each of caraway and cumin to your vegetables.

3. Cut open 3 Thai chilies and collect the seeds. Add them to your ingredients. Chop the skins of the chilies and add these, too.

4. Follow steps 3 through 8 in the classic sauerkraut recipe on pages 68–69.

THE CROWDED
NORTHEAST

*There was no answer to this beside the usual answer life gives
to the most complicated and insoluble problems, which is: you must
live according to the needs of the day, that is, forget yourself.*
—Leo Tolstoy, *Anna Karenina*

I. Megalopolis May

The Northeast megalopolis, dense with condominiums, heavy traffic, and the hustle and bustle of my life prior to Oregon, was eating up the surrounding area of my next destination, Potomac Vegetable Farm. The once-rural farm, established in 1966, was now urban as a result of Washington, D.C., sprawl. My connection to the farm was through Caitlin of Number 1 Sons, a fermentation business based out of Arlington, Virginia. Months before she'd e-mailed me:

> I write this with arms that are usually caked with kimchi paste—the smell of onion and bright red color—is quickly becoming my signature look! Please make a stop in the Washington DC area!

Since then, she'd put me in touch with several food-justice experts, starting with Casey, the farm manager of Potomac Vegetable Farms. He had driven an upside-down double-decker school bus for the White House Organic Farm Project years before. My first workshop would be at his farm. Then, in collaboration with Arcadia Center for Sustainable Food and Agriculture, there would be two workshops in D.C. The encore to my stay would be a potluck at the Number 1 Sons pickle factory; they are known for their District Dills, a delectable fermented cucumber pickle.

Having left my Northeast corporate routine years ago—where I coordinated hundreds of thousands of dollars' worth of shipments daily—I was now returning with a very different kind of success. Driving my bus and teaching fermentation was beginning to feel like a real job. It had always been playful, but now the stakes felt higher. The workshops were growing in size and frequency; I was collaborating with and teaching people who had more fermentation experience, from professional producers of fermented goods to farmers who had been fermenting well over a decade. I didn't think of myself as an expert, but people expected me to be one.

Fermentation on Wheels set out as a project to teach fermentation, but the mission was much more than that: to bridge communities, to link people to a vanishing do-it-yourself culture, and to energize positive change in the food system.

I didn't want to get hung up on other people's expectations, letting them mold my values or mission. Mary Morris, a travel writer, wrote on expectation, *We try to direct the scripts in our heads and are miserable when we fail.* It was best to travel without expectations, which was practically impossible once they were there. I couldn't control what others hoped I would bring, but I set these standards for myself: to be a good teacher, inspire connections, and enliven the food movement.

I parked in front of Meaghan and Shane of HEX Ferments' home, in their quaint wooded Baltimore neighborhood, a week after Washington, D.C. Right away a neighbor greeted me and offered a cup of tea. My fear of the bus's being a source of neighborhood controversy vanished after that. I invited the neighbor to come back for a tour later, and to bring anyone else who might be interested.

Meanwhile, I released Franklin into the neighborhood, which was nestled in a large wooded area, so he could get his outdoors fix and I could prepare in peace for the bus tour. Within half an hour, I had adorned my fermentation station with kimchis and sauerkrauts, dairy kefir, and a fizzy ginger beverage. My illustrations leaned along the windows as a background display, and my then meager library sat atop the workshop bench. I left my door ajar, and shortly after, four neighbors stopped by to check out my operation.

As we made small talk, I offered tastes of my ferments. Everything was going well until Franklin entered the bus with a bunny in his mouth. One of the neighbors screamed. I assured her it would be fine; kneeling down, I gently removed the creature, still alive, from Franklin's mouth. The woman covered her eyes as I examined the rabbit and walked it to the door, Franklin close behind. He let out a disappointed meow as I held his scruff, released the bunny, and closed the door. I washed my hands and went back to serving ferments. The hands-over-eyes woman asked, "Is that normal?"

"Well, yeah—it's a cat thing," I replied.

I met Franklin in Manhattan when I was twenty-four. He was rescued from an abandoned building in Queens and his human foster mother fed him by bottle the first six weeks of his life. When we met she made a list of food brands and told me I should feed him one part raw rabbit or venison and one part canned chicken. I asked no questions. Instead, I committed to having a very opinionated and healthy cat. And he can certainly shake me up on occasion.

My biggest Franklin scare was in Baltimore, my second day in, after a workshop at Whitelock Community Farm. The door was open and Franklin jetted to the farm. I thrust myself into workshop mode, trusting he would be fine.

After the workshop, I leisurely strapped down, then called Franklin for our departure. No Franklin appeared.

So I called his name again, in my loudest, sweetest voice.

Again, no Franklin.

I hopped on my bicycle, calling his name—traveling a mile radius around the neighborhood. Residents noticed and asked, so I told several, including Whitelock's farm manager, who helped me make and print flyers to hang around the area. I couldn't spend the night there. While I was taping the first flyer to an electrical post, a man I'd spoken to earlier called me from a distance.

"Hey! I found your kitty! He was over here yonder, nappin' in the bushes."

I turned to see a curled-up gray ball in the man's arms and squinted to get a better view. It was Franklin, and he was sleepy. As the man approached, Franklin looked at me, stretched an arm out, and yawned.

"Thank you . . . so much. I don't know how . . . "

"It's nothin'—I was worried 'bout you. You seemed frantic. Cat knows how to sleep."

Franklin and I have an understanding: He gets to be outdoors and I have to keep trust that he won't leave me. If anything, he'll be passed out on a pleasant spring day, curled up in the bushes.

Carrot Kraut-Chi with Turmeric, Ginger, and Chili

YIELDS 1 GALLON, 2–3 WEEKS

After the long day, Meaghan and I pulled an all-nighter fermenting in the HEX Ferments commercial kitchen, using leftover ingredients from their cooler storage. We carted fifty pounds of carrots to their small workstation and used a continuous-feed food processor to slice half the carrots as thin coins and to finely shred the remainder. This recipe is much less time intensive if you have a food processor with a chopping attachment. This kraut-chi, or sauerkraut-kimchi fusion, is golden orange and has anti-inflammatory health benefits with its dose of turmeric, ginger, and chili. HEX Ferments named the ferment Fermentation on Wheels to spread awareness of my project, and they generously donated the proceeds to my project. This one is dear to me.

INGREDIENTS

7 lbs carrots—rainbow carrots if you can
    find them

1 small bunch green onions

2 inches ginger

2 inches fresh turmeric

1–5 Thai chilies

3 tbsp sea salt

MATERIALS

Grater

Blender or mandoline

Gallon glass jar or crock

Weight and cover

PROCESS

1. Shred half the carrots with a grater and finely chop the other half with a knife, mandoline, or Cuisinart blender attachment.

2. Chop the green onions and mince the ginger, turmeric, and chilies.

3. Combine all the ingredients in a bowl and add salt. Massage the ingredients until a brine comes forth, then pack into a jar so the ingredients are submerged below the brine.

4. Choose a weight to keep the vegetables below the brine and cover with a tea towel and a rubber band. Transfer to the fridge after 2 to 3 weeks.

II. Searing Late May

Philadelphia, where I lived in my early twenties, unfurled its red carpet for us (Franklin, bus, me). I parked in my old neighborhood of Northern Liberties and went for a stroll. Outside the warehouse where I once sweated day in and day out was a pack of guys, gangly and familiar looking, smoking. "Wait, Tara?" one asked as I approached them.

"It is me! I'm back and I'm with a bus! Is Kip still around?"

Kip and I managed inventory at the warehouse five years before. I had a hunch he'd still be around—he was a highly promotable guy. I walked toward the back, arriving at Kip's desk. We chatted for half an hour, about our lines of work, per usual. He quickly offered me the spare key to the warehouse parking-lot gates.

"Bring your bus—then you can come and go as you please and you'll know it's safe."

It felt good to reconnect with some part of my youth, especially a part that reminded me of my tough twenty-one-year-old self, faring in a sea of burly warehouse dudes. Though I'd been an efficient, hard worker, nothing stopped my peers from treating me like an underling. Then, one evening, fed up with the "sweeties" and the occasional grubby hands touching me as some dude pretended to squeeze through an aisle, I shaved my head.

No one touched me from there on out. Nor did anyone call me sweetie.

So, of course, driving my forty-foot bus into the back lot felt amazing.

Franklin and I stayed with a friend two blocks from the warehouse while the bus sat behind locked gates, giving us a break. It wasn't much compared to the laid-back days of brewing, drawing, and cashier night shifts in Eugene a year before, but I was grateful to feel a little more land-legged.

I had to take care of my starter cultures and vegetable ferments though, and in the midst of a searing late May, the bus was turning into a hot metal box. Temperature extremes were a regular concern in the heights of summer and the depths of winter.

Temperature in Fermentation

Fermentation speeds up in higher temperatures
- Use more salt to slow fermentation
- Cut the fermentation time
- Use breathable lids, especially with beverages
- Use antimicrobial elements, such as garlic

Fermentation slows down in lower temperatures
- Use less salt to speed up fermentation
- Increase fermentation time
- Ferment on an appliance, such as your fridge, to keep a warmer and more consistent temperature.

I dived into a full week of events: a kimchi demo at historic Reading Terminal Market, an event in Northern Liberties, youth classes in crunchy-road Camden, a vegetable-fermentation workshop at West Philadelphia's food co-op, and a potluck in suburban Germantown. The tristate fermentation revolution was in full swing.

III. Witchy Magic

The week in Philly whipped me into shape for farming and fermentation adventures in New Jersey. I taught five youth classes in collaboration with Isles Youth Institute, a nonprofit in Trenton that starts gardens at and brings food education to public schools. Every kid, ignited by the wonder of life-giving fermentation, enjoyed the mild weeklong-fermented sauerkraut. They were excited to taste it after discovering how simple it is to transform foods, direct from the vegetables in their garden, into something tangy and packed with life. Even more fascinating to them was the idea of living foods and their role in our bodies—that fermentation populates our inner ecosystem and helps strengthen our immunity and digestive health.

Youth always question the waiting part: Won't food spoil if it sits out for weeks? The traditional mind-set in American food culture encourages us to steer clear of microbial mishaps and, in doing so, diverts us from do-it-yourself food processes and making time to grow beneficial bacteria. Instead we put more trust in packaged and pasteurized foods, most of which are nonliving and instantly fill our bellies.

I like to emphasize the importance of community and illuminate the reward that patience brings. Microbes collaborate over time to produce something nourishing and tasty. When we work steadily and together, the fruits of our labor come forth. Like the kale in their school garden—it started as small seeds, and it took many hands, lots of love, and patience for that seed to become the kale. Fermentation, like gardening, is a community project with a delicious and nourishing outcome. Who wouldn't want to wait for that?

At the end of classes I reserve ten minutes for kids to ask me anything about my lifestyle or the bus. Many kids ask, "Is this all you eat?" (I assure them I enjoy a diverse selection of colorful and hearty foods.) One of my fourth-graders, a young Hispanic girl, raised her hand and politely asked, "Do you plan on getting married soon?"

The kids giggled.

"Nope," I said.

The girl responded, "Whoa . . . that's awesome!"

Marriage isn't something I've ever concerned myself with, and I guess some part of that makes me a good role model for a nine-year-old girl who feels obligated to follow a familial cultural norm.

That's something I want to achieve with my bus and brand of education: break the deep-seated norms that make us believe there is only one type of success or one route to happiness. We have to step out of the box and find out who we are, regardless of what the world is, to truly discover ourselves. Kids recognize that I live a little differently. Though some of them think I'm a little strange (children never hesitate to share their opinions), they're always respectful and respond thoughtfully to my project. They can see I'm comfortable being a little different.

From Trenton I was referred to a farm in Pennington, New Jersey. The farmers offered a stay in exchange for a fermentation class. No problem, I thought. Upon arrival I parked in a large concrete lot next to several idling trucks. After three hours of buzzing midsummer heat, I was asked to park next to farmhand lodging. I spent the remainder of the day walking the fields and initiating small talk with farm employees, our language barriers keeping us from deeper exchanges.

Turnips, radishes, mint, and basil were my fermentation workshop agenda. It was early June and summer flavors were stacking up. Mint, basil, and cucumbers embodied summer the way green alliums did spring. The workshop took place next to a few large oaks surrounding three picnic tables, and forty or so people showed. Students squeezed in to grab chopping action, and at least three people cornered me to ask questions. Three were asked at once: "Why are we fermenting radishes and turnips?" "How much salt do we need to use?" "How long does it have to sit for?" I thought, "One at a time, please?" I appreciated their enthusiasm, but was stifled by the surprisingly large crowd.

The bus-tour announcement sent attendees to my door. I followed and a woman with a baby joined me. "Hey—I'm sorry, but I need to get home soon. I didn't expect so many people to show up to your workshop! May I get a kombucha SCOBY from you? I brought you a quart of honey, made by my bees."

It was my first barter transaction since the South. I love getting homegrown goods—it's the best type of exchange. Like my starter cultures, her honey was tended to with a special touch, unique to her environment and bee-friendly flowers.

We walked in, and the front of the line quickly followed behind her—something that had never before happened—and the bus was suddenly over capacity. "Good luck," whispered the honeymonger, glancing back.

The workshop left me feeling overwhelmed, and I had seven days of uncertainty before my next workshop; the schedule had a crack after a last-minute event cancellation in New York City.

I didn't know where to go.

I fired the ignition early Sunday morning, the day after the workshop. My destination was Big Bear Natural Foods, the only natural-grocery store in a twenty-mile radius. I drove the winding Pennington road until a sign that read 10 FT CLEARANCE brought me to halt. My bus is thirteen feet tall.

Reverse was the only way out. Hitting my hazards, I switched gears and crawled backward on the curvy rural road. I'd just turned around when I spotted a large sign on the right:

BLUE MOON
—— ACRES ——
FARM MARKET
Organic produce
grass-fed meats
pasture-raised eggs

That would do. Pulling into the spacious gravel lot, I squinted as a figure in the distance ran toward me. She was familiar. She had dark hair, was in her midthirties, slender . . . I opened the bus door and she said, "You're here!" It was the honeymonger.

A week's respite at Blue Moon Acres Farm with my new family of friends—Ali, Scotty, Clara, Wynn, and Reed—seven gallons of kimchi, a honey harvest, five piglets, a fermentation-themed potluck, daily shared meals, and a host of new recipes brought Fermentation on Wheels back to the awe of farming. Our convergence said some kind of witchy magic was riding with me.

Jun

YIELDS 1 GALLON, 1–3 WEEKS

Ali, honeymonger, is partial to jun. Nature's bounty is her currency. She has a few bee-hives, an herb garden, fifty chickens, and five pigs, and her husband, Scotty, manages twenty-five acres of farmland. She knows how to utilize every part of their vegetables (carrot tops instead of parsley in her meatball recipe) and every part of her animals (Liver pâté and lard? Yes.). She's curious about food and never takes it for granted. We speak the same language.

Jun, brewed with honey and green tea, is even more luxurious than kombucha. Some sources claim jun hails from Tibet, but there is no hard evidence of its origin. It's likely a divergence from kombucha, but I find jun to have a distinct flavor in addition to its honeylike aroma. Refer to page 12 to source a jun culture.

INGREDIENTS
¾ to 1 gallon water
1¼ cups honey
4 tbsp green tea
4 tbsp herbs as you see fit for flavor and /
    or remedy (see note on page 74)

1 cup jun
jun SCOBY

MATERIALS
Gallon jar or ceramic vessel with spigot
Home-brew funnel

PROCESS
1. Heat half of the water in a pot with the honey. Liquefy honey as your water comes to a boil; once it reaches a boil, remove from heat.
2. Steep green tea and other herbs of your choice for 10–15 minutes.
3. Follow steps 3 through 6 of kombucha recipe on pages 73–75.

Love for bees—honeybees pollinate over one third of our food supply. Their work is so essential, yet their population has declined greatly from a loss of biodiversity and climate change. We can attract honeybees into our lives by growing bee-friendly flowers, such as marigolds, poppies, and roses.

Strawberries were in abundance at Blue Moon Acres. Ali had also been curious about homemade mead, so we made two gallons of strawberry mead (pages 198–199)—one for the Morgans to keep and one for me to bring on the road. This making together and splitting the ferment brought us closer together when we were apart. Months later, in New England, I drank a bottle of my strawberry mead with the Morgans in mind.

IV. The Next-Best Parking Spot

The New York City parking plan: Find several large green spaces on a map (cemeteries and golf courses are great), drive to first location, and find a parking spot (if you can't find a parking spot, drive to next green space and continue search), park your vehicle, hop on a bicycle, and scan the neighborhood for a really good spot. In the summertime, this means finding shade—essential if you live with microbes and a cat. Head back to your oversize vehicle, repark it, and have yourself a day on the town.

Finding a great parking spot is hard in urban environments, and buses are not meant for here-to-there transportation. I have a bicycle and it serves well for most of my transportation needs. When it's pouring rain or my destination is over five miles each way, I hope for public transportation. That's to say, bless New York City. I love its bike-lane infrastructure and efficient transportation system.

I found a parking spot at the northwest end of Dyker Beach Golf Course, in South Brooklyn. I announced my arrival on the Internet and reached out to my New York comrades via text messages. An outing to Coney Island was in the works.

My previous roommate and longtime friend Christina met me for rides and games the next day, along with her partner, Kellen. Perhaps the most awesome ride was Boardwalk Flight, which lifted us 110 feet in the air, bodies harnessed to bungee cords, and then let loose, hurling us back into the air at sixty miles per hour. A nice bonus was the bustling view of the Coney Island boardwalk.

Coney Island rubber ducky

It was Sunday. After connecting with our more youthful selves, Christina and I made an impromptu dinner, using vegetables from the full boxes I'd reaped in New Jersey. As I sautéed beets on my propane stove, my phone jingled.

Sebastian had texted me. He was in town and noticed I was, too. Christina, now updated on all my traveling woes, asked what I would do.

Against all reasonable urges to avoid him since Mississippi, I was coming up on a gig where I would trek twelve miles to the East Village with twelve pounds of vegetables, a dozen T-shirts, and other odds and ends for my kimchi workshop sponsored by NYC Ferments. I had been excited for the kimchi workshop since its cofounder, Angela Davis, had reached out to me during my Kickstarter campaign. It would be a big one, and I didn't want to make the trek alone if I didn't have to.

I invited Sebastian to join me at the bus on Tuesday, two hours before my workshop.

Sebastian never showed to help with the twelve-mile trek. He did arrive twenty minutes early to the workshop though, announcing he was ready to be at my service. I declined his offer—everything was ready to roll, and people were filing in. I met Michaela Hayes, a cofounder of NYC Ferments and the founder of Crock & Jar, Brooklyn's farm-to-jar fermentation company. Michaela's first words were "Are you exhausted yet?" I was exhausted, but there was no way I'd let others know that, yet. Anyway, fermentation gatherings—where I taught and connected with others—produced an enormous adrenaline rush in me. I buried my exhaustion.

An excitable attendee named Cheryl Paswater approached me shortly before the workshop, sharing her enthusiasm for the art of fermentation. She barely stopped for air, telling me about her fermentation business, Contraband Ferments, and expressed her interest in volunteering on the bus. It was the first offer I'd had for company since Austin had joined me in North Carolina. I would store her interest in the *important* section of my mind's files. The small basement of the restaurant, Jimmy's No. 43, was filled, every seat occupied. I introduced the vegetables—bok choy, turnips, and radishes—all grown a short train ride from New York City, at Blue Moon Acres Farm in Pennington.

As I described my last farm visit, and its serendipitous movement in my life, I recognized Hashem, a friend and flame from my Brooklyn days, standing in the back. Christina and Kellen sat near the back, too. Gayle, from Floyd, was in town and joined the class. With so many familiar faces, I lit up. We moved into the hands-on portion of the class, and students surrounded the tables to chop vegetables. I worked on the peppers and ginger; Hashem, my tall Queens-based dreamboat of a friend, chopped next to me. We'd met three years before when I picked up a few 20 mm rolls I had developed at his photo lab. In my youthful confidence, I pursued him the moment he handed me my film. The pursuit was successful—we had friendly and romantic history. I was excited he came to my workshop. He was so elusive that I hadn't even thought to tell him I'd be in town.

Quick Kimchi

YIELDS 1 GALLON, 1–3 WEEKS (OR LONGER)

I shared a kimchi recipe in the first chapter that takes you through the more traditional method, practiced in Korea. This kimchi recipe involves one step rather than two and is similar to the sauerkraut process, thus it takes a few hours in the kitchen rather than a few days. It's an excellent method to use when you're pressed for time.

Taste your kimchi prior to fermentation, too. The flavors begin to shine as soon as you combine them. A major misconception is that kimchi is a difficult ferment to master. The many varieties each deliver unique flavors to the palate.

INGREDIENTS

3 lbs bok choy and / or napa cabbage

1 lb carrots

2 leeks

2 bunches radishes (1.5 lbs)

2 bunches turnips (1.5 lbs)

3 tbsp salt

INGREDIENTS FOR PASTE

6 cloves garlic

2 inches ginger

1 medium shallot

2 tbsp chili powder or fresh chili peppers

2 tbsp fish sauce or tamari

MATERIALS

Gallon jar

Blender

Weight and cover

PROCESS

1. Chop the bok choy/napa cabbage, carrots, leeks, radishes, and turnips and place them in a bowl. Salt them as you would sauerkraut—massage them and let the juices come out.

4. Peel garlic, ginger, and shallot and roughly chop into smaller pieces. Toss them into your blender bowl. Add chili powder or fresh peppers and fish sauce (or tamari). Blend the ingredients and put aside until your vegetables are done soaking.

3. Add the paste to your veggies, thoroughly distributing the ingredients. You can use your hands for this task, but you may want to use a large utensil to protect your hands from the hot peppers.

4. Follow steps 6 through 8 of the cubed-radish kimchi recipe on pages 31–32 .

Hashem stayed at the table, aimlessly chopping turnips, as I brought the class to a close. While packing my bag, I exchanged information with exuberant Cheryl, sold every Fermentation on Wheels T-shirt, and answered stray questions from attendees. Meanwhile Sebastian remained seated, waiting. I sensed he was waiting to get me alone for a chat. (Later, I would learn Sebastian informed multiple people at this workshop he was riding the bus at the time and claimed to be the second-in-command of Fermentation on Wheels.)

The questions waned and I put an arm around Hashem. He warmly hugged me back and asked what I was up to for the rest of the night. I didn't hesitate to say I'd spend time with him while I could—knowing his presence and attention were fleeting. Though we hadn't seen each other in years, it was as if no time had passed. We understand each other.

Sebastian, conversing with an attendee, turned his eyes to observe our closeness. He stared Hashem down. Worried he would attempt to close in on our conversation, I said in a hushed voice, "Let's sneak out the back door."

Hashem quickly glanced toward Sebastian, without making eye contact, and replied, "Let's roll."

The back door leading to Second Avenue was slightly ajar. I looked toward Sebastian, gave a friendly smile, saluted him, and made my way to the door. Hashem followed.

"Thank goodness for back doors!" I said.

We strolled five miles, catching up with each other into the night.

Plans were manifesting. Back at the bus I drafted a last-minute message announcing open bus tours and a starter-culture swap from noon to nine that Thursday in Prospect Heights. Fans shared the message on social media, and it spread through several avenues. It would be a full day.

Thursday at five in the morning I parked on the south side of Prospect Place, a twenty-second walk from my old Brooklyn apartment, and napped until traffic vibrations poured into my small room. The meters would need feeding at nine, and then every two hours after. It was fine—I would write it off at the end of the year. It surprised me that I would spend money on meters now. I wouldn't have considered it even a year ago.

I showed my old neighbors the bus and attempted to shed light on fermentation (many were perplexed, but at least the kids were excited by the bus). Two women walked onto the bus, tasted my ferments, and silently looked around until one of them said, "I don't get it. Why are you doing this?" To which I explained my obsession with fermentation and that my goal was to spread tasty microbes far and wide. They shook their heads, still confused. Cheryl, full of excitement, arrived with a friend and two kids. She was hooked, ready to join the bus for a week. Home brewer, author, and radio-show host Mary Izett strolled on with a microphone and did a short interview with me for Heritage Radio Network. And a fermenter named Barry delivered two pounds of unpasteurized tempeh, one made of adzuki beans and the other of navy beans. The samples changed how I felt about the fermented legume—never had I thought tempeh could be so good.

The next-best parking spot was in Queens, in an industrial stretch of Long Island City on the other side of the John Jay Byrne Bridge. It was adjacent to Hashem's apartment, and there was nothing unreliable about it—no street-cleaning hours, never congested. Franklin and I hung out in Hashem's apartment while he worked long days at the New School photo lab in Manhattan. He would come home to a late-night dinner, praise it, and quickly pass out after his ten-hour workday with another one to follow. In those dinner-and-cleanup moments, I remembered the comforts of domestic life. It was nice to live it at this temporary scale, knowing I'd soon be on the road again.

NEW ENGLAND REVELATIONS

The Universe is made of stories, not of atoms.
—Muriel Rukeyser

I. Backyard River

Relief and gratitude filled my every cell as I crossed the Piscataqua River Bridge, to seek refuge in Maine's wilderness. It was the closest to nature I'd felt since leaving the Pacific Northwest. I stopped at a campground in Eliot for three nights—the first time I paid for lodging during my trip. It was well worth the $81: there was no one to entertain, with no expectations to whip out a secret recipe, and it was my first time alone in two months. One great aspect of constant socializing was that I appreciated and respected my alone time more than ever.

Franklin and I spent an entire day on the banks of Piscataqua. He climbed big trees while I read books under the sun, breaking to swim every few hours. Franklin scrambled down from his perch each time I went for a dunk, pacing up and down the shoreline, desperately meowing at me to come back to safety. At our site, on the other days, I scrubbed down every surface in the bus, reorganized my growing collection of bottles and jars, and made campfire feasts every night.

New England was an ideal place to spend summer alongside like-minded good-food advocates. Though it was warming up, it was mild compared to the late Junes of my Texas youth. Portland-area highlights included a potluck, a cooperative-farm stay in Arundel, and a workshop at Resilience Hub, a community and educational space empowering people with traditional permaculture practices. Permaculture, a term coined in the midseventies by Bill Mollison and David Holmgren, means a system of agricultural and social design that mimics or uses patterns of natural eco-systems. It's a radical, albeit practical and effective, form of agricultural and social activism along with other such struggles for environmental justice arising against industrial-farming practices.

Permaculture has many branches—from food and farming to architecture and engineering—and the purpose is to design a system that is self-sufficient, sustainable, and environmentally sound. So great is this traditional system (which is mostly an adopted collection of age-old techniques), that it has contributed a wealth of knowl-edge to modern organic farms—small and large—throughout the world.

These agricultural systems utilize fermentation, too, since fermentation is a natural, self-sufficient ecosystem worthy of simulation. For instance, fermentation is crucial in making compost, used to enhance nutrients for soil. Farmers also inoculate plants and animals with beneficial organisms to promote health, similar to how we strengthen our own health when we inoculate ourselves with the good microbes of fermented foods. An illuminating book on fermentation is *The Permaculture Book of Ferment and Human Nutrition*, written by Bill Mollison (the "father of permac-ulture")—it traverses hundreds of fermentation techniques from around the world and lends an enlightening perspective on the many bacterial and fungal species we collaborate with in fermentation.

One of the coolest principles of permaculture is that we work harmoniously with and depend on natural cycles of resilient communities—ecosystems—to enrich life. It's a social practice, too—a lifestyle, to live by standards that nourish soil, plants, animals, and humans. Whenever a chance arises to work alongside permaculturists, I jump at it.

The Northeast Permaculture Convergence furthered my journey to Unity, in central Maine, where I met Ian—cofounder of Bettie the Bus Initiative. Ian demonstrated examples of and taught alternative-energy systems. Our friendship blossomed quickly after he visited my bus and observed my long-term plans, written out on paper glued on cardboard behind my donations jar (*paint the bus*, *expand the solar system*, *build a cold storage unit*, and *liability insurance*). As a fellow fermentation lover, Ian appreciated the microbial diversity of my passengers and was impressed with the project and its mission. He expressed interest in helping me achieve some of my goals.

When the weekend-long convergence came to an end, I parked at Ian's place in the woods along rocky coastal waters. Mosquitoes were rampant in New England, so he taught me how to make do-it-yourself screens for the bus windows. He helped me with a few other maintenance tasks, too, and was keen on getting my bus a fresh paint job, one of my big goals on the cardboard sign. Ian had a way of making immense undertakings seem simple. His positive life outlook and fearless approach to projects made me feel at ease. A whiff of his energy could turn the impossible into a reality. Life according to Ian: don't worry; everything is going to be amazing. We agreed to keep in touch about painting my bus in case my schedule opened up later in the summer.

We said our until-next-times and I departed for my most northern destination: the Grange in coastal Machias, where I would collaborate with longtime heroes Beehive Design Collective. The collective's mission combines many of my passions: illustration, history, activism, and education. Beehive Design Collective is a nonprofit artists' collective, dedicated to "cross-pollinating the grassroots," using illustrated images as educational tools to connect communities with issues in globalization and capitalism. The illustrated stories engage audiences with imagery that gives deeper insight into the struggle for environmental and social justice worldwide.

I held a sourdough-pancake brunch and sauerkraut demo at the Grange, a historic hall the collective maintains. Sourdough pancakes became my go-to snack on the bus. Regular batches of pancake batter assured weekly attention for my sourdough starters. Pancakes are also a great way to get your sourdough fix if you don't have an oven for baking.

Sourdough Pancakes

YIELDS 14 PANCAKES, 12–24 HOURS (OR LONGER)

This recipe is so simple, and the slightly tangy sourdough flavor pairs well with both sweet and hearty flavors (see note below). You can also integrate sweeteners such as honey, molasses, or maple syrup, hearty ingredients, and sauerkraut or kimchi brine into the batter to give it a fermentation boost. I ferment mine for up to twenty hours before adding the eggs—for maximum tanginess. Listed below are several toppings I love and fun ways to combine them. Sourdough pancakes are versatile, funky, and encourage creativity. They were well received at the Grange brunch and have continued to be a favorite potluck item of mine as well as a tasting option for youth classes.

INGREDIENTS

1 cup sourdough starter
2½ cups flour
2 cups water or whole milk

2 tbsp sugar or honey
2 eggs
½ tsp salt
½ tsp baking soda (optional)

PROCESS

1. Combine sourdough starter, flour, water or milk, and sugar or honey in a large bowl. Cover and let sit for 12 to 20 hours at room temperature, stirring occasionally.

2. When you're ready to cook, whisk the eggs in a small bowl. Then add the eggs, salt, and optional baking soda to the batter and whisk to combine. If you feel the batter is too thin or thick, adjust accordingly with flour or water.

3. Use a ladle to pour batter onto a preheated and greased medium-heat cooking surface, flip, and enjoy.

Sourdough pancake toppings are the best because sourdough pairs well with sweet and hearty, catering to both sides of the palate spectrum. My favorite topping is a combination of tahini and honey. Yogurt, maple syrup, fresh berries, and berry compotes are lovely sweet additions. On the heartier side, I like to roll sauerkraut into a pancake and eat on the go. Another delectable and more robust topping combination is kimchi and peanut sauce.* When serving to large groups, I set out a large spread of topping options, so everyone gets his or her fix.

*Simple peanut sauce recipe: blend ½ cup peanut butter, 1 inch ginger, 1 garlic clove, 2 tbsp soy sauce or tamari, 1 tbsp lime juice, and 1 tbsp honey. Makes 4 servings.

II. Botanical Intervention

In working with nature, I am assured of a collaborator who starts erasing my traces as soon as I begin my retreat. And in keeping with the spirit of open source, I know too that other people will take over what I have begun; negotiating for themselves the terms of the relationships that connect us to each other, and to the ground beneath our feet.

—Oliver Kellhammer

Vermont would host two big-league events: a presentation at Sandor Katz's Sterling College class (I decided if I could speak on fermentation in front of Sandor, I could speak on fermentation in front of anyone) and workshops at SolarFest, a three-day festival known for its long-standing celebration of sustainable-energy solutions.

Crawling up a dirt road to Sterling College after a one-night camping excursion in New Hampshire, I lost reception. The day was breezy and I rode with my side window open, not paying any mind to the wind-vulnerable totems on my dash. And then, an eagle feather I'd found three years past hiking in Oregon's Siuslaw National Forest flew out the window. It was one of the many totems I kept on my dash, above the bus control panel or tied with twine to my oversize visor. It was also one of the last reminders of my life in rural Oregon, where I'd learned to find my way through the woods, forage chanterelles, harvest elderflowers, and brew with Doug fir tips.

My totems were spiritual medicine—representative of the people, places, and ideas that were meaningful to me. Prayer was involuntary in my life, partly thanks to totems, I had thought. Would my feather, now floating down some rural road in Vermont, still provide strength and courage and keep me connected to the Universe? I hoped those ideals were glued to me now and it didn't matter one bit.

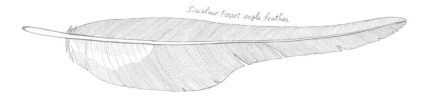

Siuslaw Forest eagle feather

I parked near the cafeteria building at Sterling College, and Sandor greeted me. Standing in the bus doorway, he invited me to lunch. I joined the class's celebratory feast of culturally diverse fermented dishes, including acarajé (Afro-Brazilian fermented black-eyed-pea fritters), an array of krauts and kimchis, and fermented sodas. My presentation, after lunch, detailed my journey as an emerging fermentation educator—mostly on the importance of being mission driven and the different programs I offered, such as teaching fermentation to farming communities, fermenting farm-fresh food with urban communities, and teaching kids about our overlooked microbes. Sandor's students took whiffs of the bus starter cultures—jun and tibicos and sourdoughs—and adopted some for later play.

We scoped out microbes under microscopes the next morning, before I started off to Tinmouth for SolarFest preparations. I stopped in front of the classroom on my way out and got a nice shot of Sandor's class with the bus.

SolarFest volunteers led me to a large grassy section of the festival grounds, near the vendor tent and outdoor theater. I started a batch of sourdough pancakes and prepared a list of workshops for the weekend, including beet kvass, nukazuke, scape pesto, and blackberry mead. Cheryl and Robin, of NYC Ferments, would join me on the bus that weekend to assist with workshops and talk fermentation to the masses. I was so excited for company and to take part in one of the longest-running celebrations of solar power and renewable energy. Solar power had increased my livelihood in ways I couldn't fathom before having it—it's cost-effective and easy to maintain. It teaches me to use more wisely, to live according to the sun's highs and lows in different regions and varying seasons. When we're plugged into the fossil fuel grid, there's no reminder that we might run out or are leaving a larger footprint than is healthy for the earth, and ironically enough—fossil fuel is finite—while sunlight, wind, and water are limitless.

Cheryl, filled with exuberance, arrived midmorning and helped with signage—making an OPEN/CLOSED sign and a sign scattered with microbes that read JOIN US FOR A TASTE BUD DANCE PARTY! The practicing New York City artist and fermentation business owner also proved helpful with her outgoing personality, selling Fermentation on Wheels T-shirts and introducing me to food vendors on the other side of the grounds, whom I maybe otherwise wouldn't have met while hunkered down in my fermentation performance space.

My main fermentation workshop, Fermenting by Season, drew a crowd of nearly fifty people. I taught at a table in front of the bus, microphone in hand, while attendees sat on the grass. SolarFest had an especially fervent fermentation crowd. My workshops were just a handful of shindigs giving kudos to agricultural and food-related aspects of sustainable living. Sandor Katz gave a keynote speech and hosted a workshop on the last day of the festival.

Cheryl introduced me to a community of bakers and farmers from Manchester, Vermont, at a food booth with a mobile wood-fired oven. They churned out fresh pizzas and breads by the hour. We became quick friends and traded sauerkraut and kimchi for decadent lunches. We liked each other so much I ended up going home with them after SolarFest, spending a week at their community farm, Earth Sky Time, nestled at the foothills of the Green Mountains.

At Earth Sky Time I played in-house fermenter for the week. The farmers gave me full access to their walk-in vegetable cooler. It was late July and cucumbers were aplenty. I took advantage.

Basil Mint Cucumber Kimchi

YIELDS 1 QUART, 1–2 WEEKS

Cucumbers can be tricky to ferment in the heat of summer—when they ferment too quickly, their innards break down fast, sometimes resulting in an unpleasant, mushy texture. To keep them crunchy, I ferment them at room temperature for a short period and then at cooler temperatures. You may also add natural tannins, such as grape or oak leaves, to promote crispness. This summery recipe features the cooling, bright flavors of basil and mint. I make it spicy with ginger and garlic, turning it into a tasty summer kimchi of sorts.

INGREDIENTS

2 cucumbers
1 tbsp salt
⅓ cup basil
⅓ cup mint
¼ cup green onion
3 cloves garlic
1 inch ginger root

1 tsp chili powder
1 tsp fish sauce or tamari

MATERIALS

Mandoline or sharp knife
Blender
Quart jar
Weight and cover

PROCESS

1. Rinse and destem cucumbers and slice them in thin rounds. A mandoline is an ideal tool for the job, but you can use a knife instead. Add salt and gently toss the cucumbers. The idea is to let the salt slowly pull water from the cucumbers rather than massage them with salt, so the cucumbers keep their form.

2. Finely chop mint, basil, and green onion and mix with cucumbers in a bowl. Gently toss ingredients again.

3. Combine garlic, ginger, chili, and fish sauce in a blender. Add the paste to the prepared ingredients and gently mix. Let sit for an hour.

4. The ingredients will have produced a salty puddle when you come back to them. If the puddle is minimal, wait another hour or simply pack into a jar and top off with water. If you top off the jar, place a lid on top and give the jar a few thorough shakes to disperse the salt.

5. Add a weight, cover with a cloth and rubber band, and leave the kimchi for 3–5 days at room temperature, then chill in the fridge 1–2 weeks. Enjoy when it's to your liking.

Fermented Cucumber Pickles

YIELDS HALF GALLON, 1–2 WEEKS

This cucumber pickle is a favorite go-to snack—well suited for lovers of traditional cucumber pickles, whether they are naturally fermented or pickled with vinegar. (To read about the differences of vinegar pickling versus fermentation, see page 67.) The addition of a grape leaf is optional to promote maximum crispness, but I find the fermentation times and temperatures to be effective in benefiting the texture.

INGREDIENTS

3 cucumbers (whole or quartered)
6 cloves garlic
¼ cup chopped onion
1 tbsp peppercorn
2 sprigs dill
2 sprigs fennel
1 tbsp coriander
½ tbsp mustard seed
½ tbsp salt (>2 percent salinity)
1 qt water
1 grape leaf (optional)

MATERIALS

½-gallon Ball jar
Quart Ball jar
Weight and cover or plastic Ball-jar lid

PROCESS

1. Place all ingredients in the ½-gallon jar, save cucumbers, salt, water, and grape leaf.

2. Destem and cut the cucumbers into quarter spears or keep whole and arrange snugly into the jar with an optional grape leaf for tannins to promote crispness.

3. Make brine in quart jar—add water and salt, seal the jar, and give a good shake to dissolve the salt. Pour the brine over the ingredients.

4. If you find a pickle protrudes above the brine, add a weight and cover with a tea towel. If the pickles are snug to the walls of the jar and stay below the brine on their own, you can simply add a plastic Ball-jar lid (or a tea towel, if you prefer) to the jar and let it ferment at room temperature for three days, transfer it to the fridge, and wait a week or two before digging in.

Barely a month in, I decided to extend my New England tour. Originally I thought I'd bumble around the Finger Lakes region after a scheduled event in Albany, but now plans were taking me to western Massachusetts and back up to Maine, where I would paint the bus. I wasn't ready to leave New England. It was an oasis of sustainable communities: my newfound friends reveled in nature's bounty, made all their meals from scratch, and believed in the power of fermentation. They were a testament to sustainable and self-sufficient lifestyles. I finally felt that I really fit in some place far from home. So I made plans to paint my bus in Portland, alongside Ian and Bettie the Bus. The paint job would give Fermentation on Wheels a more professional look. I wanted Fermentation on Wheels to be taken more seriously—I craved it. And I believed a fresh coat of paint would be the ticket.

"What thoughts or words come to your mind when I say bacteria?" I asked six teenage students on my bus, parked outside the Sanctuary for Independent Media in Troy, New York.

The students, exchanging smiles, searched for the right answer in one another's eyes and shyly looked back at me, unsure what to say. Most teenage students had been indoctrinated to a bacteria-free lifestyle, complete with antibacterial soap at every sink. The question always surprised them.

Then a female student softly said, "When I think about bacteria . . . I think about the beginning."

"Yes! The beginning! Bacteria are little history holders, made of essential building blocks for life. The human body is made of ten times more bacterial cells than human cells. The foods I work with help rebuild and populate a living flora inside of us, promoting a more robust gut, or … inner ecosystem, keeping us closer to the bacteria that surround us, everywhere, keeping us in sync with our outer ecosystem—with the earth."

"Wait, what does this food or our bodies have anything to do with ecosystems?" a male student asked. They were summer interns at the garden and had learned a bit about outer ecosystems.

"Because fermented foods and our bodies rely on the smallest pieces of life, just like the earth does. Microorganisms play a huge role in soil health, for example, which affects our food, which in turn nourishes us. If we pasteurize, or kill, all of the microorganisms that were responsible for that beneficial growth in the first place, then we miss out on some of those bacteria-rich nutrients. We neglect the microcommunity that lives within us. So, I work with plants to further develop the beneficial bacteria that they carry."

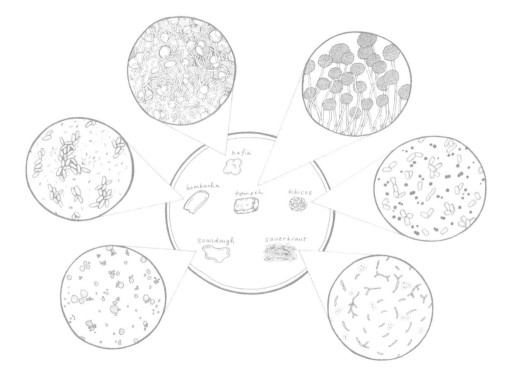

"Whoa . . . cool. How do you do that?"

I lifted the lid to a tortilla basket containing freshly cooked sourdough pancakes and filled a sampler plate with five types of fermented vegetables. The students joined me at the fermentation station, and we tasted and savored the tangy flavors of fermentation. One of the students observed, "I didn't realize sauerkraut could pair well on its own or with pancakes. It's easy to make at home?"

After, we made a batch of sauerkraut for the students to relish in a few weeks.

That evening an ecological artist named Oliver Kellhammer gave a presentation on botanical intervention at the Sanctuary. He introduced slides of nature bursting through concrete-laden city scenes; the images spoke to the importance of community engagement, and of the single initiation made by the individual artist, but also to the incredible resiliency of the plants themselves.

His presentation, like mine, emphasized the power of the smaller things that make up plants, animals, and us: microorganisms. We can't deny their super powers.

III. Work Partying

Unleash your hardworking hands along with your creativity and go home with delicious fermented gifts. With the support of our new friends Cooperative Fermentation, Resilience Hub, and Bettie the Bus Initiative, we will be painting the Fermentation on Wheels bus in Portland, ME!
—Fermentation on Wheels, Paint the Fermentation Bus!

Two big gifts awaited me in Troy. Most notably, an intern named Harley from New York City. I also received two stainless steel kegs as a donation and thus said good-bye to my grueling bottling days. Both proved essential in the coming weeks of work partying and completing tasks on a tight schedule. Harley arrived the day after my adult workshop, at the Contemporary Arts Center at Woodside. She excitedly popped out of a cab, sporting bright red hair and a huge smile. We unscrewed the maple tabletop of the fermentation station, brought it to the center's woodshop, sanded it down, and repolished it with mineral oil. I went straight to two-person work mode—there were, after all, so many things I couldn't do on my own.

The kegs—sturdy aged stainless steel—were a gift from a workshop attendee. When I expressed thanks, he said, "Thanks to you. You taught me how to make naturally fermented pickles, finally!" It was a big tip for an hour-and-a-half-long fermentation class.

How to Bottle and Rack Wine

Wash bottles, jugs, carboys, and tubing with warm water and dish soap, using a bottle brush. Follow with sanitizer when bottling beer.

(Sanitizer is available at your local home-brew store. I recommend Star San.)

You will want roughly four 750-ml bottles per one gallon of home-brew.

For especially mucky vessels, first immerse the soiled surface in a brewery wash for ten minutes.

(Brewery wash is also available at home-brew stores. Oxygen Brewery Wash is my preferred wash.)

Buy or recycle corks. Soak them in a bowl of water to soften before bottling.

Important! If you have used the recommended high alcohol tolerance yeast strains in this book and your wine is not yet dry, or at 0 percent ABV according to your hydrometer, there are still fermentable sugars. This means your brew is still fermenting and will continue to gas off CO_2 that will build up in the bottle and possibly cause it to break. If you want make an effervescent wine, seek out recycled champagne bottles and purchase plastic champagne stoppers and wire hoods from a home-brew store. Simply use a hammer to plug the stopper into the bottle and secure the hood. If you want to bottle a still, sweet mead, read more about yeast alcohol tolerances and ABV percentages on page 7.

Place your racking cane and siphon in the fermenter as shown, careful not to disturb any sediment, and hold the flexible tubing at a high point with one hand and extract wine by sucking the end of the siphon. Once wine passes the high point, place the end in the bottle (or another fermenter), drop the high point, and let gravity do the work.

Once the wine is low, quickly and gently tip the carboy to avoid the sediment and siphon as much wine as possible.

If you can manage to organize a work party and get an assembly line going, don't forget to share the fruits of your labor!

Floor corkers cost about $70 and pay for themselves quickly—they make the bottling process much faster and are easy to use.

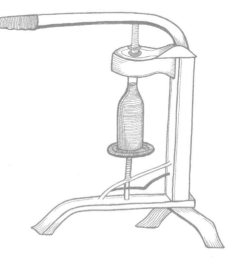

Back at the bus, I put my ducks in a row. Harley and I drafted two e-mails: one to upstate New York for my last wine-bottling party and another to Maine for my bus-painting work party in Portland. The bottles of wine would be gifts for people who came out to paint the bus. The kegs wouldn't be the end of my bottling days just yet. Four of the artists in residence at the Contemporary Arts Center offered to help bottle, and two people from the mailing list joined the party. We scrubbed and sterilized twenty-five wine bottles and organized an assembly line: one to siphon, one to cork, one to hand over to the labeler, and multiple people to switch out. It was a mint, lemon-balm wine, fermented in Oregon a year before. We did what would usually take half a day in two hours. I explained the process while we worked, then we split a bottle between the eight of us.

Harley and I arrived at Neverdun Farm, south of Portland, with a few days' rest before the work party. Jonah, good friend, resident at Neverdun, and founder of Cooperative Fermentation, greeted us upon our exiting the bus. We wolfed down chicken tacos with a mess of fermented vegetables after our two days of nonstop travel.

Jonah helped organize the impending bus-painting party. Like Ian, he has unswerving energy. He's created multiple food and farming cooperatives, consults for worker-owned businesses, and also practices activism through his love for food: foraging, fermenting, cooking, and feeding. That weekend, for our Paint the Fermentation Bus! party, Cooperative Fermentation would provide the meals.

That evening Jonah and I put together a feast of tempeh marinated in tamari, fried squash blossoms, and sautéed chicken of the woods. The next day, with Harley, we visited a u-pick blueberry farm, where guests paid a discounted price for as many blueberries as they could pick. Jonah and I made blueberry mint ale.

Blueberry Mint Ale

YIELDS 5 GALLONS, 7 PERCENT ABV, 2 WEEKS

Beer is more particular than wine and cider—you must use a sanitizer with your equipment (see listed materials). Beer involves grain fermentation, and most of the ingredients below must be sourced from a home-brew store. You can buy these grains in bulk and then crush them upon purchase with the store's grain crusher. I've found that most employees at home-brew stores are eager to help novices and will share knowledge and recipes. This is a delicious late-summer brew with a creative flair, featuring fresh-picked blueberries and mint. You can replace the berries and herbs with local and seasonal flora.

INGREDIENTS
½ lb Carapils
½ lb Crystal 60L
½ lb roasted barley
½ lb black patent
4 oz chocolate malt
6.6 lbs dark malt extract
3 oz Columbus hops
3 oz Calypso hops
½ gallon blueberries
1 cup mint leaves
1 yeast packet (Wyeast London Ale or
    Nottingham Dry)

MATERIALS
5-gallon pot
5-gallon carboy
Air lock and bung
Grain bag
Thermometer
Hydrometer
Star San sanitizer
Home-brew funnel

PROCESS
1. Crush the grains (Carapils, Crystal, roasted barley, black patent, and chocolate malt) and steep them in 2 gallons of water at 165° F for half an hour using a mesh bag.

2. Pull grains out and let drain in a large bowl. Don't squeeze the bag, but collect as much liquid as you can.

3. Add 2 more gallons of water to the pot and bring to a boil. Turn off the heat and gently stir in malt extract. We now refer to this liquid as the wort.

4. Before bringing the wort to a 60-minute boil (described below), make sure to sanitize all materials that will come in contact with it. This includes stirring utensils, home-brew funnel, air lock and bung, and hydrometer. I keep a large bowl or gallon bucket of sanitizer solution and dunk materials in it regularly. Do not rinse materials after sanitizing.

5. Bring wort to a boil, making sure not to let it boil over, and let it boil for 60 minutes. Add 1 ounce each of Columbus and Calypso hops in first five minutes (at full boil), and repeat, adding the same amount of hops twice more—at 45 minutes and 55 minutes.

6. Add blueberries 40 minutes into the boil; add the mint leaves after you turn the heat off, at 60 minutes.

7. Let the wort cool, sanitize 5-gallon carboy, and transfer the wort into it using a home-brew funnel. Top off with water, leaving at least 6 inches of headspace. Add the yeast, note the specific gravity with your hydrometer, and seal with air lock and bung. Ferment the beer for 2 weeks and then bottle or keg.

Friday afternoon I parked at Resilience Hub for our work party. We had twelve people scheduled on the first day and seven on day two. I was hopeful with the manpower we would finish in no time. Ian showed with Bettie the Bus at the crack of dawn, and we crafted the weekend agenda.

Most of the tools and materials we needed were on the buses. The biggest expenses were a paint gun and paint. I quickly discovered there was no amount of research I could have done to prepare for the weekend—with every item we bought, we needed another. To do the paint job right, we needed a clean, rust-free surface to paint; to apply the paint, we needed a paint gun; and to use a paint gun, we needed a compressor (an expensive and energy-intensive tool), which we didn't have. After scrutinizing our resources, Jonah's brother loaned us a compressor. We started by sanding the rusty and chipped bus exterior.

Large holes in the exterior, filled with only putty, revealed themselves after a few hours of strenuous sanding. Not long after the discovery, a man from an auto body shop conveniently located across the street walked our way. He was impressed with our undertaking. Ian showed him the holes and asked for advice. The man left and returned with a large piece of sheet metal and a rivet gun. He expertly taught us how to conceal the holes.

Each step revealed a new issue, and I looked to Ian for guidance. He was the backbone: jovial, organized, and persistent. When day two rolled around, the bus was ready to paint. It looked like a toy, with sheets of paper hung by blue painter's tape covering the windows and bumpers. My side mirrors had been unscrewed and were sitting to the side of my bus. (Ian promised he would screw them back on once we finished.) Clearly, no driving would happen until the bus was painted. The only way out was through.

Ian readied me with goggles and an air mask and held the gun with his hands on top of mine, guiding me with slow, even sprays back and forth. After an hour, I was barely a quarter of the way through painting one side of the bus. My right arm felt as if it would fall off. The bus would obviously need a second coat, too. The work party was also coming to a close.

The next day, Monday, it was just Harley, the compressor, and me. As I fired up the compressor to paint, a man came out from a neighboring bakery, upset that the freshly painted bus was stinking up his place. It was a perfectly good reason to ask us to leave. There were a couple issues, though: aside from no mirrors, my windows were covered with paper.

I gulped, ripped a hole in the paper so I could see, and asked Harley to help guide me to the parking lot next door, where we'd befriended a kombucha company. (I had friends all over the neighborhood—I was "fermentation-bus lady.") They had told us the day before we could use their lot as a backup plan. I moved the bus to the lot, pulled out the compressor, and started to paint.

Again I was asked to leave. The landlord wouldn't have it, so I haphazardly set up in the street. I couldn't take the paper off now. Ian would come after work to help put the mirrors on. Everything was going to be fine, I kept telling myself, in the spirit of Ian.

But no one would have me. The fumes were too much, and as much as I wanted to believe it was no big deal, I also knew they were too much. So with each person who wanted me to move along, I moved along. As I moved my bus down the street for the last time, I snagged an electrical cord. I anxiously stepped out, and on the ground under my rear right wheel, I patiently untangled the cord, as I'd done with my mom's necklaces as a kid, letting the world fall away. I was good with my hands. I was good with delicate things. It was meditative. And then I was back, lying on the concrete, covered in paint and dirt, sweating my ass off under my forty-foot bus.

I rolled out from under and Harley recommended we make our way toward upstate New York, where we had an event the next evening. Maybe that was the most reasonable thing, but I didn't want to give in to what was reasonable. I wanted to finish. I combed my fingers through my long hair until they met on top and threw my head back, face to the mid-August sun, letting out a wave of curses.

Minutes later, looking defeated, as I walked toward the bus with one of my side mirrors in hand, planning to install it myself, a voice called out from across the street, "Where are you going? You can't put those on yet."

"I don't have a choice. I've been kicked out of every lot," I said.

"But I've been watching you all weekend. You can't stop now." The man hadn't suspected I was the owner of the bus until he saw my maneuvers that morning, right down to untangling the snagged cord. He said he'd convinced his boss to let me pull into their driveway and finish painting.

You never know who will come out of the woodwork when you need them most. I pulled into the contractor's lot. I finished the paint job. Ian came over after work and put my mirrors back on. We crawled under the bus to seal a cracked exhaust pipe, too. We checked the fluids. The bus looked great, and everything was in tip-top shape. Harley and I left an hour later for our upstate New York event.

At a gas station in Massachusetts, fifty miles west of Boston, I stepped into the store to pay the regular $120 in cash for a tank fill. Walking back, I noticed a steady blue-green stream spewing from my radiator. I stopped and stared, in disbelief, for what must have been a full minute and wondered why the summer had taken such a heavy turn.

FALL
RESTORATION

I believe in God, only I spell it Nature.
—Frank Lloyd Wright

I. Reflecting with Water

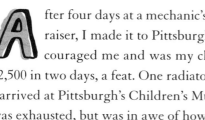fter four days at a mechanic's garage and organizing an impromptu fund-raiser, I made it to Pittsburgh. Bonnie, from my Asheville workshop, encouraged me and was my cheerleader through the fund-raiser. I raised $2,500 in two days, a feat. One radiator richer and one radiator to the salvage yard, I arrived at Pittsburgh's Children's Museum early in the morning for Pickle Day. I was exhausted, but was in awe of how sharp the bus looked and loved the enthusiasm from parents and kids.

The Children's Museum was also my first paid gig. At the end of the day, with a few days between classes, I parked on the north side of Frick Park and explored every nook and cranny of its six hundred acres. I had two more workshops before leaving the city, no connections, no way to shower, do laundry, or fill up my water tank to do my dishes. Charging money meant there was no obligation for the gig to provide such comforts. I understood and expected that, and it was worth every penny. It allowed me to indulge in some well-deserved leisurely adventuring.

After Pittsburgh I took a real end-of-summer vacation. I visited Frank Lloyd Wright's Fallingwater, a decadent and historic home built partly over a waterfall in rural Pennsylvania. I went camping for an entire week at Ohiopyle State Park, where after a steep uphill climb with my slow-moving machine, I asked the ranger, "Do you know where the kayakers camp?" She jotted down a campsite number.

I settled in and walked to the recommended site. I wanted adventure bad. "Hey," I said, arms crossed, and nodded toward the kayak on top of some strangers' car, "y'all wanna go out for a trip in the next few days?"

I hadn't ever touched a kayak until two months earlier and had only ever been out on ponds and bays.

They told me they planned to go out on the lower river, the toughest river, the day after tomorrow. "Cool," I said. We exchanged info and agreed to meet at the river entrance, nine A.M. sharp.

I hiked miles from my campsite to the nearest kayak rental place early morning. The cashier gave me a quick course: "Just paddle like hell if you enter a turbulent section" and "Don't ever stand in the river if you fall out of your kayak," among other important guidelines that escape me now. I walked to the meeting spot. Mora and Bob, the kayakers, along with another couple in their midfifties, arrived. We walked to the river together, and as we got in, they asked, "So what other rivers have you kayaked?"

I played it cool, "Oh, Oregon rivers, you know—the Willamette River. Otherwise, I haven't really kayaked much."

Mora got a look. "You sure you're ready for this?"

"Yeah. I'm ready for it."

Regardless, Mora and Bob made me walk two of the rapids: Cucumber and Dimple. They would have made me walk more of the high-grade rapids if I hadn't been so die-hard into it.

I invited them to dinner to show my appreciation for the all-day traverse. I made lamb burgers, a salad, grilled zucchini, and served wine on tap and beet kvass. Mora and Bob looked around the bus—they took in the fermentation station filled with glass jars; my tall cat, who slinked in through the side window after jumping from the roof to my hood; my woodstove, extensive spices and herb collection; and the notes to myself on my chalkboard on my paint-covered cupboard: *koji is super cool*; *8/26 feed water kefir*; *hang out at river*; *find organic apple orchard*. Mora eased into the comment "You really are the most camouflaged crazy person I've encountered on the road."

II. Seasonal Shift

If more of us valued food and cheer and song above hoarded gold, it would be a merrier world.

—J. R. R. Tolkien

I didn't feel crazy, though. I reserved September for farming, hiking the Appalachian Trail, and the Mother Earth News Fair. Though a part of me wanted to hold on to those last days of bare arms and legs and jumping in rivers, I looked forward to hibernating, planning, restoring, and making improvements through the fall. It had been my most active summer ever, and fall reminded me it was time to slow down.

The Sweet Farm, in central Maryland, hosted my last August event: a workshop, potluck, and pig roast. Fifty people showed for the hands-on event. After my brush with paid teaching, going back to a by-donation class didn't feel so much like work. I sold shirts and tapped one of my kegs next to a tip jar, and students donated enough to get me to my next few destinations.

As the roast was winding down, I stood with my new friend Rachel, one of Maryland's fermentation torchbearers and my hostess, eating pig brain and saying with awe, "Whoa, pig brain is *really* good." Then, looking under the table, we noticed three farm dogs passed out and covered in pig grease, with floppy tongues rolled out to the sides of their mouths. I felt their tummy aches and their unemployed joy.

The Sweet Farmers and I bonded quickly. I rested one week before heading to Pennsylvania's Mother Earth News Fair, a festival I'd been somewhat roped into. Hearing good things, I had wanted to scope out the scene, but knew it would be swarming, so thought I'd volunteer rather than bring the bus. The organizers wanted the bus. They offered me a "deal" to park it—$700 for the weekend.

I laughed and declined.

"How much would you pay?" the organizer asked.

"I don't know—maybe one hundred dollars?"

"Great, we'll take it."

And that was a wrap. I knew it would be packed, but the challenge was compelling. My expenses: fuel, printing T-shirts, and time. My revenue: starter-culture samples, T-shirts, and donations. Dollar-wise I'd probably break even.

The bus was full all weekend. Franklin sat in the back napping and avoiding people, unlike his usual social self. I had been warned about having a cat on board. As at all festivals, only service animals were allowed. I also had to keep a low profile and choose carefully when offering tastes of my creations, as I didn't have insurance or a food license then.

The Mother Earth News Fair is one of the largest and oldest sustainability fairs in the country—there were roughly twenty thousand people in attendance and the bus was packed all weekend. It was a naturally exhausting affair. Most memorably, while I was speaking to a group of fifteen people on the bus, a woman announced her presence by yelling from the doorway, "This stuff?! Doesn't this stuff cause stomach cancer?" I was taken aback and explained that fermented foods certainly don't cause stomach cancer. I wouldn't recommend someone drink six tall glasses of kombucha and eat half a gallon of sauerkraut every day to heal all their ills, but fermentation promotes diversity and represents life. Eating sustainably raised and grown foods, without the use of chemicals, is good for you. Fermented foods fall into the good-for-you foods group, raised and grown by powerful and responsible little life forces known as microbes. Everyone was on board with the sentiment.

At the festival it became clear that a sliding scale for starter cultures didn't make the pricing more fair. After accepting a $20 bill from a young farmer next to two crinkled dollar bills from a woman who said she was sorry but she was "saving for a new flat-screen," I fixed the price at $10 apiece.

It made me feel silly, as if I wasn't running my business well. I almost always felt taken for granted and taken advantage of by people who had more money. The wealthiest communities were often the most demanding and the least generous, and I was starting to be put off by it.

I left the fairgrounds late Sunday evening for a campground. I bent my bike on a big tree and was without my preferred form of transportation. The next day

I parked in an oversize parking lot, unsure of my next move, opened my heavy trucker's atlas, and let the realization sink in: I wouldn't be making it home at the end of the year. I knew it well by then.

I stayed at trucker stations and rest stops for several days. I e-mailed farmers I'd met in Virginia and Maryland, asking if they wanted an extra hand in the next month. I called Ali and Scotty of Blue Moon Acres in New Jersey, inquiring about Halloween festivities. I reached out to the New York City fermentation crew.

Then I called Hashem. "Hey, I miss you."

"I miss you back. How's my cat?" Hashem has a thing for Franklin.

"He's good, could be better since he's been cooped up. We'll be in the Northeast this winter. I'm thinking about New York City. What do you think?"

"I got you! Both of you."

We had been in touch during my travels after I left New York City and had discussed the possibility of me staying through winter. Hashem had my back. I knew for certain we would have a lot of fun, and that he'd enjoy the homemade food. And we'd enjoy eating it together.

Virginia turkey feather

Farm plans manifested, too. I made my way to Chilly Hollow Farm in Berryville, Virginia. I'd been introduced to the young farmers—a male duo in their midtwenties—through a pig roast I'd attended at the Number 1 Sons pickle factory earlier that month. (Late summer was pig-roast season.) I helped on their three-acre farm in exchange for rest. Potomac Vegetable Farms, where I'd held my first Northeast workshop, was twenty miles away. I was quickly getting better acquainted with the greater Virginia farming community west of Washington, D.C.

Maida of Potomac Vegetable Farms, a farmhand I'd befriended in May, visited Chilly Hollow regularly while I was there. We hiked a section of the Appalachian Trail and attended a bluegrass music festival, and she gifted me five one-gallon bags of high-heat chili peppers. Among them were ghost peppers, jalapeños, and Fatalii. She knew I'd put them to good use in kimchi. Three years later, I am still working through the dried chili peppers. Every time I use them, I'm taken back to good times with Maida and the three days of drying peppers in the garage at the farm, its air filled with pungent and sneezy spice.

I also made a batch of fermented hot pepper sauce.

Fermented Hot Pepper Sauce

YIELDS 1 PINT, 3 WEEKS

This easy fermentation is perfect for adorning morning eggs, perking up a bowl of greens, or adding to marinades. Fermented hot sauce is a must-have ingredient in the bus kitchen, since I love my food spicy.

INGREDIENTS
3 cups whole chili peppers
3–5 garlic cloves
¼ cup diced onion
½ tbsp salt (2 percent salinity)
½ qt water

MATERIALS
Quart jar
Weight and cover
Blender or food processor

PROCESS

1. Destem hot peppers of your choice—you can use one variety or multiple kinds—peel garlic cloves, and chop the onion. Place ingredients in a quart jar.

2. Make brine with ½ tbsp of salt and ½ quart of water and pour over chili peppers, onion, and garlic. Let the mixture sit with a weight and tea towel on top for 2 weeks.

3. After two weeks, strain the brine and reserve in a cup or bowl. Blend the fermented peppers, garlic, and onion in a blender or food processor until the ingredients are finely chopped. Slowly add some of the reserved brine, starting with a few tablespoons, to thin the sauce and help further break down the ingredients. If you discover you'd like the sauce thinner, add more brine.

4. Store in the refrigerator and enjoy for 2 years (or longer!).

Apples were on my mind as they were every autumn—for my annual cider and cyser recipes—so I searched for an organic orchard. The task was more difficult than I imagined. Eastern fruit growers face far more diseases and pests than their western counterparts, so organic orchards were a rarity.

I got a tip from Millstone Cellars, a cidery I'd connected with earlier in the year while visiting Baltimore. Millstone's owner told me point-blank: Country Pleasures Farm was the place for an organic-apple work-trade. They specialized in cider apples—it was my dream match. I contacted the farm immediately and they invited me for a weeklong stay.

The farm boasted over eighteen hundred varieties of apple, cherry, pear, peach, and apricot trees. They also had an enormous greenhouse filled with a dozen fig varieties. I collected hundreds of pounds of apples each day on the sprawling property, with trees that seemed to pop out of a Brothers Grimm fairy tale. I'd gather a truckload and haul them back to the barn a few times each day. I waded through the greenhouses for figs, too. Many were beginning to ferment on the trees, after being picked at by wasps. I'd harvest both—tossing the fresh ones in the fridge for the weekend farmers' market and the others in a growing bag I kept in the freezer.

I received two hundred pounds of apples for the work put in that week and drove to the Sweet Farm for one last visit. They had a press, so I conducted another trade—apples for use of their press. At the pressing party I made five gallons of wild-fig hard cider and played around with some remaining apple juice, making nonalcoholic fizzy beverages.

Fig Cider

YIELDS 1 GALLON, 7 PERCENT ABV, 1–3 MONTHS

Choosing apple varieties is one of the most important parts of making hard cider, especially when working with the local, wild yeast already present on the apples (over a store-bought yeast variety)—you will always get an expression of what you start with. If you decide to brew with pasteurized apple juice, you will need to add yeast. I've included two good cider yeasts below.

INGREDIENTS
¾ gallon apple juice
1 lb figs
1 packet of Lalvin EC-1118 or
    Wyeast 4776 (optional)

MATERIALS
2 one-gallon jugs
Home-brew funnel
Hydrometer
Air lock and bung
Siphon and racking cane

PROCESS
1. If using store-bought yeast, dissolve it in 1 cup of lukewarm water a few hours before adding it to the wine.

2. In a large pot, gently heat apple juice with the chopped figs on the stove, stirring occasionally for 10 minutes. Make sure to keep the heat on low if you plan to work with the local, wild yeast of the juice (high heat will destroy the microflora).

3. Use a brew funnel (sans strainer) to pour the figs and apple juice into your gallon jar.

4. Check and note the ABV with a hydrometer. Let the wild bacteria and yeast go to work or add the suggested yeast strain and insert bung with water-filled air lock. Give the gallon container a few good shakes to aerate.

5. After a few days, you'll notice activity in your air lock, indicating that the yeast is consuming sugars in your brew. In 1 week, after the yeast activity settles, rack the cider (according to pages 138–39) into another gallon jug, leaving the sediment and figs behind.

6. Taste along the way. If you prefer a sweeter cider, you can bottle or imbibe within a few weeks. If you prefer a dry cider, determine the ABV of your brew with a hydrometer as it ferments. When the hydrometer reads 0 percent, there is no more fermentable sugar and a dry cider is ready for drinking or bottling. You can age cider for 3 months for optimal flavor.

Apple Fizzy

YIELDS 1 QUART, 24–48 HOURS

INGREDIENTS
1 qt apple juice
1 tbsp tibicos

MATERIALS
Quart jar
Cover or Bell-jar lid

PROCESS

1. Pour apple juice into quart container and add the tibicos. Cover with a loose-fitting plastic Ball-jar lid or cloth and rubber band. Airtight lids can result in explosions (read about tibicos safety on pages 61–62).

2. Strain the tibicos from your apple fizzy, place in a jar of sugar water, and store it in the fridge for later use.

3. Pour the apple fizzy in a sling-top jar and transfer to the fridge. Enjoy the apple fizzy once it's chilled.

III. Re-visiting Blue Moon Acres

Save for a few paid gigs in Delaware, my big events to wrap up the year were a Halloween festival at Blue Moon Acres Farm and the Brooklyn Fermentation Festival in my old haunt. I paid more mind to money now, with my four-month stay in New York City coming up. My winter survival would depend on dollars rather than my working hands or ferments, so I decided what my services were worth and did my best to abide by it.

The affluent Princeton area was a hotbed for food education—eager to take in the wisdom of fermentation—and would be a testing ground for me to shake my moneymaker. In nearby Pennington, Ali and Scotty of Blue Moon Acres Farm offered a three-week respite. Their New Jersey was different from the New Jersey I knew from my early twenties while living in the Northeast. Though industry comes to mind for many who have only visited briefly—usually along the Philadelphia to New York City trek—New Jersey is home to rivers, forests, mountains, wetlands, Atlantic Ocean beaches, wildlife, and more. I was grateful to experience a snippet of New Jersey from the perspective of the Delaware Valley farming community, visiting small towns, the woods, and historic farms speckled along the Delaware River.

Amid New Jersey explorations I was offered a few compelling teaching opportunities in Princeton that would fund most of my New York City winter stay. Blue Moon Acres Farm prepared for the Halloween festival, OktoberFEAST, which would donate proceeds to Fermentation on Wheels and the local watershed association. I felt hugely supported in the Delaware Valley; there, the community treated Fermentation on Wheels like an educational staple.

At OktoberFEAST Scotty offered hayride farm tours, Ali told stories to young people, and I decked out my bus. Our friend and local potter, Debbie, brought her fermentation crocks and sold them alongside the bus. Two local chefs made pasture–raised-pork bratwurst, veggie burgers, and a plethora of sweets. The ferment table had Bloody Kimchi and Black Soldier Fly Sauerkraut made by me.

The Bloody Kimchi had no blood; it was just a scary name. The Black Soldier Fly Sauerkraut was named after a sauerkraut in the fermentation station that became infested with a top layer of black soldier fly larvae. I thought it was supergross, but

Ali, Scotty, and the kids—brave homesteaders they are—devoured it. (Their argument was that black soldier flies are beneficial and used to compost and convert waste into animal feed.) The bus stayed in theme with the post-apocalypse from the year before. My welcome sign read:

> All aboard the bus of the post–apocalypse! Meet a real life survivalist. Discover the flavors, mystery, and resistance of living foods. Prepare yourself for a sensory explosion featuring our bacterial comrades Kombucha, Sauerkraut, and Tibicos. Learn about micro–diversity, and how it can help us reach our full potential feel–good selves and survive in the new world!

The five piglets from May had grown into full-size pigs. Scotty and some of the farmhands did the slaughtering and hanging. Ali's younger brother and I, along with Ali and Scotty, butchered, bagged, and labeled the meat. The work was satisfying, involved long hard hours, and seemed appropriate in exchange for the life that was lived. Ali and Scotty's family of five lived off half a pig for the entire year, protein-wise.

Ali, Debbie the potter, and I made adzuki-bean miso (pages 52–53) together and a gallon of amazake, a naturally sweet fermented-rice porridge.

Amazake

YIELDS 6 CUPS, 8–12 HOURS

Amazake can be made in many ways, according to the recipes online, in books, and on koji containers. The most successful and delicious recipe I've found uses a one-to-one ratio of rice to koji and triples the amount of water to rice. I do add a little more water toward the end to get the consistency just right. Amazake is simple, but it requires a warm temperature range and thus a bit of attention during fermentation.

Below are some tasty flavor combinations for your amazake, too—you can throw the ingredients in a blender to make amazake shakes. Amazake is usually pasteurized so it keeps longer, but I prefer to leave it alive.

INGREDIENTS
1 cup rice
3 cups water
1 cup koji

MATERIALS
½-gallon Ball jar
Thermometer
Cooler / incubator (see page 164)

PROCESS

1. Bring rice and water to a boil on the stovetop, then cook on low for 45 minutes until the ingredients have a souplike texture. If it's thick, add ¼ to ½ cup of hot water and stir, until the ingredients resemble porridge (like freshly cooked oatmeal).

2. While the rice cooks, preheat your half-gallon jar with hot water, as well as a small cooler. I simply heat water in my kettle, pour a bit in, and pour it out.

3. Once the rice is done cooking, check the temperature with a thermometer and let cool to 140° F, then add the koji and stir.

4. Pour mixture into the half-gallon jar, place a lid on top, and incubate for 8 to 12 hours between 120° to 140° F. You can incubate with hot water or hot-water bottles surrounding the half-gallon jar. Check the temperature every few hours in case you need to pour out a bit of water and bring the temperature back up.

5. It's finished once the flavor is earthy, tangy, and sweet. Place in the refrigerator and consume within 3 days. You may also heat it on the stovetop to pasteurize and keep your amazake for up to a week.

AMAZAKE SHAKES
suggestions for a super gourmet experience

The Morgans understand my work. We walk a similar line—we do what we love, reap the rewards, and experience the immense challenges that come with following our dreams. It's hard to work at what you love. The stakes are high—every downfall puts you in a serious rut just as every milestone brings immense joy. To understand someone's suffering is no small gift. Understanding is love's other name.

RE-WILDING
NEW YORK CITY

I live with carpe diem engraved on my heart.
—M. F. K. Fisher

I. Heart-Stirring Momentum

I didn't want to touch the bus those next few months. I was longing for the nostalgia of my past life—walking the streets of my beloved Brooklyn, taking the train to nearby foreign places, and immersing myself in conversations among the multifarious community. I believed validity was at the other side of the Verrazano-Narrows Bridge. Merging my past self with my current self would generate inspiration for the next leg of my tour. That is, I needed to mastermind a logistics strategy while flexing my grassroots renegade might. New York City—of all places—would embrace such synergy. I believed no other place would help build as much exposure and momentum for Fermentation on Wheels' future.

I parked in front of my old apartment building on Washington Avenue for my last event of 2014, in collaboration with home-brew shop Bitter & Esters, owned by old acquaintances John and Doug, who'd visited the bus in May. Kombucha, mead, and beer taught by local fermenters were offered by donation in their home-brew shop. The bus was open for tastes and tours and fermentation talk.

The Live Cultures, a local folk band known for its fermentation-themed jokes and songs, performed at a nearby bar for the occasion, too. The quirky bar, known for its TARDIS bathroom, served kimchi-brine cocktails in theme with the day.

We called it the Brooklyn Fermentation Festival. Fellow fermenters from NYC Ferments showed, including Cheryl. John wrote a blog entry for Bitter & Esters praising Fermentation on Wheels—I knew then that John and Doug really got what I was doing. They understood that my business, like theirs, involved hard work, courage, and support. John also recognized that much of my project was about getting out into the public eye—showing people the joys of a sustainable and healthy lifestyle and, most of all, inspiring people to follow their dreams.

I left for Long Island City the next morning and received another warm welcome: keys, bed, kitchen, and pillow talk. I built a small nest in Hashem's apartment. I worked often but felt isolated with the encroaching bitter cold in his apartment surrounded by industrial Queens. It was loud and a twenty-minute walk from the nearest subway station. Though we lived together, I rarely saw Hashem after moving in.

I took to the kitchen to curb the feelings of isolation. I made a beer that steamed up the entire apartment and ended up tasting like feet. Many a bird was roasted, mussels steamed, and sourdough loaves baked. I rejoined the Park Slope Food Coop, shopped weekly, and worked my monthly shifts. In my culinary frenzy I couldn't eat as much I cooked, so after not having seen Hashem for five days, the next time he walked through the door I asked, "Where have you been?"

"Work."

Hashem was a photo technician, and though I'd known him to be a serious workaholic and spend the night at his previous workplace, I always found it strange.

"Where are you sleeping?"

He alluded to staying with friends in Manhattan, but there was never a clear answer.

This conversation would mark the theme of my winter stay with him; it was reticent. I swept it off—buried myself in books, organized events, bused to Flushing for roasted-duck ramen, and networked with New York City's food people. Feelings of disappointment prodded me occasionally, but I had to stay vigilant, determined, and organized. My successes didn't come out of luck. I needed to reenergize my social life.

Gathering with members of NYC Ferments one Monday evening, at their monthly meeting, I was reminded of a lone-wolf fermentation expert I hadn't yet connected with: Barry Schwartz. The tempeh aficionado. He wasn't at the meeting, so I decided to seek him out. His kitchen was in Long Island City, near Hashem's apartment. I e-mailed him asking if he'd be at his kitchen soon, and if I could help make tempeh.

We met up soon after, and Barry greeted me with a hug and his calm, it's-all-good vibe. He was different from most characters influenced by the hustle and constant stress of New York City. Barry's main extravagances were his enthusiasm for high-scale foods (he considered buying a civet cat to start producing kopi luwak, the most expensive coffee in the world, processed via the cat's digestive system) and his deep love for expensive kitchen gadgets, such as industrial nut-butter makers and Robot Coupes. He also loved to dine out in New York's abundant ethnic restaurants and wanted to share it all with me. I joined him that weekend at the Greenpoint Farmers Market to help with his tempeh booth. After the shift, we went to his favorite South Indian kitchen, Ganesh Temple Canteen in Flushing. We feasted on a glorious array of dosas, accompanied by pakoras, samosas, and chutneys. I was instantly hooked on his recommendations.

Shortly after, Barry and I were inseparable; our friendship and the tasty things we made felt, at times, like the reason for my winter in New York City. I worked every tempeh production shift and learned the entire large-scale process—from cooking the beans in a vat with vinegar to drying them in an industrial centrifuge and inoculating the beans with help of a commercial baker's Hobart. Barry introduced me to Queens' vibrant and less frequented food scene, including his favorite authentic tamale spot, Nixtamal, in Corona. We feasted on Vietnamese, Szechuan, and Thai food at a dozen other ethnic holes-in-the-wall.

Barry and I worked markets together every weekend. After a shift one evening, we went for dinner and had an idea: an illustrated educational fermentation series called *Fermentation Illustrated*. The zine series would share the cultural and historical stories of fermented foods and empower people to ferment in their home kitchens.

The idea was so cool that we decided to throw a release party for the first issue, *Tempeh Demystified*. A tempeh workshop and vegan dinner would accompany the release, while all proceeds would go into production and continuation of *Fermentation Illustrated*. The *Village Voice* claimed our event was one of the "Weekend's Five Best Food Events."

While I was in my illustration fury, a food journalist named Rachel Wharton e-mailed me, expressing her interest in Fermentation on Wheels. She wanted to pitch a piece to a local newspaper. She thought she'd heard, from a few local home brewers (Doug and John), that I was in New York City. I gave Rachel the lowdown on my entire schedule for the next month. She said she'd make sure to attend the *Tempeh Demystified* party.

A great write-up gives you a special kind of high. At that point, I had a few under my belt. It had never occurred to me that I might get exposure in a New York City newspaper, but the idea sounded nice. I consider journalists to be some of the most effective activists on the scene.

Tempeh

YIELDS ABOUT 28 OZ (THREE 9.5 OZ TEMPEH BLOCKS), 24–32 HOURS

Tempeh is a challenging ferment, but once you have it down, the results are so stunning, delicious, and rewarding that you will find a way to integrate it into your kitchen routine. I first fermented tempeh in a cooler in a bus, and I sometimes slept with the cooler next to me, waking in the night to check on the precious mycelium growth. I have practiced so much it's now near impossible for me to mess up a batch. Here's what I've learned: don't skip the vinegar or hair dryer, and use a thermometer with a probe. I don't want to scare you away from this magical ferment, but it takes commitment, discipline, time, and practice. Refer to page 13 to source *Rhizopus oligosporus* or *Rhizopus oryzae*, the culture required for tempeh fermentation.

INGREDIENTS

1 lb soybeans

½ cup vinegar

½ tsp to 1 tbsp *Rhizopus oligosporus*
    or *Rhizopus oryzae*
    (amount will vary based on
    concentration of culture)

MATERIALS

Scale

Thermometer with probe

Blender or food processor

Mesh strainer

Hair dryer

Ziploc bags

Incubator, dehydrator, oven, or cooler

PROCESS

1. Soak soybeans for 8 to 12 hours. I recommend soaking in the morning and cooking the beans in the evening. Tempeh is most difficult to regulate at 12 hours into incubation, so it's best to be awake and nearby during that time.

2. After soak, rinse the beans and blend them quickly to break them down a bit. I blend so they are roughly a quarter of the original size.

3. Transfer the beans to a pot. Add the vinegar and enough water to cover your beans by three inches. Bring the beans to a boil and then cook on medium high until the beans are al dente, for roughly 45 minutes. As the beans cook, you will notice the hulls float to the surface—scoop them out with a mesh strainer. You won't get all of them—that's fine.

4. Once the beans are cooked, drain the water and transfer the beans back to the pot or a large bowl.

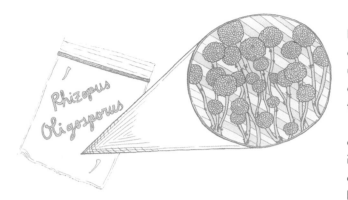

5. Dry the beans with a hair dryer while stirring vigorously. This takes 10 to 15 minutes. You don't want them too dry, just dry enough so that they aren't wet. Damplike.

6. Introduce your starter culture once the temperature is below 90° F. Distribute the culture evenly throughout the beans using a spoon.

7. Take two Ziploc bags and poke small holes with a fork throughout each of them. Don't be shy—these are breathing holes for the beans as they come to life through the power of fungus. Start with the sides and the corners, then work your way along the entire bag.

8. Spoon equal amounts of bean into each bag. I like to use a scale for accuracy. Seal the bags and gently flatten each with your hands.

9. Place the pre-tempeh in an incubator for 24 to 32 hours (read about incubator options on next page). The temperature should range anywhere from 85° to 95° F. It will take longer to ferment on the lower end of the spectrum and faster on the upper end. If your tempeh reaches 105° for longer than an hour, you will lose it to heat. After 12 hours, tempeh starts to produce its own heat. At this point, remove the tempeh from the incubator and keep the bags separate from each other to discourage too much heat.

10. The mycelium growth creates a unique soft white field with the slightest fuzz. There may be black spots, too—that's sporulation, which is great. I recommend digging in right away. There is absolutely nothing like tempeh fresh out of the incubator. Even pasteurized tempeh from the grocery store doesn't get close to this flavor experience.

11. Store the tempeh in your refrigerator and consume within three days or keep in the freezer for long-term storage (up to 3 months). This storage method will keep your tempeh alive and full of flavor. It takes 2–3 hours to defrost tempeh.

INCUBATION

fermenting in temperature controlled enclosed spaces

BASIC

Use your oven with the light turned on. Temperature usually ranges from 85° to 95°F.

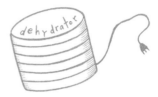

EFFICIENT

Many dehydrators can be set between 95° and 158°F.

DO-IT-YOURSELF

Fill a cooler with heated water or hot water bottles. Flexible temperatures, but can be high maintenance for lengthier fermentation periods.

ADVANCED DIY

Build an incubator with an old freezer or mini fridge, thermostat, and light bulb. Extremely reliable with very flexible temperatures.

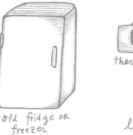

old fridge or freezer

thermostat

light bulb

There I was, spending winter in New York City, and hosting a sold-out dinner and workshop in Brooklyn's Windsor Terrace with Barry. I printed forty copies of the zine that morning, after pulling an all-nighter. Most of the food was already prepared at Barry's home kitchen—mung-bean tempeh, sprouted daikon, shio-koji cocoa, and fig rosemary mochi. While Barry demystified the tempeh process for the audience, I prepared the rest of dinner: black garlic miso dressing with salad greens, roasted beets in cardamom rose water, and black-and-tan rice. We started dinner and I tapped the keg of my fig cider, brewed in Maryland. I talked about the cider, the food, and the bus and announced upcoming educational events. We were so happy.

The morning after our success, I received e-mails from five attendees who fell ill. Each person was surprisingly cool about it—they explained they had had a great time despite the aftermath. Luckily, the majority of attendees didn't get sick, but it was unsettling. I immediately apologized and refunded them, then e-mailed Barry.

Barry took a long time to respond. The aftermath of the *Tempeh Demystified* party revealed the inequality of our partnership, which had long been surfacing. We struggled to feel supported by each other. Barry was afraid that the resulting illnesses would affect his business. However, prior to the release party we had been struggling for the primary ownership of *Fermentation Illustrated*, and that wore us down. Everything I heard started with "You should . . . " I began harboring resentment and feelings of guilt for wanting to do things my way. Our strong personalities clashed with an intensity that could be sensed by every person standing in a room, similar to how our love for each other could once be sensed by every employee in his small kitchen. Barry always reminded me, "Life is full of contradictions."

In late January I had a message from Rachel, the journalist: *That was such a cool event. It actually reminded me of what I loved about Brooklyn when I first moved here in ye olden times of 2000.* We arranged a visit. That Friday, upon her entering my bus for the first time, she told me I'd be in the *New York Times* Sunday paper. I was at a loss for words.

Back at Hashem's I took a bath to ease a head cold from the changing weather and stress. I tried not to dwell on my falling-out with Barry. I'd planned to take the train to Pennington and visit Ali, Scotty, and the kids, but I simply couldn't do it. Everything was moving too fast—I had just gotten back from an 18° F photo shoot with a *New York Times* photographer on the bus. It was cold and uncomfortable and I didn't feel ready for big press then.

I called Ali from the bathtub and told her I couldn't make it—I had some kind of bug and the thought of trekking to Penn Station made my stomach curl.

"Just come—I'll heal you," she said.

I arrived that afternoon sniffling, after a short and rather painless train ride—the hardest part was getting to Penn Station. Ali picked me up in Pennington and we drove to the farm. She offered an acupuncture session, her main trade, for my bug. I rarely trusted medicine via needles, but I always trust Ali. I exited her office and six-year-old Wynn, the middle child, was dressed in a snowsuit. I joined him outside and we rolled down banks of snow piled outside the Blue Moon Acres rice shed. He laughed so hard his eyes squinted. After the laughter, he lay on his back and made snow angels with his mouth open and tongue catching snowflakes.

Inside we made pork meatballs and greens. Ali had a client and I curled into a bed with Clara and Wynn, where we watched Weird Al Yankovic videos, crying with laughter at the immense and purposeful ridiculousness.

Sourdough English Muffins

YIELDS 18 MUFFINS, 24 HOURS

In the morning, Ali served sourdough English muffins with farm-fresh chicken eggs. She'd learned the recipe recently and used the sourdough starter I'd gifted her in May. The muffins are an especially good breakfast food for Ali's busy mom-meets-acupuncturist-meets-farmer lifestyle. She makes a few dozen at a time and freezes them. Another plus: no oven is needed for this recipe.

INGREDIENTS
2 cups warm water or milk
2 tbsp honey or sugar
1 cup sourdough starter
5 to 6 cups flour
2 tsp commercial yeast (optional)

2 tsp salt
½ cup cornmeal

MATERIALS
Widemouthed Ball-jar canning-lid ring
Plastic, glass, or ceramic bowl
Wax paper

PROCESS
1. Combine water (or milk), sugar, and sourdough in a bowl. Slowly add 5 cups of flour and mix with a wooden spoon—include the commercial yeast if you choose to use it. It will result in a faster rise.

2. The dough should be slightly wet. Sift roughly ½ cup of flour into the dough and knead with your hands, forming a nice round ball. If you find the dough is dry, dunk your hand in a bowl of water and gently pat the ball so it retains moisture.

3. Place dough in a bowl and cover with a cloth and allow the dough to leaven, or rise, for 12 to 24 hours. The longer it rises, the more sour flavors will develop.

4. Punch down the dough and fold in the salt, kneading 5 to 6 times. Transfer the dough to a well-floured surface and roll out so the dough is ¼–½ inch thick.

5. Use a ring from a canning-jar lid as a cutter for the muffin shape and transfer each round to wax paper that has been dusted with cornmeal.

6. Cover the dough and leave to leaven once more, for 2 to 4 hours.

7. When the dough has risen, cook the muffins on a griddle or pan on medium-low heat with a little bit of butter. Cook them for 4 minutes on each side, and after first flip, give the muffins a press with your spatula to encourage a traditional English-muffin shape.

8. Enjoy the muffins fresh. You can also freeze them for up to a month.

The next day, I made my way back to an intense alternate reality that was coming: my face on the front page of the Metro section of the Sunday *New York Times*.

What I loved most about the piece, titled "The Johnny Appleseed of Pickling," was the credit it gave to the New York City fermentation crew: Michaela of Crock & Jar, Cheryl of Contraband Ferments, Zack of the annual potluck Ferment! Ferment!, and Angela of Just Food NYC. They were people who needed to be seen in the *New York Times*—to shed more light on the food and fermentation movement in New York City. Also, to emphasize that fermentation is not a solo endeavor, but a community project.

It provided heart-stirring momentum for Fermentation on Wheels, too. The response to my mission on wheels was staggeringly positive. E-mails from fans and potential venues flooded my in-box for a month. The biggest challenge was accommodating requests from the Midwest. It would be easy to overexert myself if I didn't choose a wise route. My workshops in New York City tripled in attendance overnight and became lectures rather than hands-on classes.

II. Miniature New England Tour

Here's to another year of feeling free, fermenting, giving, loving, walking the talk . . . happy 2015. I think it's going to be a good one.

—Journal, January 1, 2015

Without small-scale do-it-yourself classes I felt out of my element, and then an escape from the city to do them emerged. I was invited to teach at several Northeast Organic Farming conferences in New England, a region close to my heart.

I organized workshops along my route to Vermont's Northeast Organic Farming conference. It was the coldest I'd ever weathered, though, and I was reminded of my Texas roots and poor winter-survival skills. I taught in New Hampshire and then in Brattleboro, Vermont, where I stayed with author and fermentation enthusiast Leda Scheintaub.

Leda hails from New York City. We met during Sandor's Sterling College class the summer before, where she taught students how to make dosas, a traditional Indian pancake made with fermented rice and lentils. I had been invited to stay with

Leda and learn the Indian pancake's intricacies from her partner, Nash, who runs a small kitchen on wheels called Dosa Hut. Dosas are thin and hearty—feast on them with whatever fillings your heart desires.

Dosa
YIELDS 12 DOSAS, 18+ HOURS

INGREDIENTS

2 cups rice (preferably short-grain white rice, but any will get the job done)

1 cup split urad dal

3 tbsp chana dal

1 tbsp fenugreek seeds

2 cups conserved soaking water (see below)

2 tsp salt

High-heat cooking oil (coconut oil or lard are my favorites)

MATERIALS

Large plastic, ceramic, or glass bowl with a lid (plate on top will do)

Blender or stone grinder

Ladle

Griddle or cast-iron pan

PROCESS

1. Soak the rice, dals, and fenugreek seeds for 8 hours or overnight. After soak, conserve 2 cups of the soaking water. Rinse the soaked grains a few times.

2. Blend or grind the ingredients—you may need to do this in 2–3 batches. With each blend, add some of the conserved soaking water (roughly ¾ cup total) to thin the ingredients, making a thick batter.

3. Once the ingredients are thoroughly blended and resemble thick pancake batter, pour into the large bowl and cover loosely with the lid for 8 hours.

4. After fermentation, stir in salt and transfer to the fridge or use immediately. Your batter is ready to work with.

5. Heat a nonstick griddle or cast-iron pan on medium-high heat for cooking the dosas.

6. Put a dollop of cooking oil on the pan and spread it about with an oilcloth or by shaking the pan. Quickly ladle the batter into the center of the pan and then use the bottom of your ladle to flatten and spread the batter into a thin round layer (see illustration on next page). Cook for one minute on each side.

7. The first dosa is almost always imperfect—maybe even the first few—it's part of the process! Don't fret. They don't need to be perfect, anyway.

8. If batter burns onto the pan at any point, add water to steam it off, then generously oil the pan before the next dosa. You will use oil often, sometimes before each dosa.

How to Cook Dosa

ladle roughly half a cup of batter onto a well-greased non-stick pan

quickly flatten batter with the bottom of the ladle, pressing in a circular motion. cook for 5 minutes on each side

How to cook dosa / Whitsitt '16

Fermented Cranberry-Ginger Chutney

YIELDS 1 QUART, 2 WEEKS

My most-loved combinations with dosa are chicken marinated in yogurt and grilled, lentils and potatoes, roasted eggplant with garlic, tamarind chutney, and mint cilantro chutney. And any type of fermented chutney, of course! You can use the cranberry-ginger chutney recipe below for inspiration.

INGREDIENTS
½ cup red onion
3 inches ginger
3 cups cranberries
2 cinnamon sticks
1 tbsp anise
½ qt water
¼ tbsp salt (1 percent salinity)
½ tbsp whey (optional)

PLUS
1 inch ginger
3 tbsp honey

MATERIALS
Quart jar
Blender or food processor

PROCESS

1. Chop the red onion and thinly slice the ginger, then distribute evenly in a quart jar with cranberries, cinnamon sticks, and anise.

2. Make brine with ½ quart of water and ¼ tbsp of salt and add whey if you wish to jump-start fermentation. Pour brine over ingredients in the jar. Let the mixture sit with a weight and tea towel on top for 2 weeks. With whey added, ferment ingredients for 1 week.

3. After 2 weeks, strain the brine and reserve 1–1½ cups. Discard cinnamon sticks and blend the remaining fermented ingredients. Add ginger and honey to the blender and slowly add reserved brine as needed to thin the chutney. Add as little or as much brine to get the texture you desire.

4. Transfer to quart jar and store in the fridge for 3–6 months.

With the windchill, the temperature in Burlington, Vermont, was in the negative thirties. I visited Rhapsody Natural Foods, a fermentation company specializing in koji ferments and tempeh in rural Vermont, and their first words were "Did you have to choose the coldest week of the year?" It was painful to breathe in. At the University of Vermont, where the conference was held, I dollied vegetables and materials from one building to the next on a freshly shoveled walkway with a scarf over my mouth. (Later that week a public-radio broadcaster quipped Vermont winter was a time that tested people.)

My last stop in New England was Great Barrington, Massachusetts, nestled in the Berkshires near the Appalachian Trail, where I would spend time with fermenter friends Michelle and Tehd. It was 10° F, a dramatic improvement from Burlington.

I had a missed call from Jesika in Eugene. We were bad at staying in touch, save for occasional texting. I called back and received gut-wrenching news: our communard Noah had disappeared two nights before, leaving all his belongings and his shoes in the front yard. I was shocked. She said he was distressed the night he went missing. I had recently talked to Noah and hadn't a clue. I suddenly felt so far removed from my loved ones.

Noah was a part of Fermentation on Wheels; he believed in me when many people weren't sure if I was in my right mind. He also fronted money for the bus when I was in dire straits. Shortly after I paid him back, he approached me, sat on my bed with me, and told me how excited he was for my journey. He was leaving for a monthlong trip to Russia to visit his dad the next day and that was our goodbye. Before leaving, Noah carefully slid a check into my hands. That check would fund the first six months of my journey—fuel, the beginning of my solar system, and much more. I wouldn't have gotten through Texas without his help.

At twenty-three years old he was a philanthropist. He was a good listener. He was a bacteria whisperer. Most important, he loved and believed in his friends, no matter how wild our dreams were. Jesika's phone call sparked fear in me because I couldn't fathom Noah leaving us. It didn't make sense. He loved us too much to put fear in us. Jesika and I spoke regularly after that day. Noah's disappearance consumed our community. He had been fiercely loved in the greater Eugene community, too—his immense network of friends emerged out of the woodwork to strategize a means to find him. Part of me wanted to be home, searching for him with the rest of the crew.

I stepped out of the car, parked in Michelle and Tehd's small lot, and felt cold and heavy. I trudged up the icy outdoor stairwell with a box of fermented vegetables; amazake and unpasteurized tempeh from Rhapsody; a bag of ginger, garlic, radishes, spelt crackers; and my Swiss-army suitcase. Michelle greeted me. The warm apartment felt good. I had to hold my fears in and let the snacking begin.

At Heart and Spoon Community, we cook when we're happy and we cook when we're down. Food is our core community ritual. When words are inadequate or difficult to choose, we express ourselves through food. The most powerful love statement I could make in that moment, for Noah, was to throw down in the kitchen.

Tempeh with Ginger and Sesame

YIELDS 12 OZ OF TEMPEH (3–4 SERVINGS), 30–45 MINUTES

Under Barry's expertise, I had learned how to captivate even the most finicky eaters with tempeh, a fermented legume unfortunately more commonly known as a mediocre meat alternative. This recipe also wows the palates of tempeh-loving connoisseurs. I spruced up a few pounds of Rhapsody's tempeh, cubed with a ginger sesame marinade, and after 20 minutes quickly sautéed it on the stove. The spicy and nutty flavors of ginger and sesame make this a warm savory winter dish.

INGREDIENTS

1½ inches ginger
2 cloves garlic
6 tbsp sesame oil
2 tbsp tamari
2 tbsp rice vinegar
1 tbsp water
1 tsp honey
½ tsp miso
1 tsp coriander powder (or crushed seeds)
pepper to taste

PROCESS

1. Finely chop ginger and garlic. Combine all above ingredients and stir well. Pour over finely sliced or cubed tempeh in a shallow baking dish and marinate for 20–30 minutes. Toss the tempeh in the marinade once in the first five minutes and again half-way through time of marinade.

2. Bake the tempeh at 350° F for 40 minutes, turning it over after 20 minutes, or sauté tempeh on high heat with coconut oil (or other preferred high-heat oil) for 5 minutes—if any marinade remains, pour it in the pan, deglaze with a few splashes of rice vinegar, and pour on top of tempeh.

III. Wild Spirited

Back in New York City I finalized my Midwest route. Though I pined for the understanding and safety of my Eugene community, I remained committed to my work. I would depart for Ohio after Ferment! Ferment!, an annual fermentation potluck in late March. I had looked forward to the potluck every year when I lived in New York. Now, I would be part of it.

The city and winter had been hard on me, but I learned invaluable lessons. Though New York City had embraced Fermentation on Wheels and offered un-matchable exploration opportunities, my place was on the road, where my ability to explore reached even more extreme heights. I missed a healthy combination of nature and city life. Thoughts of walking into my first field thick with vegetables—kale, squash, cabbage—gave solace. And that thought brushed the surface of a much-bigger wild-spirited place: the woods. Both farm and forest were teeming with microbes and had inspired a deeper love of fermentation in me. I was looking forward to getting back on the road.

New York City was big and wild spirited in its own way, with a side of chaos. Rachel and Cheryl joined me for a last Flushing food excursion—a dangerously filling outing for three bona fide gastronomes. Flushing is an epicenter of authentic Asian cuisines. At Ganesh Temple Canteen we ordered idlis, three kinds of dosa, and a spread of chutneys and pickles. Eating until near our limits (we were starting to hurt), we packed the leftovers and headed to the basement of New World Mall, where I ordered duck ramen and fermented tea eggs from my favorite ramen spot,

Lan Zhou. I had no room for it, so I took it to go. Then we followed Rachel through a nearby underground food-court labyrinth until we came to a spot with flat noodles; I ordered mine with lamb. On the way out, I stopped by my favorite Peking duck window and ordered half a bird.

That winter brought out the glutton in me. In my longing for the road and missing the warmth of my slow Eugene community, I ate. My desire for the road was not just for travel and fermenting nature's bounty—now it was a desire to get back to Eugene. I had to finish what I'd set out to do so I could be home with my community and help find Noah.

While the wheels of the bus had been stuck in a heavy sheet of ice from early February to mid-March, bus visits never ceased. A Dutch television crew of three tracked me down, as well as a film student at New York University. The week before my departure, I spent time speaking with them on camera. I also ordered fuel filters, filled my diesel vessels, bought six liters of heavy rig oil, and worked underneath the bus or its hood. It was a deep reminder that the bus was an immense amount of work. Avoiding it while stationed in the city was easy, and great. But I was itching to travel again and eager to recharge my mechanical skills, which I always feared would fly away if I didn't flex them.

After the first melt, I moved my bus to Brooklyn for its last NYC appearance at Ferment! Ferment! The next morning, I began my westward route.

DISCOVERING
THE MIDWEST

Courage is found in unlikely places.
—J. R. R. Tolkien

I. Departure

As I drove toward the Brooklyn-Queens Expressway on-ramp, before I crossed Fourth Avenue's eight lanes, the light turned yellow and I braked. Instead of my coming to a stop, though, my brake-pressure light came on and my bus slid downhill through the intersection as the traffic light turned red. I entered the highway; it was my only option. A brake line had popped, or something—I couldn't brake on short notice. I drove slowly. Traffic was slow moving, so this wasn't too difficult to achieve, and once the speed picked up, I pulled off to the shoulder.

I opened the hood and immediately found the issue. A brake line was detached near the engine. I sealed it with duct tape and refilled my brake fluid.

I pushed on. The Verrazano-Narrows Bridge was my next crossing; it was bittersweet. Ahead of me lay the Midwest, land of manufactured corn and soy landscapes, the breadbasket of processed foods, where kimchi and tempeh would be largely untried, and the flavors and nourishment of fermented foods would thrill and revitalize. I'd spent little time in this big region, and I would be there for half a year. It was where people would need my bus full of tasty ferments the most, right? And then—wham! A truck swiped my left-side mirrors. I was blindsided and nearly brakeless.

II. Family Homeland

The first law of ecology is that everything is related to everything else.
—Barry Commoner

My first stop, in central Ohio, was a short ride from the birthplace of my grandpa Jerry. I would greet his sisters for the first time in five years. My reintroduction to them was in rural Bath, Ohio, before a starter-cultures workshop at the local farmers' market. A familiar voice at the door of my bus said, "Oh, great. A cat." It was Aunt Jackie. I ran to the door.

Midway into her taking her words back I lunged from the stairwell to hug her. I didn't mind the comment. I was excited to see my great-aunts again. It had become a family fact that I did things differently—whether in my tendency to drift with a cat copilot, live with intentional communities (Were they cults?), or stray from the academic format my family so deeply adhered to. They loved me anyway. To boot, the *New York Times* article helped my family gain an earnest respect for my unconventional workplace. Living in and working out of a bus didn't seem so strange after all.

About fifty people showed for the presentation, mostly women thirty-five to sixty years old. As I covered the stories, uses, and how-to's of starter cultures, then passed the jars of sourdough, tibicos, and kombucha around, the students showed curiosity. My great-aunts, strangers to fermented foods, were adorably perplexed. A young man raised his hand to ask how he should go about building a fermentation community in his hometown, Cleveland. It became more apparent fermentation was an outmoded and mysterious practice here. I told him, establish something, ferment often, and share fermentation with everyone he knew.

After class the bus was filled with people eager to ferment and feast on fermented vegetables. They bought and bartered starter cultures by the armful, literally.

The food scene of the Midwest urged me to get louder—more than ever, I felt needed. Middle America, once America's prairie land and known for its fertile soil, is now home to millions of miles of industrial agriculture. The industry—through use of genetically modified organisms (GMOs) and pesticides—encourages the growth of a single crop, usually corn, soy, or beets.

Monoculture works against nature and creates a desperate attitude toward farming and food. Fermentation, on the other hand, is a possibility-filled medium that promotes diverse and healthy ecosystems. Sure, bacteria, fungi, and yeast are responsible for some delicious and nourishing foods, but even more overlooked is the scale of microbial life in soil. Soil microbes nourish plants and animals and in turn nourish us. That we're all connected is one of the most surreal and powerful realizations of life on earth.

If we deplete our soil with monoculture and chemical applications, we squander the beauty and respect of that microbial connection.

I parked at a baseball field across the street from my aunt Jo's house in Wooster the following day. As I walked up the steep hill to her house, the door opened and she greeted me, "Hey, honey!" She insisted I bring Franklin inside and cozy up. Hell, I could stay as long as I wanted. Aunt Jo was recently diagnosed with Alzheimer's, and her nostalgia-ridden state had me captivated. She shared stories from her youth: her first time hearing country singer Loretta Lynn's voice and how it changed her life; how much she loved her dad and going for rides in his big truck; and the way she and her husband drove around town in his vintage cars with the music playing loud.

I lugged her old record player upstairs and connected it to the television speaker, to spin old country records. She went straight to cloud nine. At age eleven I spent the summer with my siblings at Aunt Jo's big house listening to Loretta's feminist-themed tunes while sipping cherry-soda floats. Now, alone in that same big house, Jo would get lost in her television or her records.

Aunt Jo's son, Cousin Jeff, would take her on errands through the week. They'd arrive back midmorning with McDonald's coffee and Egg McMuffins. Fast food was the staple food of my Ohio family members as far back as I could remember.

My well-intentioned cousin Jeff also helped me change my oil. I found a mechanic down a country road who could replace my brake line and asked Aunt Jackie to pick me up.

On the drive back Aunt Jackie made a few stops. First, my great-grandmother's grave. She had died only two years before. Living on the edge, with little funds to travel, I had been especially absent from family reunions, funerals included. Next we went to an old homestead with a dilapidated farmhouse built in the 1860s. A modern house stood behind it, and the current owners were there, getting ready to tear the farmhouse down. My great-grandmother was born in this house.

The owners were kind and chatty. The patriarch brought forth a few items he thought might be of interest—three letters written in 1912 from my great-grand-mother's great-aunt to her sweetheart. The letters spoke of crop yields and family sickness, their tattered pages and faded words uncovering something I'd rarely thought about in my first twenty-six years surrounded by concrete and glass: I came from farmers. My relatives moved from eastern Pennsylvania for greener pastures in Canaan, Ohio, to grow food. Farming had shifted dramatically since they'd landed two centuries before.

I speak to my grandfather a year later about these changes. He refers to the method his grandfather used as "mixed farming"—that means he grew a variety of plants. "Not just maize, but that and many other grains," my grandfather says. On their hundred-acre dairy farm they rotated crops and fertilized with cow manure for soil health. He tells me about his grandfather's disappointment when one of his sons took over farming operations and decided to apply chemical fertilizer.

"When was that?" I ask.

"I was young—it must have been 1950."

After that, details are sparse. In the 1970s, my grandfather visited his first cousin's farm with my mother and aunt. There had been big changes. His cousin farmed one hundred acres in addition to four hundred acres of other people's land. The cousin claimed five hundred acres was the minimum for survival as a farmer in his genera-tion. My grandfather doesn't elaborate on his cousin's survival strategy, but I suspect the crops were undervalued and subsidized.

Even though I came from farmers, I had no relationship with food or land in my youth. Farming was seen as hard, wretched work. The demand and price requires

enormous supply. If a farmer can't up her production with the help of heavy machinery, then she can't make enough money to provide for her family. Industrial agriculture drove my family away from farming.

A sentence from John Steinbeck's *Grapes of Wrath* still blares in my mind each time I encounter heaving industrial machines in the thick of a corn or soy field. He describes the industrial forces as easy and efficient, "so easy that the wonder goes out of the work, so efficient that the wonder goes out of land and the working of it, and with the wonder the deep understanding and relation."

To have a connection to and understanding of food and land now, through growing food, fermentation, and communal feasting, made me feel that I was in on an old family secret. The Midwest farming scene was once more sustainable and diverse, similar to the organic West and East Coast farms I'd visited in my travels. Because industrial agricultural is guided by an economic logic that the entire country depends on, though, there isn't an easy way to get that wonder back.

Consumer choices can help reignite the wonder of food, farming, and land. If we choose to avoid feedlot meat and foods that contain preservatives and high fructose corn syrup, then we help protest monoculture. We determine what farmers grow, and what farmers grow impacts ecosystems. To consume wisely is to make a positive change in the food system.

III. Resilience

After teaching at a brewery in Cleveland, offering bus tours at the first Forest Hill Kombucha Convergence, and giving a few talks at Oberlin College, I traveled to a community in the Chaldean Town neighborhood of Detroit. Fireweed Universe City was composed of folks, ages of sixteen to thirty-five, squatting at homes within a three-block radius. The squats had no electricity or running water. I didn't expect living situations more simple and rugged than my own.

The dwellers of Fireweed Universe City didn't need more—the community was resilient and practiced a unique type of urban self-sufficiency focused on squatting, growing food, and communal living. Mainstream urban America more or less defines self-sufficiency as having a job that takes care of the bills and provides for basic needs, such as shelter and food. Fireweed Universe City works to meet the same basic needs, but their part-time jobs involves developing them from scratch. They bring urban self-sufficiency to another level.

Squatting is a great use of resources in Detroit, where entire city blocks have been abandoned. Fireweed Universe City reclaims and restores the up-for-grabs homes, grows food in the abandoned backyards, and hosts a bike collective out of an unused garage—all with a goal to improve the local community. The neighborhood was once victim to violent crimes and a crack epidemic, thus the abandonment. The members of Fireweed struggled to withstand theft and violence themselves at first, but have since cultivated a safe space in the blocks they've reclaimed. They're now respected for the positive changes they've imparted to the neighborhood.

Our first meal was a large stir-fry of vegetables sourced from the local food bank and their garden. We cooked in an upstairs kitchen on a portable propane burner. Several five-gallon plastic carboys were lined up to one side of the kitchen, near the sink, for washing. We called twelve people from four different houses on the block for the large meal and ate at a picnic table in an abandoned lot by one of the houses. During dinner we discussed fermentation. They were excited to put away vegetables long term without the use of heat or refrigeration.

My workshop was the following day, at the Innate Healing Arts Center. The owner of the center, Dr. Bob, was a neighborhood staple. He supplied the local community with drinking and garden water. The venue was an herb shop, a chiropractic practice, and a café with a vegan menu. Attached to the café was a large enclosed sunporch, where I held my workshop.

It was a diverse group, which was notable—my Midwest workshops before this had pulled from a narrow demographic—almost always Caucasian, female, and from ages thirty-five to sixty-five. We made sauerkraut. I had smoked onion in the mix, a gift from a friend in Oregon. I passed the onion and everyone took in the aroma.

After chopping the cabbage, I asked someone who had never massaged cabbage with salt to assist. During workshops, I rarely touch the cabbage once it's been salted. The experience is too mesmerizing to not share with others. It's the beginning of transformation. It's when we understand that cabbage, with the help of salt, breaks down and releases water, creating a brine perfect for fermentation. A young man approached the table and massaged the cabbage for ten minutes with a huge smile on his face. The last time I had seen someone so immersed in a cabbage massage was at a youth class in North Carolina. I'd had a similar reaction during my first cabbage massage, too.

Before I left, Fireweed Universe City offered a parting gift. They had built a bike for me after discovering I had been without one since Pennsylvania. I needed it. They told me they had needed me, too. We exchanged good-byes and hugs and relished the moment of our mutual understanding of community support. Both sides knew the reward of helping others when they were in need. We were happier for it.

IV. Midwestern Camaraderie

Days later I arrived in the small college town of Ann Arbor, where the Brinery, a fermentation company and longtime supporter, awaited the bus. Its owner, David Klingenberger, had reached out to me a few days after I launched my Kickstarter campaign in 2013. He said he wanted to promote and support the project in any way he could.

It was April 2015 now. I pulled into the hot dirt driveway of the Washtenaw Food Hub, a massive incubator kitchen due north of the Huron River. David, a man with irrepressible energy, ran out of the building to greet me and goggle at my setup. In the building I took in the sights and smells—a room full of sauerkraut-filled food-grade plastic barrels, a bustling hot-sauce production space, and a tempeh room with a modest incubator smelling like cedar. David introduced me to MelRob, a woman in her midtwenties about my height, with an asymmetrical haircut and a

Midwestern Waspy appearance, like myself. She, the tempeh manager, would be my primary contact during my stay. As MelRob and I exchanged a few words, David handed me a spare set of keys to the hub and darted off in his constant rush. I took an overdue nap in the bus before heading out for a bike ride along the river.

MelRob and I met at the market the following morning before my workshop. We made small talk. I had been told it could be a challenge to connect with Midwesterners; it was hard to get a reading on their emotions. I longed for that immediate feeling of reciprocity and mutual aid, such as on the West Coast or in New England, where strangers were inclined to take me in after a five-minute tasting spree and wholehearted chat on the bus. As I was a constant nomad, trust of strangers became my recourse, and those moments always made the mercy of the road more forgiving.

After the market I immersed myself in a four-mile uphill bike ride back to the food hub. In the absence of human connection, I have always made it a point to connect with my body. In my youth, estranged from my workaholic parents, running and biking to the nearby lake made me feel alive and cleared the clutter of my overwhelming desire to feel needed. The mile-long trek felt like five with my eleven-year-old legs—it pushed me to exhaustion. I would walk home thrilled yet with an inkling of fear and tell my parents I had strolled to the playground. (I was not allowed to venture to the lake.) Throughout my Midwest travels, I embraced my solitariness with hikes and long bike rides, mostly along water. A river always made me feel fierce and free.

That afternoon I made kimchi with a few dozen students. We used leftover vegetables, all sourced from the Brinery's many local suppliers. It was a hot day and I gave two hours of tours after class. Finally, with sweat in the creases of my eyes and nose, I walked back into the hub to find my workshop room, recently spread with vegetable remnants, cleaner than when I'd started. MelRob had a home-brewed beer ready to share. She also had multiple starter cultures in different jars. She hadn't let it catch on yet, but she was a fermentation enthusiast of the highest order. Completely obsessed.

We drank her home brew, a delectable and special reward after an exhaustingly balmy day of work. The sun lowered, and as the bus cooled down, we moved in, I tapped a few of my kegs, and we continued to drink. We talked for five hours, at least. MelRob had a lot to say about work politics, the juicier stuff; the kind of talk

I'd been craving. The messy relationships. The Midwest was isolating, she said, with no fervor for food change or fermentation, while for her—it was life.

I feel you, I said.

We then devised a two-all-nighter plan to make miso and mead.

Red-Lentil, Soy, and Toasted Barley Miso

YIELDS 1 GALLON, 5 HOURS KITCHEN PREP AND 6–12 MONTHS OF FERMENTATION

MelRob reenergized my love for fermenting legumes. I had purchased local red lentils and barley at a farmers' market in Detroit, with a plan to turn it into miso. MelRob had Michigan soybeans at hand, so we joined forces and came up with this earthy and luxurious miso, which has become my secret weapon in wooing people into eating miso straight out of the jar.

This miso calls for more koji than is regularly used in long-term miso—I haven't altered it because the original was so delicious—I think of it as a medium-term miso. Similar to long-term miso (see adzuki-bean miso on pages 52–53), this recipe calls for 13 percent salt by weight of the koji, grains, and legumes. Unlike long-term miso, though, 80 percent koji by weight of the grains and legumes is used rather than 50 percent. Source koji online or at your local Japanese grocery store (for more details see page 12).

Short-term miso is also known as sweet miso and ferments in just two to six weeks. It calls for 6 percent salt by weight of koji and dry ingredients and a one-to-one ratio of koji and dry ingredients (100 percent koji by weight of dry ingredients).

This recipe integrates multiple legumes and a toasted grain, all with different cooking times. I recommend letting it sit for a year, when the richness of the umami flavor really starts to shine, but you can start eating it after six months, too, since the extra koji speeds up the process.

INGREDIENTS
280 g soybeans

3½ cups / 830 g conserved bean water (65 percent by weight of legumes, grains, and koji)

165 g salt (13 percent, by weight of legumes, grains, and koji)

280 g red lentils

145 g barley

570 g koji (80 percent by weight of legumes and grains)

1 tbsp mature miso (optional)

MATERIALS
Gallon jar or crock

Hand blender

Weight and cover

PROCESS

1. Soak the soybeans overnight or for 8–10 hours. After soak, cook the soybeans in fresh water, covering the beans by three to four inches. Bring to a boil, then cook on low for 2–3 hours until beans are soft. Skim the hulls as they float to the top.

2. Strain soybeans using a colander and place a bowl underneath to catch the water—conserve 3½ cups of the water in a mixing bowl. Dissolve salt in the conserved bean water. Transfer the soybeans to a large bowl.

3. Cover the red lentils with two times more water than lentils and bring to a boil, then simmer for 10–15 minutes. Strain with a colander and transfer the lentils to the bowl of cooked soybeans.

4. Toast barley in an ungreased pan at medium heat for 10–15 minutes, until it turns a dark rich brown, making sure to stir the grains so they toast evenly. Transfer barley into a pot and allow it to cool for 10 minutes. Add two times more water than barley and cook until the grains are plump and soft, about 30–40 minutes. Strain and add to bowl of cooked soybeans and lentils.

5. Add 1–2 cups of brine (the conserved bean water with salt) to the soybeans, lentils, and barley and use a hand blender to break down the ingredients. You may make it as soft or chunky as you like. I like to break down everything into a semi-chunky paste, with the largest pieces no larger than a quarter-size soybean.

6. Add koji and optional mature miso to the remaining brine and stir into a slurry, evenly distributing salt (and miso) among the koji. Add the slurry to the bowl of blended soybeans, lentils, and barley, first making sure it's in a comfortable temperature range (below 140° F), and mix well with a large wooden spoon or your hands.

7. Follow steps 6 through 10 of the adzuki-bean miso recipe on page 53.

Peach Habanero Mead

YIELDS 1 GALLON, ABV 13 PERCENT, 6–12 MONTHS

MelRob had an impressive larder in her basement—of both fermented and canned goods. Among the canned goods, she had a dozen quarts of peaches from the summer before. She also had dehydrated habaneros, which inspired us to spice up the brew. With summer approaching, we decided to use both peaches and peppers before the next harvest.

INGREDIENTS
yeast (Lalvin K1-V1116 or Red Star
    Premier Cuvée)
water
2 cups ripe pitted peaches or 1 can
    peaches
3½ cups honey
1 tbsp dried habanero peppers

MATERIALS
2 one-gallon jugs
Home-brew funnel
Hydrometer
Air lock and bung
Racking cane and siphon

PROCESS
1. A few hours before adding the yeast to the wine, dissolve it in 1 cup of lukewarm water.

2. Pit the peaches. Discard the pits and place peaches into a pot and cover with 1 gallon of water. Bring to a boil and let the peaches simmer for 30 minutes. Liquefy honey in the water and peaches.

3. Let the mixture cool, then strain liquid through home-brew funnel into gallon jug. Top it off with water, making sure the liquid is no higher than the narrow neck of the jar.

4. Check and note the ABV with a hydrometer. Add the yeast to the container and insert bung with water-filled air lock. Give the gallon container a few good shakes to aerate and distribute yeast.

5. Rack the mead (according to pages 138–39) into another gallon jug in 1–2 weeks, after the yeast activity settles, and replace bung and air lock.

6. Add the dried habaneros after 3 months and let the mead age for 6–12 months. Rack into another gallon jug once again before you bottle or drink the mead to further clarify and separate it from the sediment and habaneros.

MelRob sent me off with wild-sumac wheat ale and four kinds of tempeh—adzuki bean, black bean, millet, and sunflower seed. We made tentative plans to meet in Chicago a few months later for a full week of fermentation projects. I'd found some true Midwestern camaraderie.

Southbound, I trekked the Columbus, Ohio, metropolis and its surrounding areas. Former radio show hosts Amy Eddings and Mark Hilan, of New York City, invited me to their home, named Easter House, in small-town Ada for a potluck and sauerkraut demonstration. The event attracted a large group of homesteaders. Fresh sourdough, herbed goat butter, two kimchi varieties, kale salad, green bean salad, farmer's cheese, and my baked tempeh—all homemade—filled close to thirty plates. After eating, I stood to begin my demonstration, and Mark introduced me in his best radio voice.

At a small card table in the center of the dining room, I announced, "Wild fermentation is when we work with the wild—the local microflora of our vegetable harvest—allowing bacteria and yeast to just go!" I demonstrated sauerkraut: chopping, salting, massaging, and allowing the cabbage to sweat with the addition of fennel and smoked onion for extra zing and earthiness. The fennel-cabbage-smoked-onion combo was new. I continued to work with what was locally available or what I had on hand at events, to keep my work fresh and interesting and prove fermentation's versatility. It was my seventieth event, and after seventeen months when I'd almost started to feel as if I'd tried everything, I was reminded that the possibilities with fermentation were endless. That it was part of the joy.

After a workshop in Columbus, I felt myself coming down with something. I loaded my wood-burning stove and turned on my furnace. The warmth didn't help—that night I tossed and turned, cyclically throwing my covers to the floor only to roll myself into them minutes later.

I hadn't had the chills in so long that I had forgotten what it felt like—I couldn't believe I was sick and against better judgment worried I had contracted some serious, mysterious rover's illness. My Columbus-workshop host drove me to the university clinic the next day. The doctor was as clueless as I was. It could have been a million things—bodies are complex. "So, are you saying it's allergies?"

I asked the doctor. He looked long and hard, at nothing, and replied with hesitation, "I am . . . but I'm not . . ."

He wrote three prescriptions and sent me out. I looked through the scripts, quickly researched the pharmaceuticals with my phone, and tossed the paper slips in the trash as I left the building. I made my way to a grocery store, where I bought a pint of local honey and echinacea tea. I rested and drank six cups that day.

I left for my aunt Florence's farmstead the next morning, feeling robust and ready to travel the country.

V. Magnificent Minds and Stomach-Hearted Joy

One of the biggest lies is that food is cheap—it is a lie that dishonors life. In regards to the sacredness of food, if you don't view the pig-ness of the pig or the cow-ness of the cow as important and only view it as a sack of protoplasmic protein, you have already committed sacrilege. You cheapen the life that has been sacrificed to sustain your own.

—Joel Salatin, in interview with Food Tank

At ninety-four years old, Aunt Florence continues to live alone in her home and tend her small garden, sitting on one hundred acres northwest of Columbus. She rents out most of the acreage to a corn farmer.

Aunt Florence loves to be outside, detests Western medicine unless it's absolutely necessary, and fiercely worships God. She's quick as a cricket, engaged with her surroundings, and full of an immeasurable joy. Peering at my bus through her large glasses, she exclaimed, "Tara, you've really outdone us all now." She entered the bus and carefully observed the jars filled with fermenting vegetables and carboys bubbling with boozy liquids. Entering my room, she sat on my bed and looked at the piles of books in crates surrounding it. Her short response was "Cozy."

Her home smelled like strong coffee and ancient fabrics. We immediately got into fermentation—she wanted to know why I had decided to practice and preach a long-gone food tradition. Her memories of fermenting cabbage and the sourdough starter her mother cared for were from a distant past. She had moved to canning vegetables in her midtwenties. "They kept easier that way," she said.

I told her about microbes, that they keep all things in balance, and without them her garden couldn't flourish and our bodies would be a weaker version of themselves. Aunt Florence had been growing food for eighty years and knew well that food was medicine. She acknowledged my words. "Gary has been fascinated by fermented foods," she said of her son-in-law. It was my first conversation with a family member in which fermentation talk felt natural. Even if she didn't practice it anymore, she understood it.

Gary had recently been diagnosed with *C. difficile* after taking antibiotics for a kidney infection. While the antibiotics cleared the kidney infection, they wiped out enough good bugs to allow an undesirable bacterium free rein. *C. difficile* overruns the intestinal microbiome. He was on antibiotics as part of his treatment for the new treacherous bug, but a nutritionist was encouraging him to eat things such as yogurt, sauerkraut, and miso.

I stayed three days, and Gary stopped in regularly after he got word of the bus and its fermentations. He joined our meals, mostly Florence's standard cuisine of potatoes, meat, and pickled green beans or beets with sauerkraut from my bus as a lively addition.

Aunt Florence had always known me to be vegetarian; little things like that stuck to her magnificent mind. (I was, after all, rather distant to her as a relative—how did she remember my particulars so well?) I was two years off the vegetarian boat, feasting on free-range animals with immense stomach-hearted joy. She didn't get it. "Right, so you're vegetarian. Free-range doesn't exist anymore, sweetie," she said with a pull-your-head-out-of-your-ass certainty. We were in Ohio, after all.

We had some different views about food. (She got annoyed when I wouldn't eat from a plastic-wrapped tray she pulled out of the oven.) Unresolved food quarrels would never break our love for each other, though. Aunt Florence got me a last-minute ticket to a gala at her church my final night at her farm. Once there, she walked me to each table, holding my hand, and introduced me to her church colleagues: "This is Shade's great-niece! She heals people by educating them about fermentation, but not only that—she's taken to the road, in an enormous bus all by herself, to heal large scale." Aunt Florence was so proud. I held her hand tighter,

smiled, and introduced myself to the elderly women at her church. They were uncertain what to think about Florence's newfound enthusiasm for fermentation and perplexed about the bus. I loved her all the more for it. She was so confident in me.

Then she introduced me to Trudy, a young woman she adored for her kindness, devotion to God, and gardening skills. As soon as Aunt Florence said "fermentation," Trudy's eyes lit up. Trudy was a fermenter, and she, like MelRob, knew the isolation of that love in the small-town Midwest. "How long are you here for? May I visit your bus?" Trudy asked.

She visited after the gala, late night. Aunt Florence sat in the bus, listening to our conversations about the negative environmental impact of feedlots and the overpasteurization of food, while I packaged a variety of starter cultures for Trudy. After she left, Aunt Florence looked at me and said she guessed there was still a lot to learn at ninety-four.

I made a package of dairy kefir grains, miso, and kombucha for Gary, sifted through Aunt Florence's larder, at her request, for canned road pickles, and was almost making my way to Indiana before Florence waved me down to give me something. "Here, honey—you might want to read this." It was a Bible. She said it would give hope and light on the journey, the way my starter cultures would bring hope and light to Gary's journey.

VI. Heartland Episodes

I made my way to a rural area in eastern Indiana, where residents obsessively mowed all through the bright May day. I sneezed through the cutting frenzy. Fresh-cut grass always caused my allergies to flare up, and I imagined the lawn groomers taking their hats off and calling through the stiff hot air, "Yeehaw!" (In the spirit of my Texan father, who also loves to mow the lawn.)

Beverly and Andy McDowell greeted me at their rugged thirty-four-acre homestead, Hidden Pond Farm, mowed by cattle rather than machines. Their aged barn housed a fermentation facility, where they produced kombucha, vegetable ferments, and a fiery tonic in temperature-controlled rooms. The McDowells will tell you their goal as soon as you walk through their old farmhouse door: they're in the business of healing people's innards, including their own. They had experienced health issues in their family, and since they've taken a more holistic approach to their pains, their health has improved.

Fermented foods were healing a lot of people in the Midwest, and thus the outpouring of support. Even if people hadn't fully hopped on the do-it-yourself wagon yet, they were showing up. My workshops since leaving New York were usually filled to capacity.

Cancer had an eerie presence in the Midwest. Many students and hosts I met had either suffered some form of cancer or had a close family member who'd survived a deathly brush with a malignant growth. They were discovering that food is a form of medicine, and that fermented foods could help heal and reverse negative side effects of consuming heavily processed foods.

For years I'd been exploring, not always consciously, the interconnectedness of food and health. Now, in my travels through the Midwest regaling farmers and fermenters, that interconnectedness was blaringly apparent. Midwestern food activists are on the front lines of the food movement. Because agricultural chemicals are unavoidable, they have to be more vocal to protect their land, water, and people from industrial agriculture's overflow.

I'd love to see this form of activism—planting the seed that food is important for our beings rather than something we do out of economic logic and necessity—come to fruition in the whole Midwest. It's terrifying to know our monocultural food system is responsible for so much sickness, and that our pharmaceutical-based health system isn't designed to help us get to the root of that sickness. The bummers are immense, and change at times feels impossible, but fermenters such as Andy and Beverly are proving otherwise. They've let the bummers turn them into activists.

I dipped into Louisville, Kentucky, a brief departure from the Midwest. I couldn't resist after Laurie and Larry, my friends and hosts from southern Kentucky the spring before, told me I'd be well received. Their hunch was accurate. My first affair was at a radio show called *Mighty Fine Farm and Food*. The host aggressively assured me, "You got peoples here," referring to the supportive Louisville food scene after we discussed fermentation as a gateway to getting back into the kitchen.

Then I went and got a crush on a guy. This intense distraction was probably fueled by the loneliness of the road. Andrew ran a local market and had heard about my coming to town. He loved all things fermented and admired my mission and bus, which was parked in the lot where his market would take place two days later.

He asked what I liked to do—he wanted to show off his town.

I responded, "Rivers, pickles, beer."

He hurriedly drew a map, marking all of his favorite spots, but then looked at me. "Want to come out for pickles and beer with some friends and me tonight?"

I joined him and we clicked. The next morning he texted, asking if he could take me to lunch. Andrew brought me to a Mayan café serving locally sourced food, with dishes such as grilled cactus, fried plantains, and black-bean cakes—unlike anything I'd ever had. Our dates quickly led to his giving me the keys to his place. He said, "I have a spare room in my house. You can do your laundry. Your cat can come, too. You can park next to my bus."

"You have a bus, too?" He really had me then.

We both worked a lot the next few days—me with three events and him with his weekend-long market, so we didn't see much of each other. I stayed hopeful for a Monday make-out session.

Austin showed up for the weekend, from Tennessee, where he had recently bought property. He joined me for a fifty-person sauerkraut workshop at the grocery store in town. I had grown so much since our collaborations in North Carolina and Tennessee the spring before, when I would happily let Austin take over speaking. Now I couldn't stop once I got started with a fermentation workshop. Teaching people how to ferment at home—encouraging that empowerment through food—made me feel so alive. At times, it was all I could hold on to. It was the most reliable part of my life.

After the workshop I gave Austin the keys to my bus and insisted it could be his crash pad for the evening while I stayed at Andrew's.

Austin and I had a potluck at a historic educational farm the next day. There were three glorious salads, braised pork, an array of ferments from the bus, and at least a dozen home-brewed wines. The expansive land hosted eight acres of vegetables and a covered outdoor space with a full kitchen and dining area. The sun was shining and we mingled, drinking from the abundance of wine made by an attendee, before the fifteen or so of us sat to feast.

I rose to speak, and in addition to my usual fermentation talk—what it is and how it happens and the different formats we can use to encourage it—I talked about the importance of community. Austin's friendship was my example. He had witnessed Fermentation on Wheels at so many stages, from its slow and awkward beginnings in California to its unexpected growth and uncertainty in North Carolina to its confidence in Kentucky. Fermentation on Wheels is part of a greater community of fermentation enthusiasts and educators who believe in me, and that's what propels the project forward. My nationwide fermentation community does something that my Eugene community can only brush the surface of—these friends, also my colleagues, inspire Fermentation on Wheels to keep moving.

After the potluck Austin and I retired to the bus. He decided to make the drive back to Nashville that evening, so I made him coffee and saw him off. I had three days to myself before a lecture in Carbondale, Illinois, and would spend more time in Louisville before departing. I was tired and tipsy. With my wool blanket I hoisted myself up through the bus hatch onto the roof and fell asleep under the stars.

At five in the morning I woke up with seven hours to spare and a five-hour drive to Southern Illinois University, where I'd speak about fermentation education and community impact. It was Wednesday and I'd spent the past two days with Andrew. We rolled around in our underwear in his big bright bedroom. The sweaty body rubs and rickety ceiling fan made me feel as if I were in high school again. The house had a Texas essence. On intermittent breaks we'd hop in his truck and ride to the nearest park, lie under big trees, and then eat a feast.

But I had to let go—it was time to get to work. I started the engine and took the keys out of the ignition slot while I gathered the remainder of my belongings from his house, allowing time for the engine to warm up. About an hour into my drive, as the sun rose and my mind woke up, I noticed I was driving without my keys in the ignition. Someplace along the way, I'd dropped them.

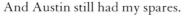

And Austin still had my spares.

I arrived at my next gig with ten minutes to spare. "Sorry," I shouted through my window to the fermentation sciences professor, "but once I turn off my bus, I won't be able to move it until tomorrow!" He crinkled his brow, worried, I could see, about getting to the lecture hall on time.

The talk at Southern Illinois University was about community, fermentation as a change catalyst, and living out our dreams. I explained how an alternative business model such as mine works: I'm afraid—always aware of the risk—but deeply committed and have learned to embrace patience. The fear drives my commitment, and the patience keeps me sane. I recalled words from my friend Guiseppi of the greater nomadic skoolie community, *The Universe will provide if you provide for the universe. It's a two-way street.* These words remind me that my mission to raise awareness about do-it-yourself fermentation is always worth it, because it represents diversity, thriving ecosystems, and collaboration. It reignites wonder in food processes and puts food back in the hands of people rather than in the machine.

I recounted stories from the road, such as my lengthy solar system installation, from California to North Carolina—I used it as a metaphor for the importance of community and trusting that good things come with time. As I told more stories, I noticed a man in a suit to the far right of the auditorium wiggling in his seat with joy and letting out occasional laughter.

I've found that with public speaking if you can spot one person in the audience who loves what you're saying, find that person and speak to him or her. There will usually be dreary expressions, too, but you can't take it personally. Seek out the lively folks. I've never been able to imagine everyone naked—that always seemed way too awkward for me.

After the talk, the previously disenchanted professor brightened up. My cheerleader, it turned out, was a history professor. We all shared lunch before my next talk.

Meanwhile, Andrew found my keys lying in the grass outside his house while Austin shipped my spare keys overnight to the university.

VII. The Arch

Everything smelled like diesel as I approached downtown Kansas City on a warm May night. I arrived at the large concrete parking lot behind the Friday-night farmers' market, hosted in a building rented out by Brooke and Dan of Badseed Farm. As I backed into the parking spot Dan directed me to, I noticed a dark liquid trail in front of the bus, clearly coming from my engine.

I got out, grabbed a bucket from my understorage, and placed it under the leak as it slowed. That was the most I could handle or do then. It was dark and I was exhausted. I wanted to focus on my hosts and prepare for my workshop the next day.

The large downtown-warehouse venue was a community space for farmers and food events. It was an ambitious undertaking for the two full-time young farmers of Badseed Farm who had close ties to the Kansas City Food Circle, the nonprofit that organized my events for the weekend. Its clear interest in food and support for farmers was strong. At my workshop the following day, the spacious light-filled room quickly reached capacity. After I introduced my project and fermentation, the audience got up to taste from half a dozen jars of ferments I'd brought in. The line to taste curled around the room. After, we fermented a gallon of turnips, carrots, and green onions, slicing them thinly and adding just salt. I love this method of fermentation—salting and massaging to create concentrated vegetable brine rather than adding brine. It's a more typical method with cabbage, but any vegetable will sweat enough given we chop finely enough and massage it with salt.

At my last Kansas City event, a potluck, I met a diesel mechanic. It was uncanny—never had a man with an oil-stained shirt and overworked hands, grease thick under his nails, come to one of my events. He was there to support his girlfriend's newfound love of nutritious foods. He realized I had a bus and lit up. When I gave a tour, he was the first on board. He butted in the occasional bus question, such as "How many miles to the gallon does she get?"

When the fermentation fury waned, I took him aside and asked if he could help me locate a diesel-fuel leak. He was happy to do it—excited even—and offered to come back on his lunch break the next day.

───────────────

"*Hold up!* There it is! Turn her off!" my new diesel-mechanic friend yelled over the roar of the engine.

I hopped out to take a look. He pointed to a rigid stainless steel fuel line with a hole dug into the side, caused by the rubbing of another piece against it over time. I could already visualize the maze of auto shops I'd approach to locate the vintage fuel line.

The mechanic then rolled under the bus, tugging on different structural parts. He rolled back out and made a list of things I should take care of over the next three hundred miles. The list gave me a deep sense of dread. Maybe I wasn't going to make it home with the bus after all.

"Well, this is all devastating news," I said, devising a proposal for the guy in my head.

"Let me know if you need help finding the fuel line." He wrote down the address of the International parts dealer in town, I thanked him, and he took off for work.

The International dealer was in a grungy, truck-covered part of town. I was by then familiar with the feeling of being the odd one out. I arrived by bike, wearing a skirt, and felt tiny next to all the truckers in the dealership. Holding the fuel line the mechanic had unscrewed from my bus, I approached the desk, and the serviceman said he couldn't help me. They didn't make that type of fuel line anymore.

"Well, that seems off. Aren't there other options?" I was determined.

"Sorry, ma'am. Can't help."

I stood, planted to the floor, and pleaded with him. There had to be another fuel line that was similar to mine. I could order multiple fuel lines and test them out. Finally, the man wrote down three different item numbers, told me to do some creative thinking, and come back when I was ready to order.

A hefty blond-haired saleswoman overheard my conversation with the man; she seemed to feel for me. I gave her a big friendly smile, one of woman-to-woman camaraderie. She approached me from behind the desk, just off break, and asked to see the fuel line.

After examining it, she wrote down three addresses of machinists in the area. She told me she was sure one of the shops could clone my fuel line.

I crawled through the machinist labyrinth for my poor part. The first two shops where unable to replicate the piece, and my heart sank to my stomach. I realized the task might be more complicated than I'd thought and that I might be stuck in Kansas City. Then, at the third machine shop, my heart nearly jumped to my throat. They made the piece.

I canceled my Omaha, Nebraska, workshop. Kansas City Food Circle generously put out a call for help to their list of local farmers. Responses rolled in and I found a great match: a farm en route to my next destination that practiced fermentation. I also cut a deal with the mechanic from my potluck. He would come that weekend and replace the parts that he had doubts about.

My home that week was Fair Share Farm, a Community Supported Agriculture farm (CSA) in Kearney, Missouri. The farmers, Rebecca and Tom, were a bookish couple with backgrounds in community organizing and environmental engineering. They'd met in upstate New York over a decade before, where Rebecca worked the fields of a CSA farm that Tom was a member of. They met, fell in love, and moved to Rebecca's home state to start a farm of their own. Their website has a great description of how any CSA model works: It's "an association between farmers and eaters who join together to build a sustainable local food system. Eaters pay for their share of produce in advance of the growing season, thereby protecting the farm from the erratic nature of weather and market forces. In return, the farm provides weekly shares of fresh, seasonal, organically-grown vegetables, fruits, and herbs to the membership." Beautifully put.

I helped on the farm alongside their farmhands while waiting for the mechanical whirlwind to come. We spent our days out in the field, picking strawberries, lettuce, and garlic scapes. Tom cultivated soil with his electric tractor as we followed behind sowing seeds for the fall season. We exchanged knowledge—on farming and fermentation—and shared most meals together. I felt at home and comfortable after a challenging week.

Strawberry Mead

YIELDS 1 GALLON, 14 PERCENT ABV, 6–12 MONTHS

Strawberries were in abundance. I made strawberry fruit syrup (pages 212–14) and mead to preserve the bounty through summer. Strawberry mead is perhaps one of my favorite ways to preserve the early-summer berry harvest.

INGREDIENTS
1 packet Red Star Premier Cuvée yeast
(16 percent alcohol tolerance)
½ gallon strawberries
¾ gallon water
3 lbs honey

MATERIALS
2 one-gallon jugs
Home-brew funnel
Hydrometer
Air lock and bung
Racking cane and siphon

PROCESS
1. A few hours before adding the yeast to the wine, dissolve it in 1 cup of lukewarm water.

2. Heat strawberries and ½ gallon of water on the stovetop until it comes to a boil, and simmer for 30 minutes, occasionally stirring. Add honey and stir well.

3. Let the mixture cool, then strain the liquid through a home-brew funnel into a gallon jug. Top it off with water, making sure the liquid is no higher than the narrow neck of the jar.

4. Check and note the ABV with a hydrometer. Add the yeast to the brew and insert bung with water-filled air lock. Give the gallon container a few good shakes to distribute yeast.

5. After a few days, you'll notice activity in your air lock, indicating that the yeast is consuming sugars in your brew. In 1–2 weeks, after the yeast activity settles, rack the wine (according to pages 138–39) into another gallon jug and replace bung and air lock.

6. Determine the ABV of your brew with a hydrometer as it ferments. When the hydrometer reads 0 percent, there is no more fermentable sugar and your wine is dry.

7. Let the wine age for 6–12 months to develop deeper flavor notes and taste along the way. Rack into another gallon jug once more before bottling (also on pages 138–39) or enjoying straight out of the jug.

All the mead recipes in these pages call for yeast strains with high alcohol tolerances and thus result in dry wine, or no residual sugars. If you prefer sweet mead, you may substitute the recommended yeast strain with Wyeast 4184 Sweet Mead. Read more about yeast, alcohol tolerance, and ABV percentages on page 7.

The CSA members came on Saturdays to pick up shares. I decided to open up my bus and share ferments. The mechanic would come later that day, too. I looked forward to being bubbly and social on an especially clear and sunny day in the midst of an unusually rainy season. The rain had been so heavy that Rebecca and Tom lost a fair amount of crops.

Jesika, my communard in Eugene, called early morning while I prepped the fermentation station for show-and-tell. We had been speaking regularly, to keep in touch and talk Noah updates. Her response to my hello was "Are you in a good place? Is this a good time?" Dread stirred within me and the words shot up and out: "Where is he?" I knew it was about Noah.

I've mentioned that community is about finding your people. There's a special kind of inner celebration in finding your long-lost family. They become part of you. You feel safer and more understood. When that cracks, you feel as if you've lost a part of yourself, or worse, you blame yourself out of fear that you didn't reciprocate safety and understanding. Noah went missing, mysteriously, and his body was discovered in an even more mind-crippling manner. We ask ourselves what we could have done to prevent it, but in the end we are left with a numb pain that pokes at the space in our minds and hearts where memories of Noah live. And we can't stop asking, Why?

I spoke to Rebecca and Tom and they were there for me. I was grateful to be staying with supportive people during the delivery of the difficult news. The mechanic came and worked on the bus. The next morning I packed for my departure. I had a few days to spare before a morning show in Des Moines, Iowa.

Then Tom visited the bus and told me I should stay another night if I didn't feel hurried. He and Rebecca wanted to take me to nearby Excelsior Springs for a BBQ dinner in exchange for helping out on the farm.

Excelsior Springs is a small town that rose during the 1800s as a tourist destination, home to several "healing springs." We went for Kansas City–style BBQ, where the meat was slow-smoked on a variety of woods and covered with a tomato-molasses-based sauce. We walked along the river with full bellies, Rebecca and Tom hand in hand, as they showed me their nearby town, its flora and its eccentric spots. The most impressive site was Hall of Waters, an enormous city hall erected in the early 1900s that once hosted large bathing facilities, where health seekers and visitors alike journeyed.

The Hall of Waters was no longer open as a site for bathing, and the town had declined as a tourist destination half a century before. As far as I could tell, though, the entire area, and its people, had a reputation for healing. The support and respite during that week would prepare me for the most challenging juncture of all.

SCENES FROM A MIDDLE-AMERICAN FARM

Be joyful though you have considered all the facts.
—Wendell Berry, "Manifesto: The Mad Farmer Liberation Front"

I. Far-flung

An endless view of corn, soy, and sugar beets surrounded me in Iowa, my home state for the entire month of June. As I passed through rural Iowa, crop dusters decorated the sky. Its cities were big, hot, and strip mall–style with near-impossible public transportation and bike rides that would tucker you out for a day. My host, the owner of a fermentation business in Des Moines, confirmed that the Midwest was a challenging region for fermentation missionaries.

Steve, a friend and handyman I'd met in Boonville a year and a half before, drove to meet me the morning before his oldest son's wedding in a nearby town. He and I had kept in touch. Anytime something came up—mechanical, electrical, emotional—I would call him, sometimes crying. Perhaps no one else had such a complete scope of my emotional landscape during my two years on the road. When

I was down, he always had a way of bringing me back to my senses, reminding me it was a miracle I had made it so far.

Steve also knows I'm not a cynic, so when he heard me expressing doubts about the Midwest, he came to talk sense into me. Steve is from Iowa (and always said he had moved to California to escape the unprogressive state). When I told him I worried I wasn't cut out for this part of the journey, he assured me, "Obviously, you are the only person equipped for this." The positive reinforcement went a long way.

At seven in the morning, thirty minutes after Steve arrived, he and I drove to the local television station, KCWI 23, where I had a morning interview.

I talked on air about fermentation's health benefits and how easy it is to do at home. In my Midwest travels, I thought, those aspects would draw people in, make them want to come out for a free workshop. The host of the show questioned this: "It's easy? I thought about trying to make sauerkraut, but the process was just mind-boggling!"

I responded, "Oh, really? What was so mind-boggling for you?"

"You had to take it, then put it in a dark area, and put some rocks on top of it. It was a pain, so I just went to the store and bought some!"

"I can clear up any misconceptions this weekend, but to be brief: you chop the cabbage, salt it, massage it, pack it in the jar below the brine, weigh it down, and give it time. It's a rather forgiving process."

"That's the part they said takes a long time—the packing."

The host was prodding me to create tension, but ultimately it was great publicity; in his television-personality kind of way, the host encouraged me to school the audience. In the wrap-up, his cohost asked,

"So, are microorganisms the bottom line?"

"Oh, not at all—these are incredibly tasty, complex foods. I don't think I can boil it down to one bottom line."

After the interview, barely midmorning, we drove to a diner. On the way Steve smoked a joint. Iowa or not, he stuck to his West Coast ways. We walked past a bar full of customers with Bloody Marys and mimosas in hand and sat at a booth. Steve ordered a vodka and tonic, and I looked at him. "Wow, that's legal? It's early."

"We're in Iowa, honey. It's never too early here."

The waitress came back and I ordered a Bloody Mary, spicy. I leaned on Steve's shoulder and he grabbed my hand. Moments like that, being and feeling close to someone—without judgment or expectation—were fleeting on the road, and they sustained me.

As I traveled Iowa, the constant landscape was enormous flat fields of corn planted in tight, meticulous rows spanning miles in all directions. The only way to keep from getting lost was to follow the road and my compass. Crop dusters sometimes flew parallel to the bus, aerially releasing fertilizer onto the crops. I grew used to it. Cities and organic farms were nestled in the cornfields, too, though the fields often encroached on both. I visited organic farms, always surrounded on three sides by corn, soy, or sugar beets and the fourth side a road. Across the road, more of the same industrial crops. Those plots were so clear-cut.

In Iowa City I posted up in the parking lot of the University of Iowa's Art Museum, a big barren lot that was hot and humid during a week of hard rain. I met a printmaker who had a studio at the museum, and I hired him to print my logo on a stack of T-shirts I'd thrifted over the past few months. Noah's memorial was that week, and I kept thinking I should train hop to Eugene—or fly, or something. Franklin would have to join me. It would be expensive and I would need to turn around as soon as I got back home. It didn't make sense. I felt lonelier than ever in that huge rainy concrete lot.

I ended up at a bar and healed myself with pub fare, red ale, and starting a conversation with the bartender, Breanne. She recognized me and knew about Fermentation on Wheels. Breanne was from upstate New York and had traveled the country with a trailer for a summer, with her art project Nails Across America. She had traveled alone, too, and knew the challenges that came with it.

Breanne wrote her name and number on a bar receipt and told me to text her if I wanted a shower or to do my laundry. I took her up on it the morning of my Iowa City workshop.

I left Iowa City with ample donations to take a break at a campsite before Chicago. I also had thirty freshly printed T-shirts and twenty-five limited-edition prints of the Fermentation on Wheels logo on card paper. (I would continue to be a terrible saleswoman. One year later, I still have twenty of the prints. I sold two and gave three away in my travels.)

Feeling drained after two more workshops north of Iowa City, both at an industrial farm (which came as a surprise), I headed for the Mississippi River with the hope it would help me find high spirits again. It was, after all, one of the greatest physical constants in my travels besides Franklin. If something could ground me yet also propel me forward, it would be the river.

Though campsites weren't exactly tucked away in Mississippi Palisades State Park, it was empty and large enough that it seemed unlikely another camper would choose to park near me. I wanted to be alone if I couldn't be near loved ones.

I parked, unpacked, and started to build a fire in the outdoor pit. Franklin and I had a week to rest up in the outdoors—just the two of us and the Mississippi Palisades. I went for a hike, crossing the expansive campground. I hiked along the palisades and looked out on the biggest river of the United States. I felt so far away from everything I knew. Beyond the river was corn.

Back at my bus an RV had parked next to me, and they ran a generator—beyond noisy. I decided to walk four and a half miles to town and find a bar.

I was working hard to blot out the pain of my grief and loneliness, and having grown up with alcohol as a coping mechanism, I could turn to it on a whim assuming it would get the job done. I decided alcohol had a lot of work to do.

Since the Bloody Mary in Des Moines with Steve, I was on a path that felt far off from the real me yet strangely familiar, from the holiday gatherings when my family would polish off a case of wine, several six-packs of beer, and maybe a few bottles of liquor. I had struggled to put it behind me, years before while living in Brooklyn, but now grief had me inching back.

Three hours later I was seven beers in, riding with twenty sloshed Illinoisans on a flatbed trailer. A tractor pulled the trailer along a scenic trail of the Upper Mississippi Wetlands. I was sitting next to a new acquaintance—a sixty-year-old ex-cop who had taken a liking to me. He'd bought all the beer. He thought I was hilarious and fascinating. The loudmouth Texan in me always came out when I drank. My stomach started to curl as I began to recognize the suspicious predicament I was in. I was too drunk and needed to get back to the bus.

Once the party was over, I hopped off the tractor to the bar where it had taken off. There was music and I wanted to dance for just a few songs. I convinced myself I had the situation under control—I told the ex-cop I didn't want him to buy my drinks anymore and started buying my own. He got it, and I thought to myself, "It's cool . . . he gets it . . . he's an ex-cop." The things we tell ourselves when we aren't in our right minds. I decided, "Just one more dance to finish off this drink." I danced with the ex-cop and he went in for a kiss. The memories are smoke now, but shortly after, I made my way up the hill, back to the state park as the sun went down. It turned into a two-hour walk in the dark.

The next morning I called Steve. I recounted my drunken afternoon and told him I wanted to get away from where I was.

"Where are you, exactly?" he asked.

"Savanna, Illinois."

Steve's parents, Darleen and John, were a twenty-five-mile drive south of Savanna in Clinton, Iowa. He said, "Pack up and drive there now. I'll tell them you're coming."

The bus fit nicely on the side street of Darleen and John's large house and they greeted me with warmth. Little Steven was there, too, Steve's ten-year-old son, whom I had met in Boonville. He recognized my bus immediately and smiled. "Hey, it's you. The girl with the bus and all the stinky food."

Steve's dad was a born-again vegan interested in fermented foods. I was surprised to meet a vegan health nut in corn country. Strict diets require diversity if you want to stay alive. It seemed an incredible challenge to eat a wide array of fruits and veggies in Iowa, and it was—John knew better than anyone else.

The vegan diet was John's path to healing when he was diagnosed with cancer a few years before. He had watched his first wife pass from cancer and was determined to not fall victim to it, so he changed his diet. It worked—he's now cancer-free. Besides being an old-timer railroad engineer, the town informally thought of him as the go-to naturopath.

It was incredible luck to link up with the town's preacher of holistic healing. In a place where pesticide use is heavy and all the plants grown are shipped out as food for feedlot animals or processed into sugar, it's important to have a guy like John. He was happy to sit at home and drink his smoothie of kale, spirulina, and protein powder while Darleen, Little Steven, and I went out for ice cream. John was tempted by nothing.

Noah turtle / Clinton, Iowa

This year I'm thankful for the kindness of complete strangers, the hospitable human spirits who make me feel at home when I'm actually far-flung.

—Noah DeWitt

Something about Darleen and John and their open arms reiterated the strength of the human body and mind—how quickly we can break down addiction or suffering and rebuild ourselves. I broke my drinking binge while with them and prepared for my trip to Chicago, where I had no inner-city hosts or workshops. I would meet with MelRob though, so I'd have great company. It was time to get to work.

II. Transformation

That Saturday at five in the morning, before the blistering July sun met my metal walls, MelRob and I made my way to Logan Square Farmers Market. There was no traffic at six, when we arrived. I parked on the then-empty North Milwaukee Avenue, where hundreds of people would pass by on their way to the market hours later. The doors stayed opened from ten to five. MelRob estimated fifty people walked in to observe my setup. Many were afraid to try fermented foods. At least two were fermented-food fanatics. Everyone thought the bus was awesome.

The next day, MelRob and I made our way to Radical Root Farm for a stay with bacteria-friendly farmers north of Chicago in Libertyville. The farm was tucked into a wooded uphill drive surrounded by agriculture and suburbs. The glorious spot had a brightly painted purple egg-mobile on-site, wild berries and flowers galore, and six acres of vegetables ready for harvest. It was hot and getting hotter. It was also time to yank out the kitchen carpet and put more wood down. On top of a new floor, MelRob and I had a mission to make elderflower mead, black-bean miso, tempeh, and koji pickles. It would be a very full week.

Elderflower Mead

YIELDS 1 GALLON, 12 PERCENT ABV, 6–12 MONTHS

Elderflowers were in full bloom and we spotted several trees on the property to harvest from. The small white flowers can be found in the summer all over the United States. You can harvest the berries in the fall—they're an equally exciting treasure for foragers. Both the flowers and the berries are powerful medicines. They are immunity boosters and have anti-inflammatory properties.

INGREDIENTS
1 packet of yeast, Lalvin K1-V1116 or
    Red Star Premier Cuvée
Water
½ cup dried elderflowers or 1 qt fresh
    elderflowers
3 cups honey

MATERIALS
2 one-gallon jugs
Home-brew funnel
Hydrometer
Air lock and bung
Racking cane and siphon

PROCESS
1. A few hours before adding the yeast to the wine, dissolve it in 1 cup of lukewarm water.

2. Bring ½ gallon of water to a boil, remove from heat, and steep dried or fresh elderflowers for 5–10 minutes.

3. Add honey to elderflowers and water and stir to liquefy. Strain the liquid through a home-brew funnel into gallon jug.

4. Follow steps 3 to 7 of strawberry mead recipe on pages 198–99.

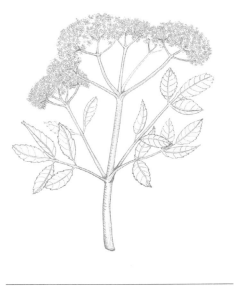

Nonsoy tempeh excites me so much, and it's not because soybeans are bad—it's just that there are so many delicious bean varieties. Why not ferment them? I'd purchased several pounds of dried heirloom beans from a farmer north of Portland, Maine, the summer before and was eager to use them for something special. We fermented one of the varieties, Jacob's Cattle bean, with roasted barley—it was hearty and nutty with a roasted aroma. MelRob always inspired legume experimentation.

I encourage you to expand your tempeh repertoire once you master soybean tempeh. Black beans, adzuki beans, and navy beans are easy to find and delicious bean alternatives in making tempeh. You can also integrate grains, such as brown rice, barley, quinoa, and buckwheat. I advise going heavier on the bean ratio because they promote better adhesion for the mycelium.

Navy-Bean and Brown-Rice Tempeh

YIELDS TWO 13.5 OZ OF TEMPEH, 24–36 HOURS

Navy beans and brown rice are excellent for your first approach to nonsoy tempeh. Not only are these ingredients very accessible, but they're a reliably delicious blend and well-loved by *Rhizopus oligosporus*, the fungus responsible for transforming legumes and grains into tempeh (source it on page 13).

INGREDIENTS

12 oz navy beans
½ cup vinegar
4 oz brown rice
½ tsp to 1 tbsp *Rhizopus oligosporus* or
  Rhizopus oryzae

MATERIALS

Scale
Thermometer with probes
Blender
Mesh strainer
Hair dryer
Ziploc bags
Incubator, dehydrator, oven, or cooler

PROCESS

1. Soak navy beans for 8–12 hours. I recommend soaking in the morning and cooking the beans in the evening. Tempeh is most difficult to regulate at 12 hours into incubation, so it's best to be awake and nearby during that time.

2. After soak, rinse the beans and break them down in a blender. I blend quickly so they are roughly a quarter of the original size.

3. Transfer the beans to a pot. Add the vinegar and enough water to cover your beans by three inches. Bring the beans to a boil and then cook on medium high until the beans are al dente, for roughly 20 minutes. As the beans cook, you will notice the hulls float to the surface—scoop them out with a mesh strainer. Once the beans are cooked, drain the water and transfer the beans back to the pot or a large bowl.

4. Bring the rice and 6 ounces of water to a boil and then simmer with lid for 30 minutes. Transfer the rice to the bowl with the beans.

5. Dry the beans and rice with a hair dryer while stirring vigorously. This takes 10 to 15 minutes. You don't want them too dry, just dry enough so that they aren't wet. Damplike.

6. Follow steps 6 through 10 in tempeh recipe on pages 162–63.

MelRob and I are still close friends. She understands that the bus and flowing is part of my package, and I understand that being stationary and feeling grounded is part of her package. And most important, we always inspire each other to grow, consume, and transform.

My dearest Tara,
   Thank you for always inspiring me to grow, to consume and transform beans, legumes, and grains.
   Few humans and microbes understand my art, but you get me.
      Love Always,
Rhizopus Oligosporus
   XOXO

DRIFTLESS

My fault, my failure, is not the passions I have, but in my
lack of control of them. —Jack Kerouac

I. Clarity

It is so important to be accessible and approachable. Invite others to the
stage; make people feel like they are on the same level. If there is any looking
down or any looking up, we won't be as effective.

—Journal, July 11th, 2015, Madison, Wisconsin

Wisconsin-bound and relieved with the new floors that lifted heat and mugginess, I could almost smell Eugene. When I closed my eyes and tried to seek it out, I was cooking with my friends in our small community kitchen, setting the outdoor table on a cool summer evening with the scent of Douglas fir and plum in the air. It was so close.

In Madison I parked by a community garden, lined by a bike path that traced from the northeast to southwest sides of town. To my right was an apartment building. A ten-year-old boy ran out from the complex to jump on a trampoline twenty feet from my bus door. I pretended not to notice. I stood from my seat and stretched after the long drive. Franklin did the same, and I fed and watered him. I glanced back at the trampoline, and the young boy's mother, a stunning woman no older than thirty, was standing nearby. They were curious.

I invited them inside and we became quick friends. Jessica and Skylar lived next door to my scheduled hostess, Rebecca Wilce, a fermenter and activist I'd met through word of mouth. Her schedule, between farming, milking cows, fermenting, and bringing her goods to market, was extrabusy, so we rarely saw each other. Jessica was fascinated by fermented foods, and Skylar was obsessed with my "bus house." They conveniently became my stand-in hosts. We made sauerkraut together and went on day adventures. Jessica recommended a region west of town called the Driftless, known for its unique topography and good food scene, where people would appreciate the bus.

A day later a woman from the Driftless contacted me, after hearing through social media I was in Madison, and urged me to stop by Viroqua. She was the owner of Fizzeology Foods, a local fermented-foods business. I took it as a sign that I had to go and started to organize a visit to the city, dubbed the Town That Beat Walmart for its efforts in keeping small local businesses strong.

Simple Syrup with Fruit or Herbs

YIELD VARIES, 10–30 MINUTES

Fruit-heavy trees and bushes scattered the Eastside neighborhood of Madison. I picked cherries, black currants, and raspberries to make sweet syrups for my beers and wines. Fruit syrups are excellent jump starts for booze while it's fermenting. Not only do they add flavor, but they also introduce more sugar, or food, for the yeast. The sweets will give your ferments a second burst of life. They are great to use with water kefir and kombucha for secondary fermentation (see page 62).

I am a proponent of mindfully winging it when it comes to putting sweet syrups together. This is partly because fresh berries, herbs, and the like are fleeting in their shelf life—making a quick syrup is an easy way to preserve the bounty and use it over a week or two.

INGREDIENTS

1 part water

1 part sugar or honey

½ part fresh berries or herbs

MATERIALS

Home-brew funnel

Quart jar

PROCESS

Simple syrup is made with a 1:1 ratio of sugar to water, resulting in 45 percent sugar. You may also make what's known as rich simple syrup with a 2:1 ratio of sugar to water (63 percent sugar). I almost always integrate fruit in my syrups and use the 1:1 ratio, resulting in a sugar content between 45 and 63 percent, depending on the sugar content of the fruit. You can substitute the syrup for the amount of sugar called for in any recipe by using twice as much syrup. Simple syrup can last up to a month (usually longer) in the fridge, but the addition of fruit and/or herbs shortens that time to about 2 weeks.

SIMPLE SYRUP

1. Gently heat the water, making sure not to boil. Boiling will result in evaporation and change the ratio. Add sugar or honey to the hot water and stir until it dissolves. Pour into a clean airtight jar and store for up to 1 month.

WITH FRUIT—FOR ROUGHLY 1.5 QUARTS

Note: This is a twist on common simple syrup and helps for accuracy. I am rarely so accurate with my measurements when making fruit syrup, though, and often play around with fruit quantity. It's hard to mess up, but making sure you have at least a 1:1 ratio of sugar to water will assure longevity.

1. Measure out 1 quart of sugar.

2. Heat 1 quart of water with ½ quart of fruit and bring to a boil. Simmer for 20 minutes.

3. Strain the fruit from the water using a home-brew funnel or strainer into a quart jar. Fill the jar with water, so it is equal to the 1 quart of sugar.

4. Pour the liquid back into the pot and add the sugar; heat gently to dissolve the sugar. Store in an airtight container in the fridge for up to 2 weeks.

WITH HERBS—FOR ROUGHLY 1.5 QUARTS

1. Bring 1 quart of water to a boil and remove from heat. Add herbs immediately and steep for 5–10 minutes.

2. Strain the tea into another container and add sugar while it's still hot. Stir until the sugar fully dissolves then top off with water. Store in the fridge for up to 2 weeks.

II. Yogurt Fermentation

I made my way to Mount Horeb, Wisconsin, to visit Branden Byers, a fermentation author I'd been in touch with after appearing on his *FermUp* podcast a year before. The hot concrete road had long stretches with fast speed limits and occasional traffic lights. In Houston they call this type of roadway a "death trap."

One hundred and fifty feet from a traffic light, a semi truck snuck in front of me, and the light turned yellow. The truck hit its brakes. My vintage bus brakes couldn't react as quickly, so I swerved to the right shoulder, with my foot hard on the brake pedal. Two carboys flew to the front cab. The first carboy smashed to pieces. The only thing that protected Franklin and me from flying glass was the second carboy—it didn't break, and in doing so it blocked the glass shards.

I shifted into neutral, pulled down the parking brake, closed my eyes, and took a deep breath. Disbelief. Another close call—it was the price of my lifestyle. Maybe all that fear made it more exciting, but I knew then I was rushing it—not strapping down as I should have; I overlooked the little things as I inched toward the end of my journey.

Branden has a deep love for yogurt-starter cultures, especially mesophilic varieties. These starter cultures are a little more elusive than the yogurt we find at the store and are easier to keep up at home because they ferment at room temperature. I loved all of the yogurt-starter cultures in Branden's mesophilic collection because of their simple needs, ropy textures, and mild flavors.

Mesophilic Yogurt

YIELDS 1 QUART, 24-48 HOURS

A selection of tasty yogurts that ferment at room temperature (68° to 76° F),
these are prized for their pleasant, mild flavors and easy fermentation.

The local microflora in raw milk will overpower the bacteria in these yogurt strains, so it's important to use pasteurized milk. Inoculate 1 quart of whole milk with ¼ cup of mesophilic yogurt and stir 2–3 times a day for 24–48 hours at room temperature until the yogurt thickens. Yogurt strains are prone to culture crossing. Milk kefir is especially aggressive in culturing nearby yogurts. Ferment your yogurts in designated areas far from one another.

långfil
Swedish free-flowing texture & mildly acidic in taste

MATSONI
Armenian slightly thick texture & gentle clean flavor

See page 13 to source mesophilic yogurt cultures.

villi
Finnish ropey consistency & mild flavor

Thermophilic Yogurt

YIELDS 1 QUART, 6–24 HOURS

Thermophilic yogurt varieties are more common and are found at your local grocery store. They are typically thicker and more acidic than mesophilic yogurts. They ferment at temperatures between 110° to 115° F for 12–24 hours. You can make your own yogurt at home using most local yogurt brands, though some may not reproduce indefinitely. You can source yogurt cultures online, too (see page 13).

INGREDIENTS
1 qt whole milk
1 tbsp live-culture yogurt

MATERIALS
Quart jar
Thermometer
Small cooler or heavy pot with lid

PROCESS

1. Gently heat milk on stovetop, stirring often to avoid burning, until bubbles form or the temperature reads 180° to 200° F. Heating the milk improves the consistency of yogurt—it denatures the whey protein and results in thicker texture.

2. Let the milk cool until it is warm to the touch or the temperature reads 110° to 115° F. Add yogurt (or yogurt-starter culture) and 1 cup of the heated whole milk to a bowl and whisk gently to thin the culture.

3. Transfer thinned culture and remaining heated milk into the quart jar. Incubate the jar of milk with hot water (not too hot! 110° to 115° F), surrounding it in a small cooler or heavy pot with lid for 6–24 hours.

4. Each yogurt culture will vary slightly in the time it takes to set. If the yogurt seems thin to you after 6 hours, let it ferment longer. I find that most yogurt sets in 12 hours; however, you can let it ferment longer to further set or encourage a tangier flavor.

5. Place the yogurt in your fridge once it has set and enjoy for 2–3 weeks. Save some of the yogurt as starter for your next batch. If you find that the culture weakens over time, you may want to source a long-lived heirloom yogurt culture (see page 13).

III. Wild-crafted Meditations

The Driftless area was hailed as such because the land escaped glaciation during the last ice age five thousand years ago. The region includes parts of Illinois, Iowa, Minnesota, and Wisconsin along the Mississippi River and is marked by rolling hills and cold-water streams, unlike the surrounding flat prairie land. The Driftless stands out.

Faith, the owner of Fizzeology Foods, organized a potluck just outside Viroqua, Wisconsin, at her homestead. I had a few days to spare before the event, so I parked by Viroqua's food co-op. It was unusually peaceful and the parking spot was a steal. I quickly researched parking laws, and noticed a twenty-four-hour ordinance. The Vernon County Highway Office was a five-minute walk, so I visited them and asked if I could stay for forty-eight hours. They said it was no problem and told me to have fun. A local motto, written on bumper stickers and magnets around town, was "Corn is not the answer." I couldn't have agreed more.

My hostess Faith and her daughter, Maya, arrived at my bus the second afternoon to welcome me to town. They both had dark brown hair and pale skin and impossibly good posture, and they towered over me like Scandinavian women warriors. "Your bus smells great," Faith said. She sat down and took in the surroundings of collected drawings, books, and food—fermented and not fermented—covering every square inch of counter space. We talked logistics for a potluck at her homestead the next evening, but quickly moved on to my visiting Fizzeology's commercial kitchen. I told her I'd meet her there in an hour.

Faith gave me the grand tour of her operation and other interesting ventures. The neighboring businesses were equally exciting: Nami Chips made crackers with dehydrated shio koji (a fermented Japanese seasoning), Kickapoo Coffee was the staple roaster in town, and Community Hunger Solutions was a nonprofit increasing access to healthy foods by gleaning from local farms. Faith had a delicate way of moving and speaking and had a deep respect for the community in her building. She also had a love for wild-crafted foods: plants, fungi, and beyond gathered from nature. It was clear her seasonal ferments were among her favorites. She added hand-dug roots, such as wild parsnip or Jerusalem artichoke, into sauerkrauts and kimchis. Faith was especially excited for her fermented burdock root, which she claimed had tested off the charts for *Lactobacillus* growth in comparison to her other ferments.

Fermented Burdock Root

YIELDS ½ GALLON, 1–6 MONTHS

Faith took the fermented taupe root and finely sliced it before serving. Burdock is found all over North America and has a long history of healing, dating back to Native culture. The entire plant has been used medicinally for centuries, and the root when ingested is known to purify blood and aid digestion. Once fermented, the root presents a mild earthiness to the palate, perfect for adding to salads and slaws.

INGREDIENTS

4 lbs burdock root

2¼ tbsp salt (3.5 percent salinity)

1 qt water

MATERIALS

½-gallon Ball jar with lid

PROCESS

1. Rinse the burdock roots and pack them into a half-gallon jar.

2. Dissolve salt in water and pour brine over the burdock roots. Top off the jar with water and seal it with plastic Ball-jar lid.

3. Ferment for 1 to 6 months at room temperature. Burdock will keep well out of the fridge, too.

4. Take roots out of the jar and thinly slice to add to salads, or even other vegetable ferments to jump-start fermentation. I love adding a few thinly sliced roots when making sauerkraut.

Faith's homestead in Westby was a twenty-minute commute from town. As I drove the wooded and hilly route, I marveled at the special terrain the Driftless is known for—steep and rugged with plenty of cold-water streams. I kept the engine in neutral, falling with great speed down a steep hill while gathering momentum that would push me back up another. As soon as I reached the top, I'd let the twisty road pull me back down again.

I arrived in midafternoon and turned onto the narrow uphill dirt road to Homestead Sanctuary, trees full of bright red sumac hugging either side of the bus. At the top of the hill the nose of the bus met a small creek. Elder trees stood in full bloom, and wildflowers were scattered among the greenery. I backed into the main drive, close-fitting to the woodshed.

Locals piled in from the surrounding area for the potluck and sauerkraut demonstration. Most of the attendees were well versed in fermentation and arrived from homesteads or intentional communities with fermented beverages and vegetable ferments in hand. The sauerkraut demo proved far too elementary for the cultured crowd, and afterward I was rushed with questions on miso, tempeh, and other ferments that require more controlled temperature settings. I realized that the visit might spur some exciting collaborations.

I stayed a week, biking alongside the cold-water streams and learning about the bountiful flora and invasive weeds—both had their place. Faith was much more of an herbalist than she had initially let on. Her herb gardens—both wild and planted—spanned the wooded and open sections of her property. If you pointed at and asked about a plant, she could name it and tell you its uses, whether for medicine, taste, or craft. The gardens and woods surrounded her solar-powered and hand-built house, hiding it from the road. Faith and her husband, Seth, were modest and humble and would have been difficult to track down. It made me all the more grateful Faith had reached out.

When Faith invited me to an ice cream social that week, I hesitated, imagining ice cream made with artificial sweeteners and other such dashes of Midwest food culture. But when days later she mentioned her hope to make a roasted-dandelion-root ice cream with raw milk, I was all ears. She had me at *roasted*. The herbal ice cream social is an annual gathering held by the Coulee Region Herbal Institute.

Hawthorn Kefir Ice Cream

YIELDS 1 QUART, 12 HOURS

I created a simple ice cream using kefir, hawthorn berries, and honey. Hawthorn berries are high in antioxidant flavonoids and promote health of the circulatory system and heart. Hawthorn is red to dark blue in color, has large seeds, and is rich, sweet, and slightly sour. Mix these delectable qualities with kefir and you will have a sweet and slightly tangy ice cream—the richness of the berry lingers softly when combined with dairy.

INGREDIENTS

½ cup fresh hawthorn berries (deseeded)
    or 4 tbsp hawthorn-berry syrup
1 cup whole milk
½ cup honey
2 cups kefir (page 58)

MATERIALS

Blender
Ice cream maker

PROCESS

1. If using fresh hawthorn berries, rinse them well, then with a knife cut the berries in half, cutting against the seed. Pull the berry apart from either side and use a knife to pry out the seed.

2. Combine hawthorn berries (or syrup), whole milk, and honey. If using fresh berries blend the ingredients together. If using syrup, gently heat on the stovetop to liquefy the honey.

3. Add kefir to the ingredients, stir together, and chill in the fridge for an hour.

4. Transfer the ingredients into an ice cream maker, and follow your ice cream maker's instructions. Transfer to a quart container and keep in the freezer.

hawthorn

The ice cream social was at a permaculture farm just off the Mississippi River, due west. Some of the ice creams were made with goat milk and some with cow milk. The unique flavors spotlighted sweet and herbal combinations such as rose hip and sumac, elderberry and honey, and hyssop flowers with maple syrup. The ice creams were so fresh, full of aroma, and made with love.

The gathering was a perfect representation of how do-it-yourself methods bring much more to the experience of food. I had landed with a special circle of people who appreciated nourishment through nature—from farm-fresh milk to wild-crafted flowers. The nourishment embraced our microbial connection.

In addition to ice cream, a few attendees brought *fizzies* for the occasion. I didn't know the term but quickly discovered they were effervescent beverages made with something sweet plus berries, herbs, or flowers. *Fizzy* is the Driftless vernacular for a nonalcoholic fermented beverage. Oftentimes a fizzy is made with the local microflora, but we can apply the term to beverages fermented with starter cultures such as ginger bugs or tibicos, too.

I was so taken by the cute term. Faith was in an especially experimental mood with my being there and the array of starter cultures from the bus, so we decided to embark on a series of fizzies.

How to Make a Ginger Bug

YIELDS 2 CUPS, 3–5 DAYS

We first made a ginger bug, which is a starter culture made by grating ginger into sugar water and repeating that for a few more days until fermentation, or effervescence, becomes visible. Ginger bugs are traditionally used as the starter for ginger beer, but they are effective as a starter in any fermented soda. You can use a ginger bug in place of tibicos (pages 61–62) in any recipe in this book. Note that ginger provides the bacteria and yeast necessary for fermentation—you will want to source organic ginger.

INGREDIENTS
fresh ginger
honey or sugar
water

MATERIALS
Grater
Jar with cover
Strainer

PROCESS

1. Grate 2 tbsp of ginger into ⅓ cup of water in a jar. Add 1 tbsp of honey or sugar. Cover the jar and set in a warm, temperature-stable location for fermentation.

2. The next day, again add ginger and honey or sugar to the same jar.

3. On the third day, repeat the above and wait one more day. You may need to repeat a few more days, until the mixture is effervescent. Once activity is present, it's an active culture and ready to use. Ginger bugs will continue to be active for as long as you feed and use them, but I've found that if you skip a few days, they will quickly dwindle. If yours dies off, they are relatively simple to start anew!

4. Use ¼ cup strained ginger bug in combination with one quart of water or juice sweetened with 2–3 tbsp of sugar or honey for a lively ginger-flavored beverage.

Black-Currant Fizzy with Ginger Bug

YIELDS 1 QUART, 3 DAYS

We used black-currant syrup and cherry syrup, both processed from my harvests in Madison, for a few of our fizzy explorations. (Refer to pages 212–14 to make your own syrup.)

To simplify the process, these recipes call for fresh ingredients cooked down with my standard sugar quantities used in the ginger bug and tibicos recipes. I use honey in my ginger bug recipes, so I've included it as a sweetening option. Tibicos is a bit more particular and doesn't usually take well to honey, so I recommend you stick with sugar unless you have extra tibicos starter and time to play. I always love to play and recommend you embrace creativity and substitute other fruits or berries that are in season in your locale.

INGREDIENTS

5 cups water
2 cups black currants
2 tbsp honey or sugar
¼ cup ginger bug

MATERIALS

Strainer
Sling-top bottle

PROCESS

1. Bring the water and black currants to a boil and simmer for 20 minutes. Add the honey or sugar and stir to dissolve.

2. Strain the liquid into a quart jar and allow it to cool before straining ¼ cup of ginger bug into the liquid.

3. Pour into two sling-top bottles and keep at room temperature for 2–3 days. Chill in the refrigerator and enjoy.

4. Open the beverage with care—when fermenting with a ginger bug, CO_2 production can be unpredictable, as with tibicos (see pages 61–62). I recommend placing the bottle in a medium-size bowl with a plastic bag on top as you open the bottle. With this method, the bag and bowl help catch any unexpected rapid effervescence.

Cherry Fizzy with Tibicos

YIELDS 1 QUART, 24–48 HOURS

INGREDIENTS

1 cup cherries

3 cups water

¼ cup sugar

1 tbsp tibicos (pages 61–62)

MATERIALS

Strainer

Quart jar

PROCESS

1. Bring the cherries and water to a boil and simmer for 20 minutes. Add sugar and dissolve. Strain liquid into a quart jar and top off with water.

2. Add the tibicos and let ferment at room temperature for 24–48 hours with a loose-fitting lid. Transfer to an airtight bottle, refrigerate, and enjoy. You may also transfer to a sling-top bottle for secondary fermentation (page 62) and keep at room temperature for a few hours. Then chill in the refrigerator and enjoy.

3. Open the beverage with care—when fermenting with tibicos, CO_2 production can be unpredictable. As with the black-currant fizzy on the previous page, I recommend placing the bottle in a medium-size bowl with a plastic bag on top as you open the bottle.

I headed for one last Driftless hurrah at the Kickapoo River, known as one of the most crooked rivers in the nation and host to three hundred species of rare plants and flowers. En route to Wildcat Mountain State Park I stopped at Organic Valley's retail store to score a few blocks of discount cheese. Organic Valley is the largest organic farming cooperative in the nation, and its headquarters sits at a bend east of the ancient Kickapoo. The more I explored the Coulee Region of the Driftless, the more I discovered the immense support for local and sustainable agriculture. It's true: a food-driven revolution is sitting in the heart of the Midwest—an oasis in the midst of corn country.

I was falling hard for the Driftless. In my peaceful, tree-abundant camp, a kayak launch site was thirty feet from my door. It was perfect. I would embark on my first river adventure since Pennsylvania the following day, with Faith and Maya.

Driftless sweetgrass

Traversing the Kickapoo River with Faith was an enlightening daylong lesson in flora and fauna. As we kayaked down the slow river surrounded on either side by bushy natives, she pointed them out, relating each to a time in her life. Boneset, she noted, was a plant she'd prepared as tea during the grueling years of building her home. It helped set her backbone and relax her muscles.

Faith inspired relationships with wild plants, in the same way she told me I reignited her passion for fermentation, with my relationship to communities of bacteria, fungi, and yeast. She said I taught her "we feed them, and they feed us." This sentiment goes for all organisms that provide nourishment. We have to take care of the earth and its unpredictable everyday gifts, so it can take care of us, too.

How can we best hold on to a moment, and the knowledge that comes with it? I took dozens of photos, I've called Faith to restore details, and I've researched the Driftless looking for more information on its abundant flora. Still there's a magical quality—the plants I learned about will never quite reach me in the same way as they did that day. The best I could do is make marks in my sketchbook to commemorate them. These weeds of the Driftless—some are native and some are invasive, and they are generally known as menaces, but they also have healing qualities. Sumac has a futuristic look with its hovering deep red bulbs speckled with fuzzy flowers and was believed by Natives to foretell the weather and changing of the seasons. Angelica, a plant with shoots of delicate snowflakelike flowers, was in one legend revealed in an angel's dream to cure the plague—and was alleged to be a powerful healer of most maladies. Burdock is a stout plant with large wavy leaves, known as one of the best blood purifiers. Mullein benefits the respiratory system, and in summer its green stalks, surrounded by large leaves

Driftless Weeds

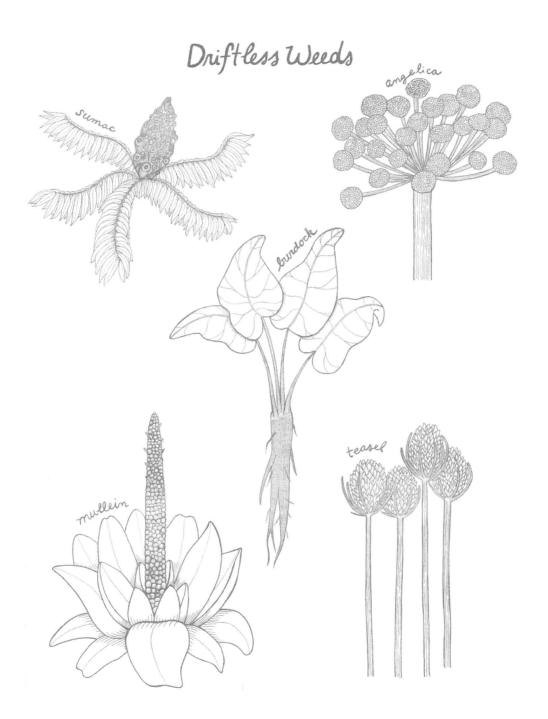

sumac

angelica

burdock

mullein

teasel

(that Faith puts in her shoes to help her feel grounded), shoot seven feet tall while the roots grow strong and deep. And finally, there was teasel—a tall thorny plant with an intense oval head, prized for strengthening and soothing sore muscles and joints and improving circulation.

The evening before leaving the Driftless, I shaved a third of my shoulder-length hair. It wasn't the first time I'd dramatically changed my appearance. The last time I'd brought an electric razor to my noggin was at Alpha Farm, when I'd left Brooklyn and everything I knew to connect with nature and find a more self-sufficient version of myself. It was more than fashion—it was about letting go.

I had to plug in to these other moments in my life to leave grief behind and move forward; and to remind myself that the universe is driven by constant change and inevitable losses. I had to accept that this life era was coming to an end. The fierce emotions of elation and fear that accompanied my journey would soon transform to lessons and cultivate the next chapter of my life.

IV. Full Moon

With wild plants on my mind I drove north along the Mississippi to Minneapolis, where Iman and Joe of Growing Lots Urban Farm greeted me. The ambitious young couple ran a CSA program from three different farm lots—two in the city and one on the city's outskirts. They were also founders of You Betcha Kimchi, a local fermentation business. I parked at one of their inner-city farm locations during my stay, where Franklin hopped off and quickly disappeared into their abundant green parsnip patch. Moments later he emerged with a rodent in his mouth. Iman and Joe were pleased and dubbed him the new head of security.

Our schedules were tight, but luckily I got to enjoy a few homemade meals with Joe and Iman, who energetically bounced from farm to farm and markets to sell their kimchi while I enjoyed bike rides along the Mississippi. The river ran between Minneapolis and St. Paul—two big, wild beautiful cities with flora I now knew by heart. It would be my last big-city stop until the Pacific Northwest, so I stocked up on food from the local co-op. I also bought kitchen supplies—cheesecloth, a

Bluetooth-compatible digital thermometer, and a digital scale—and started discovering a fancier fermentation version of myself.

Minneapolis is home to a special kind of venture—a fermentation bar named GYST (an Old English word for "yeast"). GYST Fermentation Bar specializes in all things fermented; they serve house-made and local artisan ferments and offer educational classes on the how-to's and histories of different fermented foods. I dropped in to have a snack and meet my hosts for an event we would hold days later.

GYST hosted my Get Cultured! workshop, attended by thirty food lovers from Minneapolis and St. Paul. I fell in love with at least three couples wildly smiling back at me as I spoke.

I drove back to Growing Lots that evening, tired, and pulled in to an eager Franklin. In his groundhog excitement, he had refused to join me on the bus to GYST. He wolfed down dinner while I rearranged the bus for comfort, unstrapped cords, and moved jars from the floor to my counter. As the sun went down, an August full moon shone brightly in the sky. I opened a cherry fizzy, walked into the still air, and lay down in a footpath between rows of parsnip and holy basil, with Franklin curled next to me. We were two months from home. I looked up at the full moon illuminating the sky and wondered, Was my community in Eugene gazing upon the same moon? I sure hoped so.

Before going to bed I began a new kitchen routine to sustain my early mornings and the long driving hours that lay ahead: cultured oats.

Cultured Oats

YIELDS 1 SERVING, 8–24 HOURS

Iman had praised her preference for oats soaked overnight with yogurt and water—it increases digestibility, has a more complex flavor (with its *Lactobacillus* kick), and has a creamy, luxurious texture. To boot, this process reduces phytic acid, which is found in grains, nuts, and seeds. Phytic acid blocks mineral absorption, so the soaking is especially helpful in making sure we get the most out of our ingredients. I like to soak mine in milk rather than water when I have access to good milk. You can enjoy these oats cold or gently heat them on the stovetop with a little bit of milk. I soak mine with the below ingredients, but you can stray from or add to my suggestions—all nuts, seeds, and dried fruit will add nutrition and flavor to this favorite breakfast food of mine.

INGREDIENTS

1 cup oats

1 tsp chia seeds

1 tsp ground flax meal

1 tbsp maple syrup

6 almonds (chopped)

4 dried apricots (chopped)

1 cup water or milk

2 tbsp yogurt (pages 215–16) or whey (page 57)

MATERIALS

Bowl (1-serving size)

Small plate (as cover)

PROCESS

1. Soak the oats, chia seeds, flax meal, maple syrup, chopped almonds, and chopped apricots for 8 hours or overnight at room temperature with the yogurt (or whey) and water or milk. Place a plate over the bowl to discourage bugs or dust and leave on the countertop.

2. After the soak, the cultured oats will have absorbed the liquid and should have the texture of porridge. If the oats seem dry to you, add more water or milk until you are pleased with the consistency.

3. You may eat the oats at room temperature, enjoy them cold after chilling in the fridge, or gently heat the oats on the stovetop with ½ to 1 cup of milk and enjoy hot.

Elderberry Sumac Mead

YIELDS 1 GALLON, ABV 15 PERCENT, 6–12 MONTHS

The next evening Iman and I said our good-byes with a mead lesson. We had freshly harvested sumac, elderberry syrup, and a nice supply of Minnesota honey. This brew is lightly flavored with elderberry, which has a rich, almost medicinal flavor and is a powerful immunity booster. Sumac is a citrusy, tart flower packed with vitamin C. They marry nicely for summery mead.

INGREDIENTS

1 cup fresh sumac or ½ cup dried sumac

yeast (Lalvin K1-V1116 or Red Star
     Premier Cuvée)

water

1 cup fresh or dried elderberries

4 cups honey

MATERIALS

Gallon jug

Home-brew funnel

Hydrometer

Air lock and bung

PROCESS

1. Soak fresh or dried sumac in one quart of water overnight. (The nutritive properties of sumac are damaged when exposed to high temperatures.)

2. A few hours before adding the yeast to the wine, dissolve it in 1 cup of lukewarm water.

3. Bring fresh elderberries and ½ gallon of water to a boil and simmer for 20 minutes. If using dried elderberries, boil the water and steep them for 10 minutes. Add the honey and stir to liquefy.

3. Once the elderberry honey water is cool to the touch, add sumac tea to the pot and stir.

4. Follow steps 3 through 7 of strawberry mead on pages 198–99.

STARING
AT THE SUN

I've learned that people will forget what you said,
people will forget what you did, but people will never
forget how you made them feel.
—Maya Angelou

I. Headwaters

I drove north to Lake Itasca, where the Mississippi River begins. I had crossed the river five times in my travels. I knew the lower river best from my youth, traveling to and from New Orleans, where it was a huge mass, scattering at points and then emptying into the Gulf of Mexico. Those waters were wild and terrifying, too rough for swimming. I wanted to feel the river as it erupted into existence. This was my chance.

The lake was everywhere. I spent two days on the state-park trail biking the main drag along the right arm of Itasca. And in a moment when impatience overtook me, I lumbered through the dense woods to the water, stripped, and jumped in. It was hot and the water was perfect—clean and cool and healing.

After twenty minutes I ran toward my clothing, brushing off mosquitoes, dressed, emerged from the woods, and hopped back on my bicycle. I soon reached my destination: the most northern point of the lake, where the headwaters rose. It was a simple ripple, yet responsible for so much movement and life. I walked into it and sat in the shallow water, leaning on a rock, my eyes closed. I wanted to become the river; get lost in that sacred space where life begins. If the headwaters had words, maybe they would whisper, "Anew, anew, anew." When I opened my eyes, the sun was slowly setting over the horizon.

I walked to my bike in my river-soaked shorts and shirt. To my right was a fragrant plant with pinkish-purple clusters in full bloom, joe-pye weed, a favorite of mine from Faith's lessons. The protected park was thickly covered with pine trees. I took off as the sky grew dark and the old-growth trees enveloped me in more darkness.

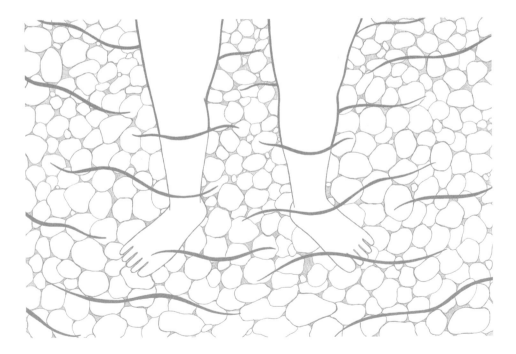

II. The Warehouse

My last scheduled event was in Fargo, North Dakota, a place that couldn't help but conjure up images of flat land covered with miles of thick sheets of snow (maybe even a wood chipper, too). It was summer, though, and the landscape was scorched and barren. In either climate, I couldn't imagine survival. I was curious about people who chose to weather such temperature extremes.

I parked at Red River Market early Saturday morning and prepared the bus for tours. The market organizer set up a tent and table outside of the bus for my demonstration. The organizer, a woman with the local floating co-op, arrived with a pile of freshly plucked vegetables covered in soil. I rinsed, chopped, salted, massaged, and stuffed vegetables into a jar in front of the audience, talking throughout. It was pure meditation for me. I had done it so many times, and now I was at the Gateway to the West. This tour, I knew, would be a distant memory soon—one big, long fermenty dream.

The co-op connected me with a farm in Moorhead, on the other side of the Red River. The Moorhead farmers, Caleb and Georgia, were a young couple in their midtwenties growing on old family land. I arrived at night, late, after getting lost on the long, straight homogenous roads. They greeted me and said they'd be at work the next day—Fargo work, not farming work.

The next morning I slept in. Shortly after rising, midmorning, I searched for the compost pile. My compost bucket had been full for a week, and I'd started to store compost in a second, larger bucket. As I walked the grounds, I came across an enormous empty warehouse—large enough to fit ten semi trucks—that smelled like death. At the end of the warehouse a field of sugar beets the size of basketballs stretched out to the horizon. There were five grain mills, too. I found the compost pile on a cement clearing near the beet field and dumped it all.

Caleb came home from work that afternoon and showed me the organic farm. It was a small garden in comparison to the hovering beet field. We walked around the rest of the property, too. I wanted to know about the warehouse, and I got the farm's history.

"This warehouse here is where it all started." Caleb said.

"What's that, exactly?"

"Georgia's grandpa housed his chickens here. This was an industrial egg farm."

"Whoa—how many chickens did he have?"

"Near twenty thousand. All stacked up in cages in the dark. He vowed to never eat Campbell's or McDonald's again."

"Why did he make that vow?"

"They were the only ones who would buy his chickens when they were on their way out. He said they were so beat-up at that point you couldn't tell it was a bird."

That satiated my curiosity.

III. End of an Era

Only the mountain has lived long enough to listen objectively to the howl of the wolf.

—Aldo Leopold

I left Moorhead at the crack of dawn the next day, traveling full speed as hundreds of empty miles stretched across the horizon, wheat as far as the eye could see.

My skin burned on my faux-leather seat as the August heat announced itself mid-morning. I thought of my engine, the cogs in the machine churning oil, lubricating its bits. I stopped at every rest stop to take out my ice packs and lay them on my face. Franklin sat on my stomach. I fried an egg on the engine for amusement. There was no way we could have pulled this off during the day hours. We'd needed to drive early mornings and late nights.

I thought about my sister in Seattle, just over the five mountain passes that lay ahead. I hadn't seen her in twenty-one months. It was the longest we'd ever been apart.

Getting back on the road one evening before sundown, I drove until I couldn't keep my eyes from shutting. It was three in the morning. Trailing into a rest stop, I passed a cattle guard and the wind picked up through my windows.

Once parked, I had to shut the windows because the wind was too much. I placed wood blocks behind my wheels for fear my bus would be blown away. The evening was pitch-black save for a star-filled sky. I instantly knew I was in an esoteric place, beyond the North Dakota wheat fields I'd been traveling through. Something was different—something massive was to be seen and I was in the middle of it.

I woke at 6:14 A.M. with Franklin by my side and peeked through the curtain. A herd of buffalo accompanied by a horse wandered past the bus. I was on national park land—the landscape was prairie among sunset-shaded badlands and intense rugged buttes. Nice territory for elk, bison, and buffalo. I hadn't seen wildlife for thousands of miles and had forgotten the feeling of awe in witnessing a herd's morning graze.

Then more than ever, I felt a connection with pack animals, in my longing for my people. I wandered into the rugged territory for a few hours and collected a large bundle of wild sage. At nine I arrived back at the lot, now filled with people, cameras in hand, coming in and out of the ranger station. I entered the station dressed in dusty black cutoffs and an oversize button-down shirt with my bag full of sage to look at maps, learn about Theodore Roosevelt National Park, and talk to the ranger at the desk.

"I saw a herd of near twenty buffalo this morning. Do they wander through the lot often?"

"Lucky you! Not too often, but we see them in the early hours at times."

"What about the horse? Does she usually stroll with them?"

"There are some wild horses out here, too. I've never seen one with a herd of buffalo."

"There was a wild horse walking alongside the herd."

The ranger wasn't sure if I'd been seeing things. It was an anomaly.

Back in the bus, I prepared breakfast and coffee. A woman with a trailer attached to her small car pulled in a few spaces from me. She had a medium-size dog in tow. She opened the trailer, pulled out a burner, and made coffee. I wondered where she was going. Why she was going there. It occurred to me then: I was thinking the same thing that countless people had probably wondered about me gazing upon my routine rest-stop moments during the twenty-two months I'd been on the road. It was something else to observe another solo traveler's food ritual. I knew those rituals so well.

I strapped down, key in the ignition, revved up my engine, and pulled out of the lot back onto Interstate 94. The farms and forests and people who'd first inspired me to embrace and share microbial awareness were ahead of me. I held on to my crystal, the gift from Bob and Gayle of Virginia, with my left hand while my other held the wheel. I was certain the bus didn't just run on metal, cogs, and fluids—that it ran on dreams and magic, too.

My journey with fermentation manifested my dreams—a community of good food-minded people from coast to coast, an intellectual space to call my home, and daily inspiration. What a rarity to wake up full of awe and wonder for what comes next! Perhaps nothing brings about mystery and chance as powerfully as travel does. These unpredictable transpirations have a message for us: they amplify the uniqueness of every experience and make us aware of every gift. Travel, like fermentation, is more than a transformative affair—it helps us build a profound relationship with hidden surroundings.

My relationship with fermentation and travel has also revealed that home is where the water is clean, the soil is fertile, and food is considered medicine. It's where I feel safe and understood.

And home is still a secret destination.

Acknowledgments

Pieces of this book began in December 2014 during an extended respite in New York City—those pieces were taken from dozens of journal entries and recipe notes. If you had asked me then whether I'd eventually publish a book about my travels and fermentation (and many of you did), I would have given you a half-smile and friendly shrug. Fermentation on Wheels was the center of my world for two years—there was little time for much else. Thanks to Rachel Wharton and her profile of Fermentation on Wheels in the *New York Times* one month later, my work was widely discovered, leading to literary industry professionals taking interest in my work and story. I'm grateful to the many journalists who have written about my work and indirectly connected me to the people of this country who needed fermentation and my variety of community-minded education.

At the end of my tour I was at the brink of exhaustion, and uncertain where I would land with my forty-foot bus full of ferments. I am grateful to my friends Laura Lee Laroux and Daniel Temple, who welcomed me back with a spot at Grow a Pear Farm on short notice. It helped me transition back to stationary life and gave me time and brain space to finish my book proposal. Thanks to my agent Danielle Svetcov, who saw the potential for a good story and helped me organize this book's proposal. I'm grateful for Bloomsbury's immediate interest in my story and then for their guidance and help in making this book a reality.

I am so grateful to those of the Eugene community who supported me while I worked on this: Heart and Spoon Community for feeding me and loving me unconditionally; Jordan Chesnut for helping me see the big picture and giving unmatchable editorial help; Lucas Nebert and Alese Colehour for offering the bus a temporary home at their farm this year and being beautiful, funny, dedicated humans; Geneva Gill for introducing me to Eugene and its greater community; and the Willamette River and its bike path for grounding me when I wanted to fly away.

Fermentation on Wheels was always at full speed. The mercy of the road proved forgiving thanks to countless hosts, venues, students, and strangers. I am grateful to all of them. I feel indebted to a handful: Steve Morely, Austin Durant, Karen Atkinson, Lauren Rhoades, Sandor Katz, Bonnie Young, Alison and Scott Morgan,

NYC Ferments, Hashem Eaddy, Ian Toal, Rachel Armistead, Luke Flessner, Doug Amport, John LaPolla, Barry Schwartz, Melissa Robinson, Rebecca Graff, Tom Ruggieri, and Faith Anacker. These folks offered immense guidance and support in the Fermentation on Wheels journey.

Fermentation on Wheels would have been impossible without those who donated to the cause monetarily, in goods, or in work—even more than the support offered, it has shown me that moving to a culture that values community good over self-interest is possible and rapidly bubbling up from under our feet. I'm lucky to have felt that ripple firsthand and to have gained a more optimistic worldview thanks to it. Thanks to these many individuals, I'm also proud to say that Fermentation on Wheels is a community-supported project—larger than its parts.

Thanks to Franklin, my cat and companion, who joined me on the journey and somehow never second-guessed staying by my side.

Fermentation has viscerally connected me to the awesomeness of life. Without running into Giles Lyon six years ago, the chance to practice fermentation may have slipped away from me. That was an especially crucial sliver in time to trust my wild-spiritedness and learn to value patience. I am grateful to Giles for teaching me how to ferment and I'm grateful for fermentation, which for me has amplified the importance of embracing wild-spiritedness, patience, and community.

Index

Index of Recipes

A Note on the Author

TARA WHITSITT is a nomadic artist, educator, and food activist. Her passion for growing food, living communally, and teaching fermentation inspired the grassroots educational project Fermentation on Wheels in fall 2013. Since then she's traveled the country with Fermentation on Wheels, teaching by-donation fermentation classes and hosting potlucks that focus on accessibility, creativity, and bringing people together.